Psychology as Philosophy, Science, and Art

Psychology as Philosophy, Science, and Art

Logan J. Fox
El Camino College

 GOODYEAR PUBLISHING COMPANY, INC.
Pacific Palisades, California

Y–6666–5
Library of Congress Catalog Card Number: 73-179008
ISBN: 0-87620-666-6

Current printing (last digit):
10   9   8   7   6   5   4   3   2

Printed in the United States of America

To

Carl Rogers

who introduced me to the
art of psychology

E. V. Pullias

who introduced me to
philosophical psychology

and

to the memory of

Ernest Thelin (1888–1945)

who introduced me to the
science of psychology

PREFACE

What is my excuse for adding another Introduction to Psychology to the large list of books already available? I am simply not satisfied with the available books, which seem to me to fall into two categories: the big, thick books which are overloaded with facts but which do not present a coherent point of view; and the so-called "humanistic" books which stress personal adjustment and neglect basic theory.

As the title suggests, this book, though brief, is my effort to describe the field of psychology as it really is, as philosophy, science, and art, and to do this with a definite, coherent point of view. Inevitably, much has been left out. But there is only so much a student can learn in one semester. A mastery of the material in this book should adequately introduce anyone to the field of psychology.

I would like to acknowledge my debt to the various scholars and teachers who provided critical appraisals and suggested additional content, resources, coverage, and approaches: Edwin Ghisselli of UC Berkeley—Measurement; Richard Thompson of UC Irvine—Philosophy; Paul Mussen of UC Berkeley—Development; John Grossburg of San Diego State—Personality; Emily Starr of Claremont College—style and examples Dean Burchett of Orange Coast College—style and examples; John Peters of San Diego Mesa College—style and examples.

My thanks to my editors at Goodyear, to Clay Stratton, and to Ann Harris, who helped put it all together. Kathryn Wissler was most helpful, as she not only typed the manuscript, but offered valuable suggestions regarding form.

OVERVIEW

CONTENTS

FOREWORD

By Carl R. Rogers, Resident Fellow
Center for Studies of the Person
La Jolla, California

Here is a book which strikes straight down the middle of the controversy which currently divides psychology into two armed camps. Is psychology a "hard" science, interested only in the prediction and control of behavior, as most of the resident psychologists of academe state, or is it a new and beginning science, endeavoring to study the person and the whole range of the human condition from both the objective and subjective points of view? You will find both points of view represented in this volume, though the author's humanistic bias, as he openly states, does show through at times.

Nevertheless it is the most broad-guage view of psychology I have seen presented in one volume. For one thing, without being boring or pedantic, he manages to put psychology into a long-range perspective. The book puts psychology into a historical perspective which comes through again and again, not as a scholarly "history of psychology," but simply as natural referent points for an understanding of what is going on today. His comments on Wundt, the laboratory man, William James the broad-spectrum philosopher-psychologist, and Freud, attempting to be the scientific clinician, bring psychology to life, even though all three are dead. I believe the book will appeal to young people.

It is as unbiased an account as I have seen of psychology as it is: meticulously empirical studies of often meaningless phenomena; richly rewarding analyses of the struggle to be one's self; and factual data about everything from genetic and hormonal influences to knowledge of behavior modification and the effects of the social milieu.

From my personal point of view the book reaches its peak in the discussion of "Being: The Art of Living" and "Psychology's Growing Edges." Here is an author who is not afraid to think, not afraid to express both popular and unpopular thoughts, not afraid to set out in the open the rifts which divide psychology today—rifts which can be resolved only by the student of tomorrow.

I have known Logan Fox for many years—mostly casually, but for a few months, very intensively. He served as my interpreter during several hard-working months in Japan, speaking the language, as the Japanese were fond of saying, "better than we do." I think that perhaps his more than twenty years of living in Japan gave him a more distant, more accurate perspective on psychology. He can view it as the hard scientist views it. He can see it very sensitively as the human science of the person. He somehow manages to bring to it a broad (and to my mind an Oriental) view which is most refreshing.

I cannot imagine a beginning student of psychology whose thinking would not be enlightened, and whose personal life would not be enriched by this book.

Psychology as Philosophy, Science, and Art

PART I
THE STORY OF PSYCHOLOGY

To write the story of psychology, do we go back 100 years or 5,000 years? Is psychology one of the youngest of the academic fields, or is it one of the oldest? How psychologically aware was the writer of this poem?

> Death is before me today
> Like the recovery of a sick man,
> Like going forth into a garden after sickness.
>
> Death is before me today
> Like the odor of myrrh,
> Like sitting under the sail on a windy day.
>
> Death is before me today
> Like the odor of lotus-flowers,
> Like sitting on the shore of drunkenness.
>
> Death is before me today
> Like the course of a freshet,
> Like the return of a man from the
>   war-galley to his house.
>
> Death is before me today
> As a man longs to see his home
> When he had spent years of captivity.[1]

Both the theme and the spirit of this moving poem are thoroughly modern. It might have been written by a French existentialist or a contemporary American poet. It comes as something of a shock to learn that it was written by an unknown Egyptian poet nearly 4,000 years ago!

Students will read, however, that psychology is not yet 100 years old, since by general agreement the beginning of psychology is dated at 1879, the year the German physiologist–philosopher, Wündt, opened his psychological laboratory in Leipzig.

How can psychology be so young and man's self–awareness be so old? The attempt to answer this question puts us right in the middle of psychology's most intense controversy. We might as well face it at the beginning of our study. The question is: Shall psychology include all of the insights into himself and his behavior that man has achieved, whether from myth and religion, common sense, philosophy and literature; or shall psychology be limited to scientifically verified factual knowledge? If we decide for the former, then psychology is as old as man's self–awareness and includes all that man has learned about himself. If we choose the latter, then psychology is limited to what has been learned through scientific investigation during the past 90 years.

Quite a case can be made for either point of view, and the decision is likely to be made on the basis of temperament. Isaiah Berlin has suggested that some men are foxes while others are hedgehogs; some like to roam freely while others prefer to move more cautiously.[2] At the beginning of modern psychology we find two men who illustrate these two temperaments. By coincidence, both were named William: one was Wilhelm Wündt; the other was William James of Harvard University.

Wilhelm Wündt was a "hedgehog." After establishing his psychological laboratory in 1879, he rarely left it until his death 41 years later. His careful experimental work attracted students from all over the West, and the textbooks he wrote and the publications he edited were the major influences that shaped the emerging field of experimental psychology.

William James, on the other hand, was clearly a "fox." He, too, built a psychological laboratory, but he rarely worked in it. In fact, he was openly contemptuous of the kind of experimenting Wündt did, saying on one occasion, "This method taxes patience to the utmost, and hardly could have arisen in a country whose natives could be bored."[3] James liked to roam. It is said that he made life difficult for the registrar at Harvard. Students signed up for psychology only to find James teaching philosophy. The schedule was corrected, but then students who signed up for philosophy found James teaching religion. Then it was logic, then ethics, then psychology, and so on. Finally, the registrar stopped trying to keep up; students signed up for William James and simply took their chances.

Every field needs both its foxes and its hedgehogs. We need our far–roaming theorists and our patient researchers. This chapter recounts the work of men representing both approaches; and the author's bias in favor of foxes undoubtedly shows through.

1

INTRODUCTION

WHAT IS PSYCHOLOGY?

According to the magazine, *Psychology Today*, "No other scientific subject

affects everyone as frequently and as deeply as does psychology."[4] The editor
gives this list of current and coming articles:

> Religion and LSD
> Behavior in Ants
> The Meaning of Suicide
> Love and Death
> Russian Psychology
> Adult Play Therapy
> Hypnosis
> The Sexual Personality
> Psychology of Painting
> The Theory of Forgetting
> ESP
> The Taming of a Wolf
> Redesigning Cultures
> The Psychology of Power
> The Strategy of Prejudice
> Dreams of Freud and Jung
> Psychology of Breast Feeding
> Creativity in Porpoises
> The Psychology of Magic
> Driving Patients Sane
> The Motives of a Soldier
> Self–Stimulation of the Brain
> Why Babies Smile or Cry
> Talking with Chimpanzees
> Psychology of the Reverse Sell
> Stimulating Executive Creativity[5]

And this is only a sample!

How, then, shall we define psychology? Is it "the science of mind," as the
word itself suggests? Some psychologists, especially in Europe, would accept
this definition, but most American psychologists would not. How about "the
study of personality" or "the study of man?" Again, some would accept one or
both of these definitions while most would not. The most widely used definition
is "the science of behavior."

But look again at the aforementioned list of topics. Does the phrase, "science
of behavior" fully encompass the variety of interests reflected? Certainly every
one of these topics refers to behavior, but the list has a flavor that the cold
definition does not. Which is the more accurate reflection of what psychology really is?

Actually, psychology means different things to different people; the field is rich in variety and alive with controversy. The definition, "science of behavior," is a least common denominator, and is therefore useful but it has a drawback. It provides a minimum ground on which all psychologists can meet, but it does not do justice to the myriad interests that psychologists pursue. An introductory textbook is more useful if it describes the field as it is. Psychology is a science, but it is also a philosophy and an art. As a science, psychology is the study of behavior. As a philosophy, it is the study of persons. As an art, it is the intuitive application of what is known about persons and their behavior.

Approaches to Knowledge

Modern man is often an uncritical devotee of science. In fact, for many people "scientific" is the same as "true." This confusion is unfortunate for our understanding of both science and truth. What is science and how does it fit into our whole effort to know reality?

Most progress in understanding occurs because someone has been bothered. Something doesn't seem right: it doesn't fit, or there is an inconsistency. While some deny this dissonance, or explain it away, the critical mind wants a better answer. It asks, "What's going on here? Why is this happening?" This attitude leads to more careful observation and to speculations about more satisfactory explanations (which we call *hypotheses*). We will consider three approaches to knowledge:

1. common sense
2. logic and philosophy
3. science

One may use common sense and intuitive thinking to reach an answer that seems "more right" (the intuitive approach). Or one may use logic and philosophical speculation to find an answer that seems "more reasonable" (the deductive approach). Finally, one may use one of the scientific methods to gather new facts which suggest a more probable answer (the inductive approach).

Whichever route is taken, the goal is a more satisfying answer. Hopefully, the search will lead to a *principle* that is precise and has wide applicability, a principle that will organize and explain a great many observed facts. Such a principle would then be called a theory.

Common sense: its values and limitations. A man's "common sense" consists of the knowledge and wisdom he has absorbed from the general culture and the lessons he has learned from his own experience. When confronted with a problem, he uses the little-understood process of *intuition* to sift through what he has stored in his mind until he reaches an answer which seems right to him.

Although common sense is belittled by those who insist on the superiority of the scientific method, the average man has a high regard for it; and while there are woeful inadequacies in this method, both the philosopher and the scientist must rely heavily on it.

Table 1

THREE POSSIBLE ROUTES TO KNOWLEDGE

Common Sense	Logic and Philosophy	Scientific Method
Intuitive	Deductive	Inductive
1. Bothered	1. Bothered	1. Bothered
2. Unsystematic observation and intuitive thinking	2. Various ideas subjected to logical analysis and tested for internal consistency as well as how they "fit" with other ideas we accept as true.	2. Scientific observation statistical methods experiment survey case study field study
3. Conclusion accepted that "seems most right"	3. Conclusion accepted that "seems most reasonable"	3. Conclusion accepted that "seems most probable"

There are many times, of course, when common sense has stood in the way of new knowledge. Things are not always what they seem. In order to reduce errors, we should be aware of some of the most common fallacies in our common sense reasoning:

1. using analogies as proof,
2. using non-sequiturs,
3. making unwarranted generalizations,
4. arguing *ad hominem*, and
5. employing words deceptively (the verbal fallacy).

Philosophy: its value and limitations. Philosophy is man's effort to organize all that he knows into some meaningful system. Every man is, of course, something of a philosopher, but some men specialize in this activity and we call them philosophers. Before science was born, it was the philosopher to whom people looked for explanations. Even today it is not inaccurate to consider all of the sciences as branches of philosophy. If we go deeply enough into any science, we become philosophers.

The philisopher's strength and his weakness is his breadth. Since his goal is to encompass all knowledge, his interests reach out to all that is known in an effort to bring it together. In this way the philosopher can become aware of inconsistencies and partial truths of which people in the narrow specialties may not be aware. This same breadth can also lead to inaccuracy and fruitless speculation. At best, a philosophy can serve as a clearing house for ideas and as a "devil's advocate" which prods us to more carefully consider the underlying assumptions of our various methods of gathering knowledge.

Science: its value and methods. We cannot get along without common sense and philosophical reasoning, for often we must act in the absence of scientifically verified facts. Yet there are values in the scientific approach which give it an authority that justifies the most loyal adherence to the demands it places on us.

To be scientific means to adopt this attitude: "I want to know the facts even though they may refute my most cherished theories." This attitude is commonly called objective or unbiased, and it is manifested in the development of methods which enable the most accurate observations as well as procedures for estimating the reliability of these observations.

Before taking a more detailed look at the various methods of science, let us understand the role of *hypotheses* in all scientific work. Science is not just a matter of gathering facts. We may spend thousands of hours observing and experimenting and amass mountains of data without adding anything important to our understanding. It is the role of the hypothesis to guide our observations, to tell us which data to gather. It is only rarely that scientific study yields fruitful results when an adequate hypothesis has not been formulated. The hypothesis is our best guess about what is going on; it is our way of staking out the area in which we think an answer is most likely to be found. Obviously, we cannot decide in advance whether a hypothesis is true or false because we are exploring an area where we do not yet have the answers. But we can judge the usefulness of a hypothesis in two ways: how well does it organize the facts we do know? and does it generate fruitful research? The latter is another way of asking whether or not the hypothesis is testable. Some hypotheses do not advance knowledge because there is no way in which they can be tested.

The most stringent scientific method is the experiment, but other methods are just as important. Generally, the following four methods are considered to be scientific.

The field–study or naturalistic method. Careful observations of natural events provide the first systematic knowledge in any area of study. Studies of animal life by the zoologist, of primitive societies by the anthropologist, and of communities by the sociologist are examples of this method. While it lacks precision and control and is limited by possible bias or blind spots in the observer, it often enables us to get facts not available any other way.

At the present stage of psychology, it is likely that the most interesting and complex questions will be studied by keen observers who study what they see going on around them "in the field." Many of the hypotheses which are later tested by experiment are formulated on the basis of field–study observations. For example, there is a famous hypothesis called "the frustration–aggression hypothesis," which states that aggressive behavior is the consequence of prior frustration.[6] This hypothesis is a more systematic statement of many observations of human and animal aggression.

The case–study or clinical method. Similar to the field–study method, but much narrower in focus, this approach involves intensive observation of one person over a prolonged time period. This method is "clinical" because it is most often used to study people in a setting where they are seeking help. It may be used with equal value, however, in any setting where prolonged contact with an individual is possible, and it has been a most fruitful approach in studying the development of children. Most personality theories, such as psychoanalysis, are based on clinical studies. Such theories must be based on a rather small number of case studies and thus tend to be quite speculative. Therefore, they must be regarded as tentative until they can be confirmed by more exact methods.

The survey method. The survey is a cross–sectional or horizontal study which compares a large number of people at one time in terms of selected characteristics. Sometimes an entire community is surveyed, as in a sociological study. Psychologists are more likely to study groups of individuals by means of various tests. The famous Kinsey reports on the sexual behavior of Americans is an example of the survey method. While a survey usually yields an imposing array of statistical data, there are many subtle and complex problems involved in interpreting them.

The experimental method. An experiment is our way of "asking questions of nature." To do this we must "capture" a small segment of nature in the laboratory and pose the questions in such a way that nature can answer them. Unfortunately, nature speaks only one word—"No;" so we must design the experiment in such a way that nature can say "No" if she wants to.

Let us suppose that we want to know the effects of coffee drinking on sleep. We first formulate a *hypothesis*, which might be: Drinking coffee interferes with sleep. Then we *design an experiment* to test this hypothesis. This process includes *operational definitions* of all important terms; a careful description of all *procedures*, especially the *controls* used; and specific *predictions* of what we expect to happen. One of the great values of the experiment is that it can be *replicated* (that is, another person may try the same experiment), but this is possible only if it is very clear exactly what was done.

Thus, in our hypothetical experiment, we would have to define operationally at least three terms: *drinking coffee, sleep,* and *interferes with*. We would define the first by specifying type, strength, and amount of coffee consumed. Sleep might be defined in terms of brain wave (EEG) readings, in terms of amount of physical movement, or by records of breathing, heartbeat, and temperature. To determine if sleep has been interfered with, we would probably state the amount of deviation from normal which we would consider to be significant.

By *controls* we mean the ways in which we try to keep track of all the factors (*variables*) which may affect the outcome of the experiment. In our experiment on coffee drinking, we might use two kinds of control. For one thing, we could take a reasonably large group of subjects and randomly divide them into two groups, an *experimental group* and a *control group*. By randomly dividing the subjects we assure that many factors are likely to be equally present in both groups—thus neutralizing the influence of these factors. We would give coffee to the experimental group and no coffee to the control group. For another, in order to control the influence of knowing that coffee was consumed, a second control group might be given coffee having no caffeine (a *placebo*—an inert substance substituted for an active ingredient).

In an experiment, the factor whose influence we are studying is called the *independent variable* and the behavior being influenced is called the *dependent variable*. The experimenter tries to keep all the variables—except the independent variable—constant (experimental control) so that the relationship between the independent variable and the dependent variable will be clear. In this experiment coffee drinking is the independent variable and sleep is the dependent variable. The experiment is designed so that we may assume that differences between the experimental and control groups in the dependent variable are due to differences between them in the independent variable. In other words, we assume that any significant differences in the way the two groups sleep are due to the fact that the experimental group had coffee while the control group did not. If the results turn out the way we predicted, we say that the hypothesis was supported. If there are no *statistically significant* differences in the sleep of the two groups, we say the hypothesis was not supported. It should be remembered, in this connection, that Nature does not say "Yes." If she does not say "No," we can only say "Maybe." Thus, hypotheses are not really proved or disproved; they become more or less probable. A hypothesis that is supported by many experiments may be called a *theory*. Those theories which may be used for predictive purposes with a high degree of reliability are generally called *laws*.

The place of statistics. A central goal of the scientific method is quantification of all observed factors. We assume that if something exists it must exist in some quantity. Therefore, scientific observations usually take the form of counting, weighing, or measuring. This practice reminds us of Sir Francis Bacon's famous statement that the essence of science is "counting the horse's teeth." In all the methods of science, mathematical calculations play a vital part. With the increasing sophistication and availability of computers, many questions are being analyzed by "mechanical brains." In such computations as *factor analysis* the computer is able to quickly find relationships which it would have taken years to work out by hand or calculating machine.

HISTORY OF PSYCHOLOGY

The Historical Background

The history of psychology is intimately related to the history of science in general. Two influences which prepared the way for psychology and helped to determine the direction it would take were the change in attitude toward nature and the world; and new knowledge of physical processes.

The change in attitude toward the world that occurred from around 1500 to the middle of the nineteenth century is now difficult to imagine. Astronomy and physics paved the way by demonstrating the uniformity of physical processes throughout the universe. It was found that the movement of the stars and planets could be calculated in the same terms used to calculate physical movement on the earth. This discovery led to the abandonment of animistic and mystical interpretations of physical processes in favor of explanations based on cause and effect. No one was more important in this change than Galileo (1564–1642) who contributed to the development and improvement of both the telescope and the microscope. It was the use of these two wonderful "eyes" that did so much to hasten the "demystification" of the physical world. This change reached a climax in 1859 with the publication of Darwin's *Origin of Species*, which signaled that even man was now to be viewed as a part of nature who could be studied by the new methods that were unlocking nature's secrets.

The new knowledge of physiological processes, which both resulted from and influenced the changing attitude toward natural phenomena, made the science of psychology possible. It is easy to forget how recently our knowledge of basic physiology was acquired. A reasonably accurate book of anatomy was not available until 1543. The theory of blood circulation was not published until 1628; and studies of the brain and nervous system did not begin to yield solid facts until the early 1800s.

Early "Giants" of Psychology

We are told in the Bible that in the early days of man "there were giants in the land." Perhaps it always seems that our heroes are in the past. There were many giants during the formative years of psychology, and 20 of them are listed in Table 2.

In most fields during the early formative period, so-called "schools of thought" arise. In psychology three major "schools" had arisen by the turn of the century, and two more, by the time of the first World War. Today, however, most psychologists do not fit into any of these classifications.

Table 2

TWENTY GIANTS OF PSYCHOLOGY'S FORMATIVE YEARS

1869	Galton publishes his *Hereditary Genius*
1874	Wündt publishes his *Physiological Psychology*
1885	Ebbinghaus performs the first significant experiments in learning
1890	James publishes his influential *Principles of Psychology*
1892	Titchener establishes "structuralism" in the United States
1895	Freud publishes, with Breuer, his *Studies on Hysteria*
1896	Dewey publishes a paper on "Reflex Arc" (S–R)
1896	Cattell develops first mental tests in the United States
1898	Thorndike performs early experiments on animal learning
1904	Spearman describes intelligence in terms of specific and general factors
1905	Hall publishes important findings in educational psychology and adolescence
1905	Binet, with Simon, devises first intelligence tests for children in Paris
1906	Pavlov publishes first results of his studies in conditioning
1907	McDougall publishes first text on social psychology
1911	Adler breaks with Freud to form school of Individual Psychology
1912	Wertheimer describes "phi phenomenon" and launches school of Gestalt psychology
1913	Watson's article on "Behaviorism" launches a new movement
1913	Jung breaks with Freud to form school of Analytic Psychology
1916	Terman revises Binet test for use in U.S. at Stanford
1917	Köhler publishes results of problem–solving in apes

Wilhelm Wündt—structuralism. Wilhelm Wündt (1832–1920), who is credited with being the first scientific psychologist, was interested in the structure of the mind, which he approached through an analysis of states of consciousness. We referred to him as a "groundhog" (p. 3). Wündt's main ideas came from Gustave Theodor Fechner (1801–87), who in 1860 published his *Elements of Psychophysics*, in which he set forth methods for measuring the strength of sensations. His basic idea was that the strength of a sensation may be determined by measuring the stimulus that evokes it. For example, some stimuli are too weak to produce a sensation. But if the stimulus is gradually increased, there will be a point where it begins to be noticed. This is the threshold or *limen* (from which we get the term *subliminal*—referring to a stimulus below the threshold of aware-ness). The stimulus can be increased a certain amount more without any corres-ponding awareness that it has occurred. However, there comes a point where there is an awareness of the increase. This amount of change is called the *just noticeable different* (jnd). Using these methods and others that he himself devel-oped, Wündt experimented with subjects whom he had carefully trained to ob-serve and report on their own awareness. These subjects were called "trained introspectionists" and they were a most necessary part of Wündt's work. Wündt's most famous student was E. B. Titchener, who came to Cornell University in the United States in 1892, bringing structuralism with him.

For 35 years Titchener (1867–1927) fought for structuralism in the United States; but before his death in 1927, it became clear that while American psy-chology would honor Wündt for his pioneering methods, it would not follow him. In a sense, each of the other four schools we shall study was a reaction against structuralism. Perhaps that is a tribute, negative though it may be, to the influence of Wündt and Titchener.

William James and John Dewey—functionalism. While structuralism borrowed the tools and methods of physics, functionalism borrowed a theory and some ideas from biology and therefore took psychology down an entirely different road. The theory was Darwin's theory of evolution, and the ideas concerned organismic function. If man is an organism, and organisms survive by adapting to their environment, it follows that *behavior is functional,* or useful for survival. This idea is the core of the functionalist argument. It is, perhaps, the most im-portant single idea to enter the field of psychology. In fact, it was soon so widely accepted that functionalism as a school ceased to exist. Every psychologist, for all practical purposes, became a functionalist.

Two men worked out the implications of this point of view—William James (1842–1910) and John Dewey (1859–1952). We have already mentioned William James, the "fox" (p. 3). It was the broader aspects of the organismic approach that interested him. Nothing irritated James more than ponderous detail which seemed to him to have no practical application, for he was a philo-sophical pragmatist. His feeling comes through in his appraisal of Fechner, whose philosophy he admired, but whose psychophysical methods appalled him.

> But it would be terrible if even such a dear old man as this could sad-dle our science forever with his patient whimsies, and, in a world so full of more nutritious objects of attention, compel all future students to plough through the difficulties, not only of his own works, but of the still drier ones written in his refutation. . . The only amusing part of it is that Fechner's critics should always feel bound, after smiting his theories hip and thigh and leaving not a stick of them standing, to wind up by saying that nevertheless to him belongs the *imperishable glory*, of first forming them and thereby turning psychology into an exact science.[7]

It was John Dewey who really formulated functionalism's principles and who, incidentally, opened the door to a more radical view which has played a dominant role in American psychology. Dewey, of course, is most remembered for his philosophy of education, which provided the foundation for "progressive education." But Dewey was a psychologist before he turned his energies to education and philosophy at Columbia University. When the University of Chicago was founded in 1892 Dewey was selected to be the head of the psychology department. Before long Chicago was the center of a vital, functionalist psychology which imaginatively worked out the implications of evolution in human life. It held the view that

> the survival of the fittest means that use and functional practicality are basic to all progress, that struggle is fundamental in the nature of human life, that kings have no divine right because individual differences exist at random and nature rules by selection among them, and that in the end the aristocracy of chance which nature establishes can be overthrown by the effectiveness of social inheritance and social evolution.[8]

In 1896 Dewey wrote a paper called "The Reflex Arc Concept in Psychology." In this paper he argued that stimulus and response, commonly designated S–R, work together as a functional unit serving the organism. Woodworth later changed the lettering to clarify the role of the organism, and S–R became S–O–R, with the O standing for organism. But it was the earlier form that was picked up by John B. Watson, Chicago's first recipient of a doctorate in psychology, and used as the symbol for his views which came to be called "behaviorism," to which we shall come a little later.

Sigmund Freud—psychoanalysis. One year before Dewey's paper on the reflex arc a book appeared in Europe called *Studies of Hysteria.* It was authored by Joseph Breuer (1842–1925) and Sigmund Freud (1856–1939). Both men were medical doctors, and the book was a medical report; but this was the beginning of "psychoanalysis," one of the most influential schools of thought in psychology as well as in all of Western thought. At the time, Breuer was far better known; but as he himself predicted, today we remember him because he was associated with Sigmund Freud.

In Freud we meet one of the enigmas of psychology. Here is a man who, along with Darwin, Marx, and Einstein, must rank as one of the four men most responsible for shaping the modern mind. If the average person were asked to name one psychologist, Freud would probably be named most frequently. Yet many psychologists do not think of Freud as a psychologist. For example, in *The Definition of Psychology* (1937),[9] Freud and psychoanalysis are not even mentioned. Again, in 1948, psychology's greatest historian, Edwin G. Boring, wrote an article for *The American Journal of Psychology* called "Masters and Pupils among the

American Psychologists," in which he traced the intellectual genealogy of the 119 psychologists listed in the first seven editions of *American Men of Science.*[10] Freud was not listed once, as either pupil or teacher, whereas Wündt was directly or indirectly linked with nearly 40 of these men. Yet Freud is left out of very few introductory psychology textbooks. The most widely read psychological books are those by people influenced by Freud, and the language of psychology is saturated with terms that come from him or his associates.

The enigma seems larger when we learn that Freud was unsurpassed in his devotion to science. He was trained as a physiologist specializing in neurology, and distinguished himself as a researcher of the first rank. He reluctantly began practicing as a physician because his economic circumstances demanded it, but his primary interest was still research. He early accepted a deterministic philosophy which insisted that all events are caused by discoverable prior events, and he enthusiastically embraced Darwin's evolutionary hypothesis.[11] Any history of psychology must recognize that Wündt, James, and Freud are the three giants from whom modern psychology has sprung.

At the same time it should be noted that Freud's imaginative speculations far outran any possibility of putting them to carefully controlled experimental tests. Many of his followers have taken his theories almost as sacred dogma. However, there is little doubt that his influence is now waning among both psychiatrists and psychologists.

We can now see Freud in perspective as a pioneering creative genius who put forth stimulating concepts and theories, and as a stubborn individualist who dogmatically propounded ideas for which there was inadequate evidence. What are his ideas which have been so stimulating and so problematical? Freud advanced three main ideas:

1. the unconscious source of neurotic symptoms
2. the importance of early childhood experiences
3. the centrality of the sexual drive in personality development

His psychoanalytic method consisted of various ways of getting at the repressed early childhood sexual experiences which were assumed to be causing difficulty for the patient. These ways were:

1. *free association*, where the patient lies on a couch and reports to the analyst everything that comes into his mind
2. *dream analysis*, which Freud called "the royal road to the unconscious"
3. analysis of the *transference relationship*, which occurs when the patient relates to the analyst as if the analyst were his mother or father.

People were offended by the declaration that most of us are controlled by forces in ourselves of which we are not aware; they thought he was silly for taking dreams seriously; and they were horrified by his notion that infants are sexually aware. Freud's ideas are controversial even today, and we will consider them more carefully in later chapters.

Two other early schools of thought deserve mention before we leave this brief historical review.

John B. Watson—behaviorism. In connection with functionalism, we noted that Dewey's S–R formulation was picked up by John B. Watson (1878–1958) and made the basis of a radical point of view that has had a profound influence on American psychology. Watson received his doctorate in 1903 from Chicago, where he was trained in the functionalist tradition by James R. Angell (1869–1949). In 1913, after he had gone to Johns Hopkins University, he published his famous article, "Behaviorism," and in 1919, his *Psychology from the Standpoint of a Behaviorist* spelled out the details of his new approach. Watson insisted that psychology should study only behavior, that its method should be entirely objective, and that its central problems should be those of prediction and control. He was particularly critical of structuralism, saying:

> "States of consciousness," like the so-called phenomena of spiritualism, are not objectively verifiable and for that reason can never become data for science . . . The behaviorist finds no evidence for "mental existences" or "mental processes" of any kind.[12]

Later he said, " 'Consciousness' is neither a definable nor a usable concept; . . . it is merely another word for the 'soul' of more ancient times."[13]   To quote Boring again,

> Behaviorism was itself too unsophisticated to last. It has now given place to positivism or operationism or whatever one prefers to call the newest psychological objectivism. The operationist argues that all the data of psychology, including the data of consciousness, are to be defined by the operations which are used to observe them.[14]

While most psychologists would not claim to be behaviorists, it is a measure of Watson's influence that today just about every textbook of psychology in America defines psychology as "the study of behavior," which is, of course, Watson's definition.

Max Wertheimer—Gestalt psychology. In 1912, a year before Watson's article on behaviorism appeared, Max Wertheimer (1880-1943) at the University of Frankfurt, Germany, published "Experimental Studies of Apparent Movement." This article marked the beginning of Gestalt psychology, which began as a protest against structuralism and then opposed behaviorism as well. The German word *Gestalt* means *pattern,* or *whole,* and Wertheimer, together with Wolfgang

Köhler (1887-1967) and Kurt Koffka (1886-1941), stressed a "molar" as opposed to a "molecular" level of theorizing. *Molar* refers to more wholistic explanations while *molecular* has to do with approaches that stress smaller bits of data.

Wertheimer's classic study illustrates how Gestalt psychology attacks problems:

> If two electric lights are placed a few feet apart along one edge of a table and an upright rod is put on the other edge between the lights and a nearby wall an equidistant from each light, two shadows of the rod may be perceived on the wall. Now, if the lights are switched on and off alternately, in rhythmical succession and at the proper rate of speed, the *shadow of the rod will appear to move back and forth between its two positions.* When the time between the two light exposures is too short, the shadows will appear simultaneously each in its own place; when the time is too long, there will be merely a succession of shadows—first one and then the other, in their respective places.[15]

This apparent movement Wertheimer called the "phi phenomenon." He insisted that it could not be explained on any molecular basis, since there was no real movement in the stimulus object.

In another experiment, in which the Gestaltists delighted because they believed it disproved the S-R bonds of the behaviorists, a chicken was trained to peck the lighter of two gray boxes to get food. After the chicken had learned this task, the lighter gray of the original pair of stimuli was then paired with a still lighter gray. Which would the chicken peck? If the S-R theory were right, it should peck the gray it had been trained to peck, since the "bond" was supposedly established between that specific stimulus and the pecking response. But the chicken did not do this. It pecked the lighter of the two grays, and, in so doing, rejected the stimulus it had been trained to select and chose one it had not seen before. This experiment seemed to support the theory that the chicken was responding to the *relative* and not to the *absolute* amount of light and to respond to a relationship is to respond to a *Gestalt* (whole situation).[16]

The Gestalt school of psychology has been particularly influential in the area of perceptual studies, and we shall study some of this work in Chapter 8.

Psychology Today

As we mentioned earlier, most psychologists today would not fit into any of these early schools of thought. While we still have "Freudians," "Gestaltists," and "behaviorists" who bear a resemblance to early members of the various schools, it would no longer be fruitful to attempt a classification on this basis. It is more informative to describe today's psychologists in terms of the kind of work they do. One study, in 1963, reported on the following categories of employment:[17]

	(percent)
Colleges and universities	35
Federal, state, and local governments	26
Schools	11
Business and industry	11
Non-profit clinics, hospitals, and other organizations	10
Self-employed	6
Other	1
	100

When the kind of work done was used as a basis for classification, the results were:

	(percent)
Behavior modification	28
Teaching and training	21
Research	18
Administration and management	17
Assessment and evaluation	10
Management consulting	3
Other	3
	100

From these statistics it is clear that teaching and counseling make up the largest part of the work that psychologists do.

Perhaps this is a good place to clarify the relationship between clinical psychology and some of the related professional fields. A *clinical psychologist* is a behavioral scientist, trained in the academic discipline of psychology. He has at least an M.A., and usually a Ph.D., and has done specialized study in the fields of Abnormal Psychology, Psychological Testing, Personality Theory, and Counseling or Psychotherapy. He must also complete a supervised internship.

A *psychiatrist* is a medical doctor who has been trained in psychotherapy and has done advanced study in the field of psychopathology or mental illness.

A *psychoanalyst* is a psychotherapist who works within the framework of Freud's theory and uses a therapeutic technique called psychoanalysis. He is usually a psychiatrist, although a few are "lay" analysts—without medical training. One requirement for a psychoanalyst is to undergo psychoanalysis as a patient. Most psychoanalysts are psychiatrists, but a relatively small proportion of psychiatrists are psychoanalysts. Most psychiatrists, however, are eclectic in that they use ideas and techniques from many different sources.

A *psychotherapist* is someone who helps disturbed people. Clinical psychologists, psychiatrists, psychoanalysts, and sometimes psychiatric social workers all practice psychotherapy.

CHOOSING A PERSPECTIVE

Points to Remember

The beginning student can easily be baffled by conflicting definitions of psychology and by controversies over methodology. Here are some general suggestions to help the student find himself and choose a perspective from which he can pursue his own study of psychology.

1. Remember that psychology is a science where the thing being studied is itself doing the studying. Obviously, this makes for the greatest possible interest and the greatest possible number of complications. In physics and chemistry consciousness (in the form of man) is studying inanimate processes. In biology and physiology, and to a greater extent in the social sciences, consciousness is studying living processes. Only in psychology is consciousness attempting an objective study of itself. Some of the processes studied by psychologists are very similar to biological processes. The knee jerk, the pupillary reflex, the salivary reflex, and simple reaction time are public responses which can be studied with little consideration of consciousness. But complex human and, perhaps, animal behavior is a very different kind of problem. Questions such as, "What are you thinking?" "What are you planning?" "How do you feel?" "How does it look to you?"—each call for a fundamentally different approach. Here consciousness must study consciousness, and this is clearly "a new ball game."

2. It may be consoling to the would-be psychologist to remember that no science is completely objective. The data gathered by machines are not considered data until someone "subjectively" determines that they are of importance; and even then, such data do not say anything until they are interpreted "subjectively."

We do want to be objective in the sense of being reasonably unbiased and open to facts, and we also prefer to deal with the kinds of facts that can be verified by other researchers. But it is no service to psychology for a conscious, purposeful scientist to pretend that there is neither consciousness nor purpose. *Subjectivity is what psychology is all about.* How to study subjectivity in such a way as to arrive at reliable facts about it is a continuing problem for every serious student in the field. (*See* Carl Rogers' article in chapter 13.)

3. Remember that anything can be studied at different levels of conceptuali-
zation, depending upon the focus of our interest. Just as we can set a camera
lense for closeup, wide range, or telescopic, so we can focus our observation
according to how specific or general we want to be. A man may be studied chemically, physiologically, or psychologically. Furthermore, we can focus on a reflex,
such as the knee jerk, or we can focus on facial expression, bodily movements,
patterns of behavior, verbal reports, inter-personal interaction, etc. We know that
a painting cannot be seen through a microscope. The pigments, the composition
of the canvas, and the brush strokes can all be studied; but the painting cannot be
seen in this way. Nor can it logically be put together from such microscopic observations.

The particular focus we choose is to be determined by our purposes. When we
are studying small parts of larger processes, we want very fine details and we insist on the greatest amount of precision. When we are looking at larger processes
or complex patterns of behavior, our attention focuses at a different level or else
we fail to see what we are looking for.

The fact that some observed phenomena, upon closer observation, are composed of smaller elements and processes involving these elements does not alter
the factuality of the original observations; and it may enrich our understanding
of them. Physics does not nullify the observations of the astronomer, nor does
chemistry negate the observations of the biologist. Neither do any studies of partial processes in man alter the observed facts about his consciousness or his behavior.

Some Axioms on which Psychology Rests

Psychology, in common with all sciences, shares with philosophy the necessity
of building on assumptions which cannot be proven or disproven. The following
are four examples of such *axioms*. There are others the student may want to
state for himself.

1. *The reality of consciousness.* We assume that we are conscious and that
   consciousness is not an illusion.
2. *The unity of the person.* We assume that persons have a unity in time in
   spite of the transient nature of the substances of which they are composed.
3. *The reality of the perceived world.* We assume that in spite of the subjective nature of our perceptions, they represent reality in some way; and
   there is a reasonable correspondence between our ideas of things and the
   way things are.
4. *The freedom of persons.* We assume, in spite of all deterministic theories,
   that persons are in some important sense free; that persons are capable of
   setting goals, of making decisions, and of expressing some degree of
   autonomy. Unless this idea is true, there is no meaning in what is

written in these very lines; nor is there any meaning in what any scientist says, including the behaviorist who tries to convince us that we ought to decide we are not free to decide! Unless, in a most important sense, he is speaking freely, then both what he is saying and our response are determined by natural causes and he is doing only what he must do and, of course, our response is not free, either, and we are doing only what we are being caused to do.

SUMMARY

The term psychology means different things to different people. Some would include in the definition all of the insights into himself and his behavior that man has achieved, from whatever source; others would restrict the field to scientifically verified factual knowledge.

Knowledge may be approached through the methods of common sense, philosophy, and science. Each has its values and its limitations. Scientific psychology makes use of several different methods. The field–study method is especially suited to studying behavior that cannot be brought into the laboratory. The case study method enables us to study a few individuals in great depth by observing them in a clinical situation over a prolonged period of time. The survey method is especially valuable for getting a cross–section of the population for comparative purposes. The experimental method's chief value is that the results of any experiment can be checked by replicating it exactly.

Psychology, as a separate discipline of study, is less than a hundred years old. Its early history was marked by such illustrious men as: Wilhelm Wündt, who studied the structure of the mind; William James and John Dewey, who helped change the emphasis in psychology from the structure to the function of the mind; Sigmund Freud, who stressed the unconscious mind; John Watson, who insisted on the study of overt behavior with no consideration of mind; and Max Wertheimer and Wolfgang Köhler, who preferred the study of wholistic rather than partial processes.

Today's psychologists do not fit well into the categories of these early schools of psychology. Modern psychologists can be classified in terms of where they are employed or the kind of work they do.

QUESTIONS FOR STUDY AND CLASS DISCUSSION

1. What are some common sense ideas that have been validated by scientific research? What are some that were not validated?

2. Can you think fo some instances when common sense would be especially useful to scientists?

3. What kinds of facts about people do you think might be learned through the field–study method that could not be learned by other scientific methods?

4. What strengths and weaknesses do you see in the case–study method?

5. What kind of psychological question would you seek to answer with a survey?

6. What is the value found in the experimental method that no other method has?

7. What do you think psychology should study? How would you define psychology?

8. Which of the "early giants" of psychology appealed to you most? Why?

9. Do you think that subjectivity can be studied objectively?

10. How is subjectivity involved in even the most objective experiments?

SUGGESTIONS FOR FURTHER READING

Cohen, John. *Humanistic Psychology.* New York; Collier Books, 1962.

Hook, Sidney, ed. *Dimensions of Mind.* New York: Collier Books, 1960.

James, William. *Psychology: The Briefer Course.* New York: Harper Torch-books, 1961.

Thruelsen, Richard, and Kobler, John, eds. *Adventures of the Mind.* New York: Vintage Books, 1959.

Wertheimer, Michael. *A Brief History of Psychology.* New York: Holt, Rine-hart and Winston, 1970.

.

PART II
PHILOSOPHICAL PSYCHOLOGY

What is the most difficult of all?
What seems the easiest to you:
To see with your eyes
What lies before your eyes.[1]

Psychology, as philosophy, is the study of persons. Most psychologists prefer to define psychology as the *science of behavior*; and many would object to our definition on one or both of two counts: it leaves out animal studies, which make up a large part of the work of experimental psychologists, and it includes experience, a subject considered inappropriate for scientific study.

Other psychologists, who favor the inclusion of subjective experience, would prefer not to limit this definition to *philosophical* psychology. They would insist that a true *science* of psychology must come to grips with persons in all their complexity.

All of these are important objections. We agree that animal studies belong in psychology, and the reader will find a summary of them in Chapters 8 and 9. We strongly agree that a true science of psychology must come to grips with subjective phenomena, and we only make the distinction between philosophical and scientific psychology as an expedient so that we may present the case for a humanistic psychology without continually trying to prove that we are being scientific. We realize that there are convincing reasons for questioning whether data should be called "scientific" until the exacting demands of scientific criteria have been met. But we do not agree that a field of study, which is primarily concerned with understanding human beings, should refuse to deal with that which is most human just because it is difficult to develop scientific methods for studying it. Rather than try to settle issues on which our best psychologists do not agree, we shall explore, as best we can, the area of the personal. We call it "philosophical," not because it is unscientific, but because so much of the best theorizing in this area has not yet been subjected to critical scientific tests.

We admit that it is extremely difficult to obtain reliable data about this inner world of persons. We also admit that there are times when important experimental studies can best be conducted by choosing to ignore what may be going on "inside" the subjects being studied. The fact remains, however, that we all know something *is* going on inside the subjects and inside the experimenter; and any general psychology must find a central place for these inner facts. As Gordon Allport, the dean of personality psychologists, insists,

> Do not forget what you have decided to neglect. If you have a neat
> S-R formula for a certain type of learning—fine; just don't forget
> that you have decided to neglect other forms of learning. If you are
> working with animal drives—fine; but don't forget that you have
> bracketed human aspirations.[2]

Ivan Pavlov, whose classical conditioning experiments stand as a model of objectivity, gives his reasons for ignoring the subjective in his work:

> This is the reason why, from the strictly scientific point of view, it
> seems to me that the position of psychology as a study of subjective
> states is completely hopeless. Certainly these states for us are a
> reality of the first order; they give direction to our daily life, they
> condition the progress of human society. But it is one thing to live
> according to subjective states, and quite another thing to analyze
> purely scientifically their mechanism. . . . After persistent delibera-
> tion, after a considerable mental conflict, I decided finally, in regard
> to the so-called psychical stimulation, to remain in the role of a pure
> physiologist, i.e., of an objective external observer and experimenter
> having to do exclusively with external phenomena and their relations.[3]

Note that Pavlov recognizes that subjective states are a reality of the first order, that we live by them and human society depends on them; yet, he believes that they cannot be subjected to scientific study and, therefore, psychology should ignore them. This is an honest statement and it tells us that Pavlov made a decision. It remains for us not to forget that Pavlov and other objectivists made a decision, and to make our own decisions.

This text reflects a different decision from that of Pavlov.

Chapter 2, *The Person*, is a direct expression of the decision to include the subjective in psychology.

Chapter 3, *The Social Milieu*, is a description of the environment in which persons must develop and live.

Chapter 4, *The Interpersonal*, is a description of the ways in which persons interact with other persons in the social milieu.

Chapter 5, *Reactions to Frustration*, explores the ways in which persons may act when they are blocked in their efforts to reach goals which are important to them.

Since we have not yet found adequate scientific tools for quantitative statements in these areas, these chapters are about philosophical psychology.

Actually, philosophy is the mother of all sciences, and it is not fitting that any science should despise philosophy. Philosophy has been defined as "man's effort to see things clearly and to see them whole." As scientific methods become available, true philosophy gladly assimilates the facts discovered. Until such methods are available, our search for understanding of persons must remain largely philosophical.

2

THE PERSON AS ORGANISM
AND AS EXPERIENCING SELF

Psychology, as we have asserted, may be thought of as the study of persons. Perhaps, as one philosopher has suggested, psychology should study all individuals, even electrons and protons. Certainly many species of animals have proved to be a fruitful source of psychological knowledge. But the individuals we are primarily concerned with are persons, members of the species homo sapiens *who are capable of achieving selfhood.*

THE HUMAN ORGANISM

A detailed description of the species characteristics of man is beyond the scope of this book. Nevertheless, it is useful to remember a few of the most notable characteristics of the human organism.

Helplessness

Man is born into the world as the most helpless of creatures. He is "unfinished" and vulnerable. Equipped with only a few reflexes, in contrast to the instinctual "preprogramming" of other species, there is little that he can do for himself but cry. Unless some "mothering one" cares and responds with tenderness to this crying, the human being does not live long. The dependence necessitated by this helplessness continues biologically for about twelve years and socially for nearly twenty years.

Neural Equipment

The most noticeable part of the newborn baby is its head, which is out of proportion to the rest of its body. Centered in a brain, which largely fills this head, the human being comes with a nervous system that is awe–inspiring. Experts differ as to the complexity of this "computer system," but all agree that the size of an electronic computer that would rival it in complexity would be somewhere between the size of the Empire State Building and the size of this planet!

Furthermore, this computing system is amazingly open to the environment. Its entire surface is vulnerable to the environment and, hence, sensitive to it. The surface sends to the inner computer a constant stream of "information bits" by means of which the environment is introjected, or brought inside.

Malleability

The combination of the "unfinished" character of man and this superior neural equipment makes him extremely malleable or shapable. There are practically infinite possibilities open for man; and, in fact, we find that there are many different ways of being human. With few instincts to guide him, but with a marvelous capacity for information gathering, storage, and retrieval, man has come to rely on learning, reasoning, and creating.

Motor Ability

There are countless activities that man cannot do as well as other animals, but in two areas his motor ability enables him to adapt to his environment in a way no other animal can match. One is manual dexterity. By walking upright, man is free to use his hands to wield weapons and tools, and the ability to oppose the thumb and forefinger gives him the dexterity expressed in his complicated technology. The other motor ability is speech with which man can symbolize his environment and communicate with his fellows in such a way as to make possible the kind of cooperative activity that has been the key to his survival.

Social Nature

Man's helplessness has demanded that he be a social animal; and his brain and speaking ability have made this way of life possible. The earliest archaeological evidence of human life reveals man as a social being. It was the only way he could survive, and it is the only way that he is likely to continue to survive.

Self-consciousness

Brain development, learning ability, speech, and closeness with his fellows—these come to a focus in man's most unique characteristic, his self-consciousness. We need not deny some dim form of self-awareness in other animals, but man is so much more self-aware that he is qualitatively different in this respect. He not only knows; he knows that he knows. And he knows himself. This is man's most precious ability which can be his greatest problem.

EXPERIENCING SELF

Experience of Self

By experience of self we mean the whole subjective realm in which persons live. Experience has to do with awareness or consciousness, in all its degrees, from the kind of awareness we paradoxically call "unconsciousness" to the most intense forms of wide-awakeness. It has to do with feeling, thinking, wishing, wanting, questioning, deciding, dreaming, planning, despairing, losing oneself, and finding oneself.

The Questionable Aspects of "Inner World" Experiences

It is not without reason that the subjective realm has been questioned or that a researcher of Pavlov's stature should say, as we have already noted, "a study of subjective states is completely hopeless" (p. 24). The history of the attempts to study psychic life does not give us much confidence. In poetry, drama, and novels we have a vast amount of keen description which we recognize as true, but all attempts to produce a science of the mind have so far yielded little that is usable. The monumental work of the structuralists, so impressive in its painstaking methodology and so sterile in its results; the reasonable approach of the functionalists, so appealing in its underlying assumptions and so promising still in its methodology; the daring and imaginative system of psychoanalysis, so influential in the popular world and so controversial among scholars; the approach of the Gestaltists, so courageous and different but so obscure and academic— these, as well as other schools of psychology, have not given us the kind of reliable data about the mind that physics, chemistry, and physiology have in their areas. Though written in 1890, and that by a man of genius who, more boldly than most, dared to attempt a description of "the stream of consciousness," the words of William James remain a true summary of the situation psychology faces in its efforts to scientifically describe man's subjective life.

When, then, we talk of "psychology as a natural science," we must not assume that that means a sort of psychology that stands at last on solid ground. It means just the reverse; it means a psychology particularly fragile, and into which the waters of metaphysical criticism leak at every joint, a psychology all of whose elementary assumptions and data must be reconsidered in wider connections and translated into other terms. . . A string of raw facts; a little gossip and wrangle about opinions; a little classification and generalization on the mere descriptive level; a strong prejudice that we *have* states of mind, and that our brain conditions them: but not a single law in the sense in which physics shows us laws, not a single proposition from which any consequences can be causally deduced. We don't even know the terms between which the elementary laws would obtain if we had them. This is no science, it is only the hope of a science. . . Something definite happens when to a certain brain-state a certain 'consciousness' corresponds. A genuine glimpse into what it is would be *the* scientific achievement, before which all past achievements would pale. But at present psychology is in the condition of physics before Galileo and the laws of motion, of chemistry before Lavoisier and the notion that mass is preserved in all reactions. The Galileo and the Lavoisier of psychology will be famous men indeed when they come, as come they some day surely will, or past successes are no index to the future. When they do come, however, the necessities of the case will make them "metaphysical." Meanwhile the best way in which we can facilitate their advent is to

> understand how great is the darkness in which we grope, and never
> to forget that the natural–science assumptions with which we
> started are provisional and revisable things.[4]

Here are some of the questions which plague us as we seek more assured know-ledge of the inner world.

1. Does a person really know what is going on within himself? Even if he is sincere, he may be deceiving himself. He may be subject to illusions, hallucinations, and delusions; or he may not have access to the important causative processes.

2. Even if a person does know what is going on within him, can he communicate his reality to another person? Is there any assurance that the meaning he is putting into words is the meaning another person will get from them? The semanticist's warning is appropriate here: "Words don't mean; people mean."

3. Even if a person can communicate his real experience, *will* he? And how can we tell whether or not he is reporting honestly? He may be deceiving himself as well as the one to whom he communicates. In other words, he may honestly think that he is being truthful but "unconscious" forces may be causing him to distort.

4. Is there such thing as "raw" individual experience? While a person may think that a feeling is his own, maybe he is just saying what he has been conditioned to say by his culture. For example, someone might actually enjoy eating snails, but he has been taught to express feelings of revulsion toward such behavior.

Just to review the difficulties is to discourage us! Is there any hope of testing the reality either of our own experiences or the reported experiences of others?

Some Tentative Principles for Testing Experience

The following principles may indicate directions in which answers may be found. Some are common–sensible, some are philosophical, and some are applications of scientific principles.

Cross-checking between sensory modalities. Here we have a common sense idea that most of us have used. If we find it "hard to believe our eyes," we seek further information with our ears or our sense of touch. Illusions and hallucinations tend to occur in only one sense modality at a time. Another common saying is, "I pinched myself to see if I was awake." Here, again, we are cross-checking.

A safe generalization is that *an experience in one sense modality which is confirmed by that of another sense modality increases in validity, while an experience in one modality which is not supported by that of another decreases in validity.*

Stability over time. All of us have felt or thought something which later seemed less real to us; while other experiences have sometimes become more real with the passage of time. In the former case we might say, "I must have been dreaming," or "It seemed that way then, but now it doesn't." In the latter case we might say, "Everything which has happened has confirmed what I felt," or "Nothing else has happened to confirm it, but I *know* it was real." Confirmation of experience may result from the re-occurrence of the same experience, from other experiences which confirm it, or from the forcefulness with which the original experience continues to seem real.

By itself stability over time does not insure the reality of an experience. There are some experiences which, upon reflection, we reject, but later find that they were valid. Nevertheless, stability over time is one of the common tests to which we subject experiences—"You think that's what you want to do, but wait until tomorrow and see how you feel then."

This principle needs refinement, but it gets at something important. *An experience which seems more real with the passage of time has more validity than one which seems less real with the passage of time.*

Consistency with other experiences. When something conforms to our expectations, we accept it more readily than when it does not. When it does conform, we get "convergent feedback"; and when it does not, we get "divergent feedback." These terms are used in cybernetics. This principle is important, but it does not prove or disprove the validity of an experience because many things turn out to be true that we did not expect and vice versa. Nevertheless, divergent feedback raises questions that we cannot ignore without losing our integrity. A man cannot, with equanimity, hear a dog speak or see a cat fly; he must become bothered or else give up the effort to know anything.

Even though this principle is not sufficient for determining the reality or unreality of an experience, it is one of the most important principles in the search for reality. *An experience which is inconsistent with previous experiences that were accepted as real, raises questions about itself and/or those previous experiences. The inconsistency results in the tension of an unresolved dissonance.*

Logical reasoning. This principle is an extension of the last one, but it is more abstract. From our experiences and the teaching we receive from others we develop a system of ideas and principles by which we understand and deal with the world. When we have a strange experience, we test it with this system. If it is inconsistent with, or unexplainable in terms of these principles, we have the same kind of problem described in the third principle above: there is divergent feedback. Again, this does not prove anything, but we cannot ignore the situation. Questions have been raised which call for answers.

An experience which is inconsistent with logical principles that we have accepted raises questions about itself and/or our logical principles. The result is again the tension of an unresolved dissonance.

Evidence from correlates. Here we have a principle which a person may use to check his own experience or to evaluate the reality of an experience reported by someone else. This principle is a specific application of the third and fourth principles which deserves a separate description. Things that go together are said to be correlated. For example, when I feel hot, the temperature in my surroundings, as measured by a wall thermometer, is high, or the temperature of my body, as measured by a doctor's thermometer, is high. Now if I report that I am hot, but neither thermometer registers hot, I would be bothered. If this happened to me, I would think, "It must be in my mind." If someone else reported it, I would think, "Either he is not telling the truth or it is in his mind." Again, if we see someone stuck with a needle or burned with a hot iron, we would expect him to cry out in pain. If he does not, then we wonder: "Is he pretending? Is he hypnotized? Are his nerves dead? Is it a real needle or a real hot iron? Am I dreaming?" If someone with a big smile says he is in great pain, or that he really wants something he is making no effort to get, I begin to question since the expected correlates are missing.

The validity of an experience increases when it occurs along with experiences known to be correlated with it. Its validity decreases when it occurs with experiences not known to be correlated.

Interpersonal validation. The term "consensual validation" refers to the method of proof based on agreement between people. A common sense example is the claim that "fifty million Frenchmen can't be wrong." If I see something that another person with me cannot, this discrepancy raises questions. How many times has a person who was frightened at a noise asked his companion, "Did you hear that?" It is heartening when the answer is, "I sure did."

What we mean by "interpersonal validation" goes much further than ordinary consensual validation. Here we are proposing what may well be a key that could unlock the inner world of experience. Psychotherapists, from Freud's first work until now, have been concerned about how to get at the reality of a man's inner world. Hypnosis, free association, and dream analysis were used by Freud. Some have used sodium pentothal (so-called "truth serum"); others have used projective tests, word association tests, and questionnaires. Carl Rogers developed an approach called "non-directive" or "client-centered" counseling, in which the therapist accepts the client in a warm and understanding way that is consistent and genuine. Rogers believes that it is in such a relationship that a person is most likely to experience his real feelings and to communicate them with less distortion.

Obviously, day-to-day relationships are not so safe as the relationship Rogers describes. Nevertheless, with certain people we are less likely to distort our feelings or the report of them, while with certain other people we feel so anxious that we don't tell them how we feel and we may even hide our feelings from ourselves. Thus it is in good interpersonal relationships that the process of validating experiences is most realiable. Sidney Jourard suggests in *Disclosing*

Man to Himself,[5] that the inner world of experience may be validated only for the person himself, and only when he feels most secure in a relationship. This same degree of reality may be reached by two people who respect and care for one another. But it may never be possible for one man to know for certain what is in the mind of another if he does not want it known. For the sake of human values and freedom, we may hope that this remains so.

The most reliable method for validating the reality of an experience is to talk about it with another person who seeks to understand and accept with warmth, and who responds with genuineness.

The implications of this interpersonal relationship and its contribution to the process by which we validate our own experiences will be presented in Chapter 4 where we consider the realm of the interpersonal.

Can Subjectivity be Objectively Demonstrated?

The only experience we know is subjective or private. We know our own experience directly, and we imagine the experience of another by listening to what he says and by making inferences from his behavior. It should be noted that any inferences we make from behavior to experience are rooted in our own experience.

As we noted before, it is the inherently subjective nature of experience that has made a science of experience so difficult to achieve. However, the principles for validating experience which we have suggested show that the subjective is not without its lawfulness. *Subjectivity* is not a synonym for *imaginary* or for *unfounded*. Some of the experiments on perception (which we report in Chapter 8) have looked at some of the simpler subjective processes with some degree of objectivity.

While we have not yet found ways of demonstrating the reality of the subjective by means of objective data, we need not deny the subjective. For that matter, there is no way of demonstrating to someone the reality of the *objective* unless he subjectively decides that he will accept the proofs for the objective. Thus it is objectivity which rests on the subjective rather than the other way around. It is as if cells were asked to prove to molecules that cells exist, but the cells are required to do so without referring to anything but molecules. The cell knows the molecule, but the molecule does not know the cell. Thus the subjective can know both the subjective and the objective, but the objective cannot know the subjective.

The evidence for the subjective is all of a subjective nature, and the principles which enable us to distinguish one subjective state from another must be found within the subjective or some higher order. Before postulating such a higher order, let us see what we already know about experience in terms of experience.

Language: The Door to the Subjective

Human language, in contrast to the more rudimentary sounds that animals make (which seem to function largely as signals), is both the product and instrument of subjectivity. Some of our language is not different from animal sounds. Our cries and grunts, our moans and groans of pain or ecstasy are not fundamentally different from the so-called language of the higher animals. But the greater part of human language is much more than this. It is a way of symbolizing our sensations, perceptions, emotions, and thoughts. Most important, for our purposes, is the language of the self—the sentences in which "I" is the subject or where "me" is the object.

"I sit here at my desk typing. I am writing a book. The thought of this book both excites and frightens me. I feel tired. My back aches. The light from the desk lamp shines on me and it feels warm. I open the window and a cool breeze blows against my face. It feels good. I know that I am doing these things, and I know that some things are happening to me. I like some of these and I don't like others. I want to stop working, but I want to finish the book."

The last paragraph is an example of the language of the self. Some of the statements are more objective than others. For example, "I sit here at my desk typing" is more objective because what I am doing can easily be verified by other people; it is public. The same is true for "the light shines on my face," "I open the window," and "I am writing a book." Other statements are more subjective. For example, "I feel tired," "it feels good," "my back aches," and "I want to stop working." When I wrote the sentences as they flowed into my mind, I did not have the feeling that I was switching from subjective to objective. I was reporting experiences, all of which seemed equally real to me. While some of the statements would be more difficult for another person to validate, I feel equally sure of them all.

The Dimensions of Experience

What, then, are the dimensions of experience as revealed by the language of the self?

I sense. I sense warmth and cold, I sense pressures and pains, I sense light and sounds and odors and tastes, and I sense movement and position.

The tactile sense differs from the others in that when I touch something I usually feel both the thing I am touching and my finger touching it. We distinguish the two aspects of this experience by saying, "I feel the table; it feels smooth."

Much scientific knowledge has been gained about the neural processes involved in sensory experiences. Some of these data can be found in Chapter 9.

I feel. It is interesting that we use the same word for both the tactile sense and for emotion. Perhaps it is tactile experience that is most likely to arouse emotions of pleasure or displeasure. At any rate, we shall distinguish sensations from emotions and use "feel" in referring to the latter.

I feel excited or calm. I feel ecstatic or depressed. I feel joyful or sad. I feel pleased or displeased. I feel secure or fearful. I feel energetic or lethargic. I feel relief or anxiety. I feel satisfied or dissatisfied. I feel angry or calm.

These feelings occur in connection with organismic changes, such as accelerated heart rate, redistribution of blood, sweating, abdominal cramping, etc. In fact, William James, in his famous theory of the emotions, proposed that emotions are nothing more than the awareness of these physiological changes. Cannon and Bard, who had more knowledge of the nervous system, demonstrated that neural activity in the hypothalamus (a lower center in the brain) is the basis for emotional experiences. Common sense asserts that there is usually some situational reason for feeling a certain way, and recent experiments by Schacter confirm this notion (see Chapter 9).

I know. To sense and to feel is, of course, a kind of knowing, and here again we see the artificiality and the impossibility of analyzing experience which is a whole. Nevertheless there are experiences designated by "I know" which are different from those designated by "I sense" and "I feel." The object of sensing is a stimulus: I sense heat, light, sounds, etc. Feelings (emotions) do not refer primarily to objects but to states of the subject: I am angry, I am sad, etc.; but knowing has an object which is *some thing.* The only way I know is by knowing about something; the only way I am aware is to be aware of something. The simplest form of knowing we call *perception*, which is the patterning (through selection and filling in) of stimuli. Something becomes defined or recognizable and capable of being responded to. Gestalt psychologists call this something a *figure*, and what is left out of this patterning they call *ground.*

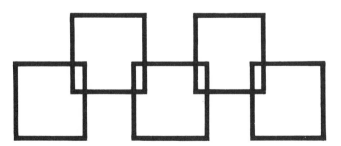

Figure 1. Figure and Ground

A more complex form of knowing might be called *knowing how* which refers to the perception of relationships. This process makes it possible to solve some problem. Köhler, the Gestalt psychologist famous for his work with apes, calls this kind of knowing *insight.* In his classic experiment with Sultan, he demonstrated that an ape, after considerable experience with the component parts, can suddenly "see" that boxes piled on top of each other can be used to reach bananas otherwise out of reach.

A still more complex form of knowing is *understanding*; but we have now crossed a most important threshold called *thinking.*

I think. By thinking we mean the process that deals with stimuli no longer present to the senses. When I perceive, that which I perceive is now present to the senses, or else I am hallucinating. But if I respond to something no longer present to the senses, there must be some *representation* of that to which I am responding. This representation may be an image, a sign, or a concept. To have an insight is to see a relationship as Sultan did; to understand is to go a step further—to see a principle which can be abstracted from the specific situation and applied in similar situations.

Once we are able to make representations of things and of relationships between things, an amazing world of possibilities opens to us. We can remember, whether it be recognition, recall, or reminiscing. We can ponder, whether by imaginary trial-and-error problem solving, careful analytic reasoning, or random exploration of possibilities just for the fun of it. We can plan, decide, doubt, and dream (fantasize).

Thinking is sometimes classified into two types: realistic and autistic. Realistic thinking includes all of the symbolic processes that deal with components of reality, including the logical processes of deductive and inductive reasoning, as well as evaluative and creative thinking. Autistic thinking includes fantasies, delusions, and other private symbolic processes which have meaning only in the mind of the thinker.

I want. Here we come to a controversial problem: Is there such a thing as motivation? For some theorists motivation is their central concept. Freud, Adler, and McDougall represent this position and are called *dynamic* psychologists. Others exclude motivation from their formulations. B. F. Skinner is the most famous representative of this position known as *operationism.*

On the surface, the issue seems clear. Of course there is motivation! When I want something, I know that I want; you can't fool me! But it is not that simple. What is it to want? Is it to need (to be in want)? Is it to desire? Does it simply refer to the likelihood that something will happen?

One writer has said,

> But to say I want something and do nothing about getting it is not to mean what I say, not to really want it, but merely to wish for it.[6]

It is this idea, too, that Skinner is expressing when he says that what we call motivation is only another way of saying that something is very likely to happen. Therefore, concepts of motivation explain nothing. In other words, why does a rat eat? Because it is hungry. How do we know it is hungry? Because it is eating!

On the other hand, we know that two occurrences of behavior may not *mean* the same thing. Doing something for one reason is not the same thing as doing it for another reason. Here we run into the question of causality and teleology. What causes behavior and what is the purpose of behavior? We usually discover meaning when we discover relationships. When we discover that eating is related to the fact that an animal has been deprived of food for 48 hours, we say that we understand why he is eating. We might add that it is because he is hungry. If a rat who has not been deprived of food is eating, we look for some other reason. Since the administration of a mild electric shock to the hypothalamus is highly correlated with eating in well-fed animals, we think that the shock *causes* the eating. In the case of complex behavior, since it is difficult to find causes, we look for *purposes*. Whether we speak of causes or purposes or motivation, the meaning of behavior is understandable only when we know something about the factors related to it.

Some writers distinguish between *push* and *pull* types of motivation.[7] Push motivation refers to what drives one to act, and pull motivation refers to what attracts one to act. Other writers distinguish between extrinsic and intrinsic factors in motivation. Maslow[8] distinguishes between deficiency and growth motivation.

Human beings report experiences most vividly in the words "I want." A thirsty man says, "I want water!" Someone faced with death says "I don't want to die." In these cases the words "I want" do not seem separate from the whole movement of the person. At other times, "I want to" is followed by an unspoken "but." This reservation leads to the question of the *will*.

Few questions in philosophy have been so controversial as whether or not there is free will, with the determinists on the one hand and the voluntarists on the other. Is there genuine freedom, or is all behavior caused in the same sense that physical reactions are caused? We shall keep questions of motivation (cause or purpose) and freedom (will) in mind as we take a look at "happenings" and "doings."

Something happens vs. I do it. There is nothing clearer in our awareness than that we move and act. But at one extreme, we perform actions for which we feel no responsibility; they just seem to happen. In this sense, we treat them as we do our bodily processes. My heart beats, my stomach digests, I blush, I flinch at pain, my knee jerks when it is tapped—all these happen without my willing that they should. On the other extreme, we perform actions for which we feel completely responsible; "I did it." We own these actions and claim that this behavior occurs because we will it, we choose it, we decide it, we want it.

Behavior in between these two extremes seems to be part happening and part doing. I itch so I scratch myself; I am hungry so I eat; I am sleepy so I go to bed. Depending on how strong the push or pull is in these cases, we feel either more or less responsible for the behavior. If the push is very strong, we say, "I did it, but I couldn't help it." If the push is not so strong, we say, "Sure, I was sleepy but I didn't have to go to sleep; I was just careless." What is it that determines whether behavior is a happening or a doing? Whatever is the determiner should be related to the questions raised above, about motivation and freedom.

The principle involved here seems to be one of mediating processes. You remember that Watson (the behaviorist) took Dewey's S-R (reflex arc) as his basic model, while the functionalists went on to transform S-R into S-O-R. Pure happenings (like the knee jerk) seem to involve simpler, older, deeper, and more direct mediating processes than do pure doings. The more habitual or reflexive behavior becomes, the more it becomes a happening and the less responsibility we feel for it. It is interesting to note that reflexive behavior is mediated by nerve centers close to the involuntary nervous system. On the other hand, behavior that involves careful planning and deliberate decision is mediated by nerve centers in the cerebral cortex, especially in the frontal lobes.[9] Behavior between these two extremes seems to be some mixture of these two kinds of mediation. Figure 2 schematically illustrates this idea.

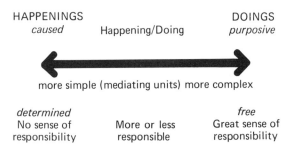

Figure 2. Happenings and Doings Compared

According to this theory, happenings are caused or determined, and do not involve a feeling of responsibility. Doings are purposive or chosen, they are experienced as genuinely free, and they do involve a feeling of responsibility.

I am. It remains for us to consider whether or not there is a genuine experience of "I am" since it may be an abstraction or derivative from other experiences such as "I act" or "I think." Descartes derived the certainty of existence from the act of thinking: "I think; therefore I am." It was also Descartes, who, perhaps without intending it, set the stage for the dualism which first clearly separated the subjective and the objective, then gave priority to the objective over the subjective. It has been against this tendency, of course, that the existentialists have objected so strenuously.

Linguistically, "I am" requires a predicate noun or a predicate adjective—"I am a man" or "I am tall." Judeo–Christian theology has insisted that "I am" without any qualifiers is a synonym for God; that God is the only complete being while all other beings are contingent or partial. This study of being is called *ontology*. We shall not go into the theological question here, but the ontological or existential question is one that psychologists must face. Is there an experience of existing?

Recent research on sensory deprivation indicates that our sense of identity is dependent on adequate sensory input. Clinical experience suggests that people feel more alive when they have good relationships with other people. It is difficult to imagine how we could feel that we exist if we did not have any sensations, whether from without or from within. It seems most reasonable to hypothesize that all of the other dimensions of experience we have so far noted are mediators of the "I am" experience and that it is a dimension within each of these. "I sense" is more accurately stated, "I am sensing" or "This is a sensing I." So with all the others: I am feeling, I am knowing, I am thinking, I am wanting, and I am doing.

SUMMARY

If psychology is to do justice to the study of human beings, as well as lower animals, it must deal with so-called subjective phenomena. If it cannot yet do so according to the strict criteria of science, then it must do so within the framework of a sound philosophical approach.

The person may be studied as an organism and as an experiencing self. As an organism, man is characterized by an "unfinished" quality at birth and a long period of development. He is equipped with a fantastic nervous system and is very much exposed to his environment which greatly influences the course of his development. The successful survival of man as a species has depended on his manual dexterity, speaking ability, and sociability. However, his most impressive attribute is his self–consciousness.

As an experiencing self, man presents an unusually difficult problem for scientific study. "Inner world" experiences, while very real to all of us, are difficult to validate objectively. There are, however, subjective principles which can be used to check the validity of our experiences. Perhaps the most important avenue to the subjective is language, especially language related to the self. Linguistic analysis makes clear that we recognize many dimensions of experience.

QUESTIONS FOR STUDY AND CLASS DISCUSSION

1. Compare science and philosophy. Is one more "true" than the other?

2. How is our understanding of man enriched by studying him as an organism?

3. How is man's helplessness at birth and his long period of dependency related to later personal problems?

4. If man's brain is such a fantastic "computer," how much of this computer capacity do you think an average man uses?

5. How did man's special motor abilities serve him in his earliest days? Are these motor abilities relied on more or less today?

6. Why did sociability have such survival value for early man? Is it as important today?

7. How would you go about "proving" to someone that you feel a particular way?

8. How useful do you think linguistic analysis is for studying experience?

9. Which seems more "real" to you, the desk in your room or the feeling you are having right now?

10. Do you seem more real or alive at some times than you do at other times? If so, what are some of the factors involved?

SUGGESTIONS FOR FURTHER READING

de Chardin, Pierre Teilhard. *The Phenomenon of Man.* New York: Harper Torchbooks, 1961.

Jourard, Sidney M. *Disclosing Man to Himself.* Princeton: D. Van Nostrand Co., 1968.

Maslow, Abraham. *Toward a Psychology of Being.* Princeton: D. Van Nostrand Co., 1962.

McCurdy, Harold G. *Personality and Science.* Princeton: D. Van Nostrand Co., 1965.

Rogers, Carl R., and Stevens, Barry. *Person to Person: The Problem of Being Human.* Walnut Creek, California: Real People Press, 1967.

3

THE SOCIAL MILIEU

The organismic view, set forth by Darwin and applied to behavior by the functionalists, states that man adapts to his environment. It is easily overlooked, however, that man's social milieu is of greater significance than his physical environment. In the past 25,000 years, the changes in man have been cultural, not biological. Whether societies have survived or not has depended on their cultural achievements.

Man is a social being, and he can be understood only in the context of his society. He might be able to live in total isolation (we have no clear evidence on this in spite of the stories about so-called "wolf-children"), but it is impossible to conceive of human life except in the company of other human beings. All human life that we know is social in nature.

THE SOCIETIES INTO WHICH WE ARE BORN

We often speak of "society" as if there were just one big force "out there" with which we must deal. Even in the simplest of cultures, a person might belong to a particular family and, perhaps, a clan, as well as the total tribe or political unit. A child born in America faces a much more complex situation. He belongs to a family, and usually a kinship group. His family belongs to a socioeconomic class, a racial group, a political party, a town or part of a city, and often to a religious group. All of these groups are part of a nation and a grouping of nations. To make matters more confusing, these various groups are often in conflict. Therefore, to speak of "society's influence" is meaningless. We must look more specifically at the various societies which influence us.

The Family

With a few exceptions, the primary group into which a baby is born is some kind of family organization. The particular way in which the family is organized differs widely from culture to culture, and even among the sub-cultures of the larger culture; but whatever the organization, no other society influences the development of personality as much as the family. The naturalist, Loren Eiseley, puts it this way:

> To the student of human evolution this remarkable and unique adjustment of our peculiar infancy to a lengthened family relationship between adults is one of the more mysterious episodes in the history of life. It is so strange, in fact, that only in one group of creatures—that giving rise to man—has it been successfully developed in the three billion years or so that life has existed on the planet. Family life is a fact that underlies everything else about man—his capacity for absorbing culture, his ability to learn—everything, in short, that enables us to call him human. He is born of love and he exists by reason of a love more continuous than in any other form of life.[1]

The influence of the family begins before the baby is born. We do not speak here of genetic influences, which will be considered in Chapter 7. Here we are concerned with social influences, such as how the family feels about the arrival of a baby, or *another* baby. Is the baby awaited with proud expectancy or is its coming dreaded because of shame, in the case of illegitimacy, or of anxiety, in the case of economic or marital difficulties?

When the baby is born, other factors determine family attitudes. Is it a boy or a girl? Is it healthy or sick, is it damaged or intact? In some primitive societies, even before the baby's first breath, a hasty examination was made to see if it was a boy. If not, it was often killed. Families in other societies, not so drastic, either shouted with joy or cried in anguish when the sex was determined. Even in our enlightened society, many a child who was born the "wrong" sex has grown up experiencing hostile attitudes as a result. The consequences of being sick or crippled can be even greater, and even a baby's physical attractiveness can affect the attitudes of those around him.

Additional factors are birth order, multiple births, age of parents, presence of other adults in the home, and many other influences which determine the way the baby is treated by the family.

Of course, the most important family influences are expressed in the close interpersonal relationships within which the child develops, and these we shall trace more carefully in the next chapter.

The Sub-cultures

The baby does not know it for some time, but from the day of his birth his lot is cast with a particular group of people with whom he will spend much, if not all, of his life. His father's occupation and/or income is one of the determiners. We call this factor economic class. His parents' parents may be another determiner. His parents may have come from so-called "better" or from so-called "undesirable" families. This factor largely determines social class. One of the most important determiners of the group in which he will move is skin color. If he is black, much of the white world may be closed to him, as will be true in some places if he is "brown," "red," or "yellow." There are also religious groupings, geographical groupings (the North, the South, etc.), and ethnic groupings that have nothing to do with color.

In cultures of low mobility a person is likely to spend his entire life in the sub-culture into which he was born. In other cultures he may move from one sub-culture to another. Nevertheless, for most people, the sub-culture into which they are born determines to a large extent the one in which they will work and live, and gives them peculiarities which are difficult to eradicate completely. As an old saying goes, "You can take the boy out of the country, but you can't take the country out of the boy."

The Larger Culture

Here we refer to more general groupings such as nation, group of nations, or even the broad distinction of East versus the West. In terms of social demands made upon him, it is a man's nation that is most crucial; but it is the long-term cultural stream into which he is born that most influences his spirit. For Americans this stream is western civilization, with its Greco-Roman background and Judea-Christian heritage.

It takes little imagination to conceive of how different one would be if he had been born in the East rather than the West, in China rather than England, in Russia rather than in America, or in the Congo rather than in Australia.

THE MEDIUMS OF CULTURE

Within the various societies we have described there are important mediums through which the culture reaches and shapes us. If Marshall McLuhan is right that "the medium is the message," then each of the mediums which we shall notice is not so much the mediator of culture as it is the culture itself. Whichever position we take on this issue, several media demand our attention.

Language

Language serves as the primary medium for culture. Every human being is born into a linguistic world which shapes the way he sees himself and others, which makes thinking possible and yet limits the scope of his thinking, and which affects him in countless other ways of which he will probably never be aware. Just as fish are probably not aware of water, the average man does not develop an awareness of the linguistic world in which he lives.

The origins of language are not known, but interesting clues are available in animal studies, archaeological remains from prehistoric man, comparative studies of cultures, and developmental studies of children.

Animal studies indicate that pigeons and doves use as many as 12 specific sounds, dogs as many as 15, cattle as many as 22, and apes as many as 30. There is not a very great *quantitative* difference between the ape's 30 sounds and the 300 words used by some men,[2,3] though qualitatively there are great differences. Recent work with the porpoise suggests that it makes use of a very complex signalling system, and even the bee utilizes a system for communicating information that is so accurate and complex as to be called a language.[4]

The language that we see in animals falls mostly into the category of *emotional expressions which come to serve as signals*. Here we do not need to hypothesize an intent to communicate, and in the interest of parsimony* we will refrain from doing so. Some animal language, however, borders on intentional communication, particularly the dance by which bees communicate the direction, distance, and amount of nectar they have found.

Archaeological remains of early man reveal a well developed sense of imagery. He drew pictures of the animals he knew and made designs on his pottery. We can guess that this capacity to "image" things led to the first picture writing and that the gestures and sounds (to which we referred above) were imitative. Will Durant reminds us that we still rely heavily on gestures and imitative sounds (like roar, rush, murmur, tremor, giggle, groan, hiss, heave, hum, cackle, etc.), and he tells the following story:

> The Englishman eating his first meal in China, and wishing to know the character of the meat he was eating, inquired, with Anglo-Saxon dignity and reserve, 'Quack, quack?' To which the Chinaman, shaking his head, answered cheerfully, 'Bow-wow.'[5]

Studies of undeveloped cultures indicate that even the simplest of these have a language, though not necessarily written.[6] We know that spoken language is very much older than writing. The vocabularies of peoples differ greatly among themselves, and these differences clearly relate to the differences in their environments and styles of life. For example, in the Arabic language there are about 6,000 names associated in some way with camel, while among the Eskimos there are about 50 words for snow.[7] It seems clear that language is functional, in that it developed in response to need.

Developmental studies of children cannot tell us anything about how a language originally developed, but they do give some clues about the sounds humans can make and the process by which a language is shaped from these sounds. For example, there are no inherent differences in the sounds of infants all over the world. While their earliest sounds are one syllable cries, within the first few days they most frequently make eight distinguishable sounds, which represent about one fifth of the sound elements used by adults. By the time he is two-and-a-half, the average child in any country uses 27 phonemes (speech sounds). As the child babbles certain of his sounds are reinforced by the response of adults. These sounds tend to be repeated and come to be associated with meanings assigned to them by the adults.[8]

Far more important than its origins, however, is the function of language in society. Four functions stand out:

---

*Loyd Morgan suggested that science should follow a policy of parsimony or stinginess in developing hypotheses. This means that in trying to explain animal behavior we should not use explanatory concepts which were developed to explain the more complex behaving of human beings.

The means of cooperation. We have noted that man has survived through the cooperation of community life. Language is the key to this cooperation: to give signals for action, to assign positions and give commands; and to communicate the subtle cues involved in playing complicated roles.

The reservoir of a community's learning. Starting from scratch, one man or a community of men can learn very little. But, once language developed, what one generation learned could be taught to the next. Thus, through language, we are heir to the learning of at least 10,000 years and probably much more. This reservoir of learning contains not only the factual knowledge slowly gleaned from experience, but, more important, the wisdom that has accumulated from the mistakes and suffering of all previous generations. Much of this wisdom was carried in the myths and legends parents told their children.

The basis for shared meaning. Man not only cooperates and learns by means of language, he experiences his humanity through talking with his fellow man. Theodora Kroeber wrote about the last of the primitive Indians who lived in California in the late nineteenth century. Using information taken from Ishi, the lone survivor of these "stone age" people who stumbled into civilization in 1911, she reconstructed the way in which these people shared meanings.

> Harvest time was friendly and gossipy and neighborly. What the men and women and children learned and experienced during the days of the big encampments would be the raw material for conversation, speculation, and philosophizing after everyone was home again, and the days drew in.[9]

We do not know how the earliest men spent the long evening hours of winter, huddled around their fires, but we can guess that many of the words and gestures used were those of one human being reaching out to another to share his life.

The means to selfhood. Language, which is the basis for society, is also the basis for the individual. The language which society teaches to all its members is the means by which the individual knows himself, organizes himself, and maintains his unique selfhood. In Chapter 4 we shall see how language serves as the basis for the self–system and how it is the means by which we interact with other people.

Customs

Customs are behaviors that are regulated by social agreement, whether or not this agreement has been formalized. Such agreement has to do with matters of food, dress, sexual behavior, meeting people, homes and property, and even on

which side of the road to travel. Failing to abide by customs which are considered matters of taste is "uncouth." Failing to comply with customs involving
right and wrong is "immoral." Other customs have been written into law and to
transgress them is "illegal." Still others have to do with national life or with
religion, and failing to observe these is "unpatriotic" or "irreligious." Then there
are the customs dealing with matters so fraught with ancient feelings that they
are enforced without speaking of them: these are the taboos.

To belong to a society is to speak its language and to conform to its customs.
Thus language and custom are identifying marks; those who speak or act differently do not belong. When people form a group, whether they are children or
adults, they usually develop a special language, style of behavior, and identifying
mode of dress.

People who are born and raised in a society and have little or no contact with
people of another society are usually unaware that they are following customs.
Instead, they feel they are acting "naturally," following "common sense," or that
they are only "doing the right thing." In a pluralistic society like America, most
of us have contacts with people who talk, act, or dress in a way different from
ours.

Institutions

Whenever people feel the need to perpetuate a code of behavior, a set of
values, or a mode of cooperative endeavor, an institution is usually established.
An institution is an important cultural medium. There are religious institutions,
such as churches, synagogues, and temples; there are educational institutions,
such as schools, colleges, and universities; there are economic institutions, such
as factories, stores, and shipping companies; and there are social institutions,
such as family, government, and armed forces. These institutions have a recognizable structure, specific functions, defined roles for members, a code of behavior, rituals and symbols, and physical traits such as geographical location, property, and buildings. People enter some institutions voluntarily, while they are
born or drafted into others.

Whatever the major function of an institution, all serve as mediators of culture and thus are partly educational. The armed forces claim that they "make
men"; without doubt, when they are successful, they make "military men."
When religious institutions are successful, they make "saints," "good people,"
"children of God." The family makes a "family man," "well–behaved children," and "homemakers."

Sometimes institutions outlive their usefulness and continue only through iner-
tia. All institutions tend to display what Gordon Allport has called "functional
autonomy."[10] Once established, they tend to perpetuate themselves without
direct reference to the reason for which they were established.

The Arts

The function of language, customs, and institutions as media for culture is rather easily recognized. In fact, these media are usually formalized and often given official status. The arts, however, usually serve in an informal and unofficial manner. Yet their influence is pervasive. Such expressions as, "The pen is mightier than the sword," and "I care not who makes the laws if I can write the songs of a people," suggest this influence. Art, music, poetry, drama, and novels—who can measure their influence?

The arts conserve, mediate, criticize and create. The values, meanings, customs, and history of a people can be seen and read in its arts. Monuments, murals, portraits, symphonies have immortalized brave men and brave deeds. By means of myth and legend, ballads, fairy tales and dramatic rituals, and poetry and novels, the spirit of a people has been implanted in the minds of individuals.

But the arts have never been content to conserve and teach. The artist has been society's sharpest critic. Blessed (or cursed) with extreme sensitivity, artists find compromise, hypocrisy, and mediocrity unbearable. As Camus put it, "The nobility of our calling will always be rooted in two commitments: refusal to lie about what we know, and resistance to oppression."[11] For this criticism society has often made the artist pay the price of poverty, ostracism, and, sometimes, death.

The greatest value of the arts lies in their creativity. They have created the beauty, truth, and visions of new possibilities for which men have striven and died.

Mass Communication Media

Newspapers, popular magazines, paperback books, moving pictures, radio and television—these may all be thought of as part of the arts or as institutions, but their influence is so great and their emergence is so typical of the modern world that they require separate mention.

The mass communication media differ from the mediums of culture which we have mentioned so far in several important respects. First, they are purely commercial; that is, they are in the communication business to make a profit. Thus mass communication is a means, not an end. It does not have cultural goals of its own but is available as a means for achieving the goals of others who pay for its use. In other words, mass communication media are for sale to the highest bidder. In this country the highest bidders are large commercial interests, while in many other countries the government "calls the tune." Nevertheless, many of the mass communication media do contribute to educational or altruistic purposes. Their directors have undoubtedly set some limits on the uses to which the media will be put. But the fact remains that these tremendous forces are argely regulated by economic interests. A concerned population has, through ts representatives, therefore legislated some controls over these media and has also influenced them by reacting negatively toward them and/or the sponsors.

In the second place, mass communication media differ from other cultural media in the scope and speed of their influence. No other medium reaches so far so quickly. On the positive side, the media can be used to create larger areas of understanding, to help in time of disaster, and to open undreamed-of doors for education. On the negative side, propaganda, unfounded rumors, advertising of alcohol and tobacco, and assaults on established values are also transmitted through the media. Thus as a result of mass communication, the rate of social and cultural change has been greatly accelerated.

In the third place, mass communication poses serious questions for individualism and the role of what Toynbee calls "the creative minority." If, to be profitable, mass communication must appeal to the lowest common denominator, it becomes increasingly difficult for all that is unique, for that which must be cultivated before it can be appreciated, to survive. Will it be possible for the little business man, the craftsman, and the innovative writer to survive the competition with the mass mind produced by mass communication?

In the fourth place, mass communication's relationship to group processes is somewhat different from that of the other media of culture which grow out of interpersonal and group activities and exert their mediating influence in these processes. Mass communication acts on the masses but without the individuals who make up the masses being in any necessary relationship to one another. This is what David Riesman has called "The Lonely Crowd.[12] Paradoxically, the question is whether improved communication is leading to imrpoved community or to more of the loss of identity which may be modern man's most pressing spiritual problem.

THE DIMENSIONS OF SOCIAL STRUCTURE

All the groups in a society may be analyzed in terms of these seven dimensions:

1. power
2. leadership
3. role
4. status
5. communication
6. ideology
7. sociometry

Power

In its simplest terms, power is what makes things happen; it is influence. Raw power is force or the threat of force. Other kinds of power come from: money, the ability to bestow favors, access to people who have power, skill, knowledge, a position of authority, etc. One cannot be in a group long before discovering who has the power and what the key to that power is.

In the family, father, mother, brothers and sisters, grandparents, and even neighbors all have power. A child soon learns where the power is and how to use it or escape from it. When it is advantageous and possible to do so, he may play one power off against another.

The average person is ambivalent toward power. When he wants something done and can get the cooperation of those who have power, he believes that power is good. When someone else, with power on his side, does something to which he objectis, he believes that power is evil. This ambivalence is especially evident in attitudes toward government and the police.

Leadership

Power and leadership need not go together. The leadership structure refers to the visible or apparent pattern of decision-making or authority. But just as many kings were dominated by a "power behind the throne," the leader often speaks for someone other than himself. This happens not only in government and politics, but in business, the church, and in the home.

There are two fundamentally different kinds of leadership: the mystical or heroic, and the functional or facilitative. The former is represented by Alexander the Great, Julius Caesar, Napoleon, Winston Churchill, Charles De Gaulle, and John F. Kennedy. The facilitators are, of course, far more numerous and really keep the wheels of the world turning. Leaders at various levels in political parties, legislative leaders, business leaders, foremen in factories, and union leaders—these, and many more, facilitate the cooperative activities of people.

We still do not understand the process by which men become capable of inspiring or commanding, for good or bad, vast numbers of people. We call the quality "charisma," but it has not yet been carefully studied. Functional or facilitative leadership, however, has been studied and some methods have been found that improve the effectiveness of group management.[13]

Role

In order for a group to function, each member must play a role; that is, each person must take a position and perform the activities appropriate to that sition. On a baseball team the roles are very carefully and explicitly structured. a friendship group the roles are implicit, but they operate with as much force if they were explicit.

Family roles include baby, child, brother, sister, father, mother, husband, fe, etc. In general, the role is defined by the larger culture, refined by the b-culture, and given specific content in each family. We first play roles that inherited and defined by others. When we mature, we have more to say about at roles we will play and participate in defining them.

There are other roles at school, in the play group, on the job, and in the larger mmunity. There is no way to escape playing some role. To attempt to play role is to fall into the role of delinquent, rebel, or madman. We shall deal re with this important matter of roles in the next chapter on Interpersonal lationships.

atus

Just as power and leadership are closely related, role and status go together. le has to do with the horizontal structure of a group: and status, with the tical structure. Role has to do with one's function in the group; status, with e's prestige. We often have some choice as to the role we will play; we have tle, if any, choice as to our status. It is assigned to us by the group.

Some roles are open only to persons of high status. Corporations often select igh status person to be chairman of the board because of the prestige he will d to the company. Some roles do not require status, but confer status instead. en someone of low status becomes famous in sports or the entertainment rld, he then has very high status. Some people who do not have high status tend that they do by displaying the status symbols of a fine car, expensive thes, or a big house in an exclusive neighborhood. These "status seekers," as nce Packard calls them, do not thereby acquire genuine status, but they may l enough people for the effort to be rewarding.

mmunication

Earlier we noted the role that language plays in creating and maintaining a iety. Every group can be analyzed in terms of communication. What are the nnels through which information flows and where does it go? In any group re will be a serious loss in efficiency if the information does not flow to the ision makers. If sufficient information is not flowing out from the decision kers, the group will have a morale problem.

The movement of people is related to communication because some important ssages must be spoken face to face. When freeways cut through communities, the resulting disruption of old communication patterns can seriously affect community life. Lack of adequate public transportation can isolate huge sections of cities and result in loss of morale, increased suspicion, and a weakening of bond with the larger community.

The words *communication* and *community* are quite similar and go together in that community results from communication. Where there is no communication, there is no community, no matter how close together the houses are. Nor can a community of nations happen until peoples can communicate more freely. Iron and bamboo curtains destroy community. Walls of creed, race, and snobbishness are equally destructive.

Ideology

Ideology embodies the purposes and values of the group. Every group has a ideology, although the extent of its influence varies greatly from group to group. We usually only use the term when the ideology is quite obvious, but it is worth noting in all cases. Every successful politician is keenly aware of the ideology of his group, and his speeches indicate his loyalty to that ideology. Powerful and otherwise effective men have discovered how limited their influence can be when they oppose this ideology. On occasion, a ruthless man may exercise great power by skillfully manipulating the symbols which evoke a people's loyalty to the ideology.

Sociometry

J. L. Moreno[14] who also gave us the therapeutic tool called "psychodrama," developed the method of sociometry. Sociometry is a systematic method for conceptualizing the way in which affinity grouping may be influencing behavior. The idea behind the method is simply that people in a group have more of an affinity (liking) for some members than they do for others. Sometimes the affinity is mutual, sometimes one-sided. Friendship groupings, "cliques," and other interpersonal patterns reflect these affinities. Figure 3 is a sociometric diagram showing the pattern of choices and rejections in a group of ten scientists for collaboration in writing a report.

Sociology and social psychology, as well as the more specialized fields of psycholinguistics, group dynamics and cultural anthropology, are rapidly expanding fields with a vast literature. At this point we can only mention the existence of these important fields.

Some of the most pressing problems we confront are of a social nature. What can be done to stabilize the dissolving family? What can we do to make huge cities livable? What can we do about delinquency and crime? What can be done

bout economic, intellectual, and spiritual poverty? How can we solve interna-
ional problems without war? How can men of all races and creeds live together
vithout war? How can men of all races and creeds live together in brotherhood?
Vhat can be done about the population explosion? Each of these questions de-
erves the most dedicated study in all of the behaviorial sciences.

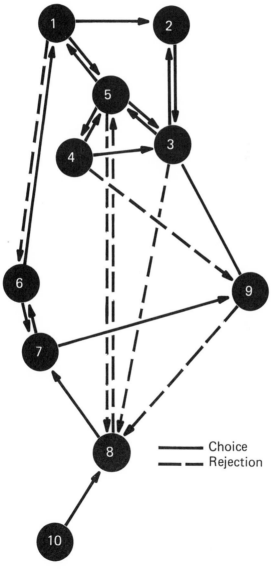

Figure 3. A Sociogram

Faced with such problems, the student may be impatient with the less drama
tic questions in this book. Impatience alone will not solve these problems; but
impatience, tempered by the knowledge that most short-cuts lead nowhere, ma
provide the energy to pursue knowledge that may lead to solutions. Perhaps we
must begin in the area of the interpersonal (Chapter 4) before we can solve the
larger social problems.

SUMMARY

We have given a brief description of the social environment in which the indi
vidual human being is born and in which he must live.

The society which constitutes man's environment may be his family, the sub
culture, or the larger culture.

These various cultures influence the individual through language, customs, in
stitutions, the arts, and mass communication.

Groups may be studied in terms of various dimensions along which they are
structured, including power, leadership, role, status, communication, ideology,
and sociometry.

QUESTIONS FOR STUDY AND CLASS DISCUSSION

1. What are some of the benefits you have had from your family that,
   perhaps, could not have been found in any other way?

2. See if you can identify all the groups or societies to which you
   directly or indirectly belong.

3. Do you play the same roles in each group to which you belong, or
   different roles?

4. Can you imagine in what ways life is different for the following child
   ren: the son of a wealthy white attorney, the son of a black janitor,
   the son of a Mexican farm hand, the son of a Chinese storekeeper (a
   of them living in or near Los Angeles)?

5. How much can you tell about someone by (1) his language, (2) his
   manner of dress, (3) his hair style, (4) the kind of car he drives,
   (5) where he lives?

6. How important is language ability in our society?

7. What are some consequences of defying customs? Which customs in
   our society require the strictest conformity?

8. What are some of the strengths and weaknesses of institutions?

9. What would we lose from our lives if there were no arts?

10. Can you identify some of the influences that the mass communication media have had in your life? How do you evaluate these influences?

UGGESTIONS FOR FURTHER READING

ies, William H., and Cobbs, Price M. *Black Rage.* New York: Bantam Books, 1969.

cLuhan, Marshall. *Understanding Media.* New York: Signet Books, 1964.

ead, Margaret. *Coming of Age in Samoa.* New York: Mentor Books, 1949.

ontagu, Ashley. *Race, Science and Humanity.* New York: D. Van Nostrand Co., 1963.

uthwick, Charles H. *Primate Social Behavior.* New York: D. Van Nostrand Co., 1963.

4

THE INTERPERSONAL

Psychologists and sociologists tend to think in terms of the individual or society and to ignore the true arena of human life: the interpersonal.

The most notable exception to this tendency was Martin Buber, the Jewish philosopher who gave us the term "I and Thou."

He said that both individualism and collectivism come from our failure to achieve genuine interpersonal relationships.

> The human person feels himself to be a man exposed by nature—as an unwanted child is exposed—and at the same time a person isolated in the midst of the tumultuous human world. The first reaction of the spirit to the awareness of this new and uncanny position is modern collectivism.[1]

He then described what happens when a real interpersonal encounter takes place.

> When imaginings and illusions are over, the possible and inevitable meeting of man with himself is able to take place only as the meeting of the individual with his fellow-man—and this is how it must take place. Only when the individual knows the other in all his otherness as himself, as man, and from there breaks through to the other, has he broken through his solitude in a strict and transforming meeting.[2]

Buber insists that the smallest human entity is not one but two: an I-Thou. I cannot be I except in relationship with a Thou. This "I-Thou" relationship is different from what Buber calls an "I-It" relationship in which I treat the other person as an object rather than another subject who remains himself while we interact.

Harry Stack Sullivan, in The Interpersonal Theory of Psychiatry, *worked out a detailed theory of how the individual develops from birth within interpersonal relationships, how he can be damaged by poor relationships, and, finally, how he can be healed by a good relationship in psychotherapy.[3]*

The interaction between the individual and his social milieu cannot be reduced to terms which derive their meaning solely from any other realm. As Fritz Heider says of the interpersonal,

> If one studies this field one soon comes to the conviction that it is profitable to conceive of it as being autonomous to a certain degree and not to reduce it to terms of a lower order.[4]

In other words, the terms individual, society, *and* interpersonal *are all basic terms which cannot be reduced to simpler terms without losing their meaning. Individuals are neither one-half of an interpersonal relationship nor small parts of society. An interpersonal relationship is neither two individuals added together nor one piece of society. Society is neither the aggregate of many individuals nor the sum of all interpersonal relationships in it. The whole is more than the sum of its parts, and smaller wholes are more than parts of larger wholes.*

THE GROUND OF THE INDIVIDUAL

If society is the milieu in which the individual lives, the interpersonal is the process by which he lives. Both Buber and Sullivan declare that the individual person, as a psychological reality, comes into existence through interpersonal processes, and continues to maintain his selfhood only in relationship with other individuals. No one has more dramatically demonstrated the importance of the interpersonal for individual integrity than Ernest Becker. In his book, *The Birth and Death of Meaning*, he builds on Sullivan's idea that the self-system is the human organism's adaptive response to anxiety, which is defined as "interpersonal insecurity." This self-system is linguistic and is developed, as the individual learns the language, for the purpose of providing "buffering processes" by which the individual protects himself from the threats which he perceives in important interpersonal relationships. From this point of view, "personality is largely a locus of word possibilities," and "words are the only tools we have for confident manipulation of the interpersonal situation." And again, "To present an infallible self is to present one which has unshakable control over words."[5]

The essential ideas we have taken from Sullivan and Becker are:

1. The self-system (the "Ego" of Freud) is a development arising out of interpersonal experiences.
2. Operationally, it is a linguistic system.
3. Functionally, it provides three essentials for the individual:
   a. A base from which to influence important others to interact with one so that one's needs may be met.
   b. A symbolic organization (self-concept) with which to identify and through which to express oneself.
   c. A buffer for anxiety: a way of maintaining self-esteem in the face of insecurity.

KINDS OF INTERPERSONAL BEHAVIOR

"Symbiotic" Behavior

Webster defines symbiosis as, "the living together in intimate association or even close union of two dissimilar organisms."[6] We can apply this term more loosely to a very close relationship between two people in which one or both cannot live without the other.[7] Such a relationship is unsound unless there are unusual circumstances which make it necessary.

In certain respects, the infant-mother relationship is symbiotic. The mother needs the baby to suckle and to fulfill (make meaningful) the processes of conception, pregnancy, birth, and lactation. The baby needs the mother's breast, her warmth, and her loving care. It is an unequal relationship in which the ability of the mother to take care of herself contrasts with the almost complete inability of the infant to take care of himself. Thus the mother largely determines the quality of the relationship. Sullivan has shown that whether or not the baby experiences anxiety depends on how his mother treats him. Erikson agrees, and says that the most crucial issue in infancy is "trust versus mistrust."[8]

Symbiotic relationships occur during normal development and in the case of therapeutic and/or custodial care for incapacitated persons. Other symbiotic relationships are usually not conducive to the growth of healthy individuality.

Manipulative Behavior

Manipulation occurs when an individual is caused to do something by another individual in the absence of genuine mutuality. The influence may be physical force or skillful exploitation of weakness, as in seduction or deception. Sometimes the influence may be more subtle, as in advertising or propaganda. Buber would say that such relationships are "I–It" relationships. The other person is viewed as an object to be manipulated rather than a person to encounter. Fromm calls this "the market place orientation," because one person is used for the profit of another.

Obviously, few people are manipulative at all times, and few are never manipulative. Perhaps our world cannot function without some interpersonal manipulation. Certainly much of the economic system now operates on skillful manipulation. While our government is, ideally, "of the people, by the people, and for the people," many people undoubtedly experience government as manipulative. What we call "good teaching" may be partly skillful manipulation, and parents must wrestle with the question of how much to manipulate their children. Even psychotherapy (Chapter 10) is involved in a controversy about how much manipulation should be used by the therapist.

Transactional Behavior

In recent years, a point of view called "transactional analysis" has been popularized by Eric Berne. This approach recognizes that many interpersonal relationships occur because one person wants something from another. In these terms, what a person is trying to get is called the "payoff" and what he has to do to get it is called the "price." Some common transactions are described in Berne's *Games People Play*.

An example of a "game" is *If It Weren't for You*, which Berne says is the one most commonly played by spouses. The wife manipulates her husband into forbidding her to do something she really doesn't want to do anyway. Then she plaintively cries, "If it weren't for you. . . ."[9]

There is no clear line of demarcation between manipulations and transactions. In fact, Shostrum, in *Man the Manipulator*,[10] thinks of the latter as forms of manipulation. If we do make a distinction, it would be on the basis of how much mutuality is involved. If one person is playing a game and the other person does not know it, this is manipulation. If both are playing the game, this is a transaction.

There is no doubt that most of social behavior is transactional, and perhaps necessarily so. By conventionalizing the most common recurring activities life becomes more predictable and less anxiety-arousing. Socialization is the process of learning the common "games" of our society. We learn the rules, develop skill, and confidently "transact" with people to meet our needs as they, also, "transact" with us to meet theirs. Viewed in this light, one of the most important aspects of social education is play. Not only does the child learn important skills he will later need, such as how to play his sex role; but he comes to understand the idea of games and develops confidence in his ability to play them.

Intimacy

The symbiotic, manipulative, and transactional relationships we have so far described may play very important roles in the functioning of the social system and, by enabling the individual to be a part of his society, they may be of great value to the individual. But, none of these qualify for the designation, "I-Thou" relationship, which Buber applies to the genuine meeting of one with another (*an other*). Customarily, we may describe as "intimate" the relationship in which two people play the game of "making love." But, unless each is meeting the other with a love that is respect, Buber would designate it as an "I-It" relationship.

In intimacy, one naked self is exposed and open to another naked self. Sexual intercourse, at its best, is the essence of this kind of intimacy, but sexual behavior often occurs without any intimacy. Then, too, there may be great intimacy between people without any sexual behavior. Erik Erikson, in his outline of the eight stages of man (see Chapter 6), relates intimacy to the crisis of young adulthood. When a person has resolved the identity crisis of adolescence, he is ready to learn how to be close to another by expressing himself with integrity and delighting in the other's expression of himself. In such moments persons discover themselves, they discover others, and they discover new meanings in human life.

SPECIAL ASPECTS OF THE INTERPERSONAL

There are many special aspects of the interpersonal:

1. the function of roles
2. contracts and commitments
3. the love relationship
4. communication
5. secrets
6. mutuality

The Function of Roles

In Chapter 3 we noted that role structure is one of the characteristics of the group and that it makes possible the cooperation without which a society cannot survive. Now we shall look more closely at role and its function in interpersonal relationships and in the definition of the self.

The word *role* comes from the theater. When we talk about roles and try to understand interpersonal behavior in these terms we are using what is called a "dramaturgical frame of reference."[11]

Thinking of life in dramaturgical terms is not new. Shakespeare said, "all the world's a stage." If this is so, one cannot be in the play without accepting some role which the drama provides. In this analogy, the drama or script is prepared by society. Some dramas are much like impromptu or open-ended productions in which the actor can be quite flexible. Nevertheless, some limits are set as to what roles are available, what people are available, the definition of the roles, and the situation in which the actors will perform. Other dramas have classical themes, familiar to all, where plot, style and roles are all well defined.

At this point one may object that he does not want to act, that he will just be himself instead of playing some role. This is a most serious objection and raises a profound question. The existentialists speak of "authentic existence." Maslow speaks of "self-actualization." Rogers speaks of "congruity." And our Christian culture teaches us to be honest and sincere, to hate hypocrisy and "put on." Why cannot a person "just be himself"? Perhaps the answer lies in the processes by which one becomes a self, the processes by which one validates his self, and the processes by which one must contribute to the selfhood of another person.

Both in the history of the species and in the story of any one life, the individual emerges within an existing society. Buber says that a man becomes a self when he is addressed by another. The self is *called* into existence by being spoken to, by being named, by being described. Anyone who has not seen a loving mother with intuitive genius "creating" a personality out of a little human animal has missed a wonderful sight! Such calling, such addressing, such describing—and gradually a self emerges that knows it is being called, that comes to accept the descriptions of itself, that knows itself in relation to others called by other names and described in other ways.

As the child develops, he begins to act on the basis of the name he has been given. He tries out behavior which has been assigned to him. He accepts the descriptions of himself which he has heard and he expects that others will accept these descriptions. In this way the child, and later, the adult, validates himself with others. If other people did not accept his name and other descriptions of him, it is doubtful that he could exist as a self, that he could believe in or even know himself. Fortunately, most of us grew up hearing reasonably consistent things about ourselves; and, when we acted on them, there was enough confirmation so that we became sure enough of ourselves to withstand a fair amount of personal attack. Very few of us could maintain our ego–identities in the face of disconfirmation from all of the people who matter most to us.

As our identity depends on others, so does their identity need confirmation from us.

For these reasons it may not be possible to be "just yourself." Rather, the process of true self-realization may be achieved only through effective role playing.

The psychiatrist, Carl Jung, developed a theory of "individuation." Where Freud understood personality development in terms of sexual growth; and Adler understood personality in terms of strategies for overcoming feelings of inferiority; Jung saw man's central striving as the effort to become "somebody," and, particularly, the somebody he really is. Jung believed that a person could fail at this (lose his soul) in two main ways. If we think of society as a great ocean, represented in the diagram below by the space under the line, a person can fail to become somebody by completely submerging himself in society (A); that is, by being only a role; or he can fail to become somebody by being so far out that he is a name without any role (B). Consider a mailman as an example of the first possibility. Everywhere he goes people say, "There goes the mailman." When he stops for lunch in the cafe where he has been eating for 15 years, everyone there greets him, "Hello, Mr. Mailman." No one knows his name. Even when he goes home, as he walks up the sidewalk to the house, his children see him coming and cry out, "Mother, the mailman is here!" His wife says, "It's good to see you, Mr. Mailman; sit down to supper." This man is nobody. He is a role without a name. On the other hand, suppose a man is walking down the street and someone asks, "Who is that?" He is told, "Oh, that's Jones." "Well, who is Jones?" "Nobody." There is nothing else that can be said about him. He has a name but not a role.

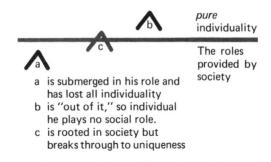

a is submerged in his role and
   has lost all individuality
b is "out of it," so individual
   he plays no social role.
c is rooted in society but
   breaks through to uniqueness

How then can one become an individual, a real somebody? Jung insists that he must have roots in the society but still break through to uniqueness (C). He must find his role, and it will most likely be a role that has been played but which he plays in his own way. A really great life appears when someone finds a great role and plays it as it has never been played before. Jung's term for these roles is "types," and he saw them as being carried in the "collective unconscious" of the race as "archetypes." Some of these archetypes release great power in the individual who typifies (fills the type for) them. For example, a *mother* taps deep roots in the racial unconscious (or, social history). However, she is also in danger of being swallowed up by the role, of being nothing but a mother. All great roles involve this danger, but when the individual breaks through such a role to uniqueness there is great self-fulfillment.[12]

To play one's role in interpersonal relationships effectively requires many things, only a few of which we shall note here. The role must be sharply defined so that others can recognize "who" one is and play their roles responsively. There are humorous occasions when someone is not quite sure how to act toward someone else whose sex role has not been adequately defined. Once a particular role is adopted in a group, its members will expect a continuance of the role; and they will not readily accept a change in role. Credibility is one of the most important prerequisites for effective role playing. It has often been said of someone, "He doesn't look like a teacher," or, "Who told her she was an actress?"

It should be added that a person need not play only one role. The really effective person plays many roles and, if they are not inconsistent with each other, this variety enriches and vitalizes him. Some of the more demanding roles can be more bearable if there are opportunities to play other roles as well. A mother wants to also be wife, lover, or career woman. A policeman wants to also be friend, sportsman, or just plain "Joe."

As we noted, the idea that interpersonal relationships may be viewed in terms of roles is analogical, and its validity depends on the amount of similarity between a person's everyday life and the world of drama. Viewing relationships in dramaturgical terms seems to throw light on many aspects of social life and even on self-identity; but certain haunting questions do remain. Given that social life may be much like role playing, cannot two people meet without playing any roles? Are there not times when the self just is or expresses itself?

In our analysis of the kinds of interpersonal behavior we noted that it is only in *intimacy* that true "I–Thou" encounters are likely to occur, and, perhaps, it is only in intimate relationships that we may step out of our roles as we step out of our clothes (which are so closely associated with roles). However, it is probable that even in the most intimate of relationships there is some "presentation of self," in Erving Goffman's terms, and some withholding of self, while in many conventionalized, role–playing situations a good deal of the "real self" is expressed.

Those wishing to read about personal encounters which do not involve role playing should read Carl Rogers, Sidney Journard, and Martin Buber. (See references at end of the chapter.)

Contracts and Commitments

A special form of interpersonal relationship is the contract or commitment. All societies require some form of mutual commitment among their members. In some societies this commitment may not be verbal; but most societies have initiation ceremonies, oaths of allegiance, and other means of renewing or confirming the covenant. John Locke was one of the first to spell out the meaning of this for a democratic society in his description of the "social contract."

One of the oldest and most familiar interpersonal covenants is the marriage contract. The covenants by which people are initiated into religious communities are probably as old. More modern are business partnerships, labor contracts, and professional commitments. Psychoanalysis is rooted in a contract between the analyst and his patient.

Erving Goffman, among others, insists that all interpersonal encounters involve some degree of commitment which must be taken for granted if social processes are not to collapse. When a person walks down the street, he assumes that other people will not put their hands on him or invade his privacy in other ways. If a person gives a proper greeting, he has a right to expect a polite greeting in return. If he offers someone a seat on a bus he expects a courteous acceptance or a polite refusal. In other words, to refuse to practice the social amenities constitutes a breach of social contract. When we act properly and the other person does not respond properly, we are not just personally angry—we feel outrage that we, as social representatives, are being treated improperly.

Here we have a problem somewhat similar to the one involving roles. How can we reconcile these social contracts and commitments with spontaneity and honest feeling in interpersonal relationships? Should I greet people with a smile even if I feel miserable? Should I keep promises even when I am sorry that I made them? Should I stay with a covenant, such as marriage, when I no longer want to?

In a sense, these are ethical or moral questions and, perhaps, cannot be settled by psychology. However, they are also interpersonal relationships and, as such, cannot be ignored by psychology. Perhaps the following principles can shed some light on this issue.

Human beings, by their nature, require that some relationships be relatively permanent. Of course, children need to be reared in a stable family setting. Erikson and Sullivan agree that true adulthood in human beings is reached only in what Erikson calls "generativity," which is the capacity to care for the young.

Human society, by its very nature, requires that some relationships be relatively permanent. There is no evidence to suggest that a society could exist in which everyone acted only on impulse. Rather, the history of man suggests that he has survived because he learned to subordinate impulse to social needs. This does not mean that society is more important than the individual and his feelings; but it does suggest that man has social impulses which have predominated.

The deepest interpersonal relationships have always had a "given" quality to them. It is only recently that people have been free to choose their relationships. A radical individualism and an unrealistic voluntarism have combined to give modern man the notion that he is free to do as he pleases. There is no question but that individualism and voluntarism have positive value. The idea of emigrating to new worlds, the dream of building a new society where a man can live by his own conscience, the optimism that there will always be new frontiers where a man can start again—all these are worthy concepts. But on the frontier men were forced to cooperate in order to survive, and their dreams were tempered by the harshest of realities.

Family relationships, neighbors, and co-workers are all usually given, not chosen. If psychology is to be of any help, it must give us principles by which we can live in given as well as chosen relationships.

The Love Relationship

No quality is so universally praised as love. It supposedly makes the world go round, and is claimed to be all that anybody needs. It is said to be the mystery of life; it is called the greatest thing in the world, and it is offered as a one-word replacement for all ethics. The problem is that we cannot agree what this wonderful quality is.

The psychologist is tempted to turn love over to poets, the song writers, the novelists, and the romantics of all ages. What can an academic discipline do with love? And, after the psychologist has finished dissecting it, will it still be love?

Here we return to psychology's responsibility. If we are not willing to attempt to deal with all aspects of human behavior, we should turn the field over to someone else. Loving relationships are most fitting phenomena for psychological study. It is true that we cannot yet do justice to such complex relationships, but we can discover some of the relevant principles involved.

Whenever we deal with something complex, it is helpful to make whatever distinctions we can. The Greeks had three words for love: *agape*, the kind of love God has for man; *eros*, our love of the desirable; and *phileo*, brotherly affection. Erich Fromm distinguishes between love of God, self-love, parental love, love between a man and a woman, and brotherly love.[14] Many writers have insisted that sexual passion and love should be distinguished. Sullivan suggests that *lust* be used, without negative connotations, to mean sexual desire; and that *love* be used for the mature, selfless caring that only healthy adults can express.[15] Sullivan also suggests that much that passes for love is really a need for love or a desire to be loved. There is an interesting analysis of love in Austin Wright's *Islandia*. In this fictional land there are four words for love: *Apia*, simple sexual desire; *Amia*, love between friends; *Ania*, the love that leads to parenthood; and *Alia*, the sharing of a place, a life, and a destiny.[16]

In Chapter 2 we distinguished between "happenings" and "doings." This distinction can help us understand the love relationship in which happenings and doings interact in the most complicated way.

First, there is a *situational aspect* which is largely a happening. As we noted before, there tends to be a "given" quality in our social environment. By and large, factors we do not control give us our families, our neighbors, and our fellows. This "giveness" has been called fate, destiny, luck, and providence; but whatever we call it, we "happen" to be in close proximity to the particular people who make up our personal world. It is these people that we love or hate.

Second, there is an *emotional dimension* which is largely a happening. Genuine emotions cannot be produced by voluntary effort. Emotions tend to happen; and while there are ways of conditioning or training them, it would seem best for psychological health to simply let them be. Someone may be surprised to discover that he is suddenly "in love" or that, in spite of pretenses to the contrary, he is "out of love." It is love's happening quality that leads many people to think that there is nothing they can do about love—that it either happens or it doesn't.

But there is also a *behavioral factor* in love which, because it is something we can do a great deal about, may be the most important. Love may be defined as a way of treating people, a way of behaving toward them. Years ago, St. Paul wrote,

> This love of which I speak is slow to lose patience—it looks for a way of being constructive. It is not possessive; it is neither anxious to impress nor does it cherish inflated ideas of its own importance. Love has good manners and does not pursue selfish advantage. It is not touchy. It does not compile statistics of evil or gloat over the wickedness of other people. On the contrary, it is glad with all good men when Truth prevails.[17]

Goethe said, "there is a courtesy of the heart that is akin to love."[18] Psychotherapists have learned, in their efforts to help troubled people, that to really care about persons means to treat them in certain ways. To dramatize the fact that helpful caring is not something sentimental, Bettelheim wrote the book, *Love is Not Enough.*[19] From my work as a counselor I have become convinced that what we try to do in psychotherapy is very close to the fundamental meaning of love. I suggest the following behavioral definition of love.

Love is recognition. Love begins by paying attention to the presence of the other. To ignore is one way of being unloving.

Love is understanding. To care about someone is to desire to know him, to understand how he feels, and to realize how the world looks to him. This kind of understanding is quite different from the effort to see through someone. Genuine understanding comes from letting the other tell about himself while we really listen.

Love is acceptance. If someone is to be loved, it must be as the person he is, not as someone different. To accept another is to be deeply willing that he be what he will be; it is to be close to him without judging or evaluating him. It is to respect his personhood.

Love is response. To love a person is to communicate our recognition, understanding, and acceptance, and further, it is to respond to him with tenderness and integrity. To be tender means to deal gently with his needs and weaknesses. To act with integrity means to be honest about how we feel. Love often requires that two people take the time, energy, and interest to resolve issues which may be seriously crippling the relationship.[20]

It is my hypothesis that if two people are willing to *do* the four actions listed above, warm, satisfying, and exciting feelings are very likely to *happen.*

Communication

In these first few chapters we have stressed the importance of language. We noted in this chapter how it is within a linguistic system that the self is organized and interacts with others to meet its needs with a minimum of anxiety. Now we will pay more attention to the communication processes involved in interpersonal behavior.

The simplest form of communication is the giving of cues or signs to which others respond. We have noted that this kind of communication does exist among animals other than man, and that it consists primarily of expressions of emotion. There are clear signs for pain, fear, anger, hunger, and sexual arousal.

There are less clear signs for irritation, boredom, pleasure and sadness. This language of signs does not depend on words, though in the case of human beings, it may make use of them.

All cooperative behavior depends on signs and it cannot function smoothly if they are not dependable. Since persons may use words to express emotions, they sometimes suppress, distort, or pretend to have feelings. On the one hand, this pretense is acceptable in situations that require us to keep our feelings to ourselves; but on the other hand, in intimate relationships, pretense leads to confusion and unreality. In public, etiquette requires us to keep certain personal feelings suppressed. In private, this same suppression makes intimacy difficult if not impossible. As Jung put it,

> ...in the long run nothing is more unbearable than a tepid harmony
> in personal relations brought about by withholding emotion.[21]

In general, interpersonal behavior is facilitated when communication follows these four principles:

Clarity. According to information theory, if the *input* is not clear, the message will probably not reach the destination. For example, husbands and wives often do not clearly communicate their wants to one another. Each expects the other to read his mind; and when the message doesn't get through, he feels hurt and angry. The receiver can help clarify a message by checking to make sure he understands what is being said.

Consistency. When we send inconsistent messages, we are misunderstood. Two forms of inconsistency have been given special attention by psychologists. One of these is the "two-layer" communication. Our words say one thing, but our tone of voice or facial expression says another. Carl Rogers calls this kind of inconsistency *incongruence.*[22]

A more complicated form of inconsistency is the "double bind."[23] Bateson first noticed this kind of inconsistency in the behavior of certain mothers toward their children. The double bind involves three elements:

1. the first message which is usually verbal, for example, "I want you to love me
2. a second, usually non-verbal, message that contradicts the first; for example, "I don't want you close to me because I am afraid of love"
3. a situation in which the child is forbidden to speak about, and may not even be aware of, the inconsistency.

Appropriateness. Communication is facilitated when the message is "fitting." This appropriateness pertains to roles, situations, and goals. Inappropriate messages are often misunderstood, and they make it very difficult for the other person to respond. Familiarity in a formal situation; joking at a serious moment; speaking "out of character"; purposeful deception—each of these puts others "on the spot" and makes for insecure relationships.

Responsibility. Good relationships demand that we accept responsibility for what we communicate. Goffman points out that we not only "give" signals, we "give off" signals. We are responsible for both, and Goffman defines *sincerity* as the intent to live up to expectations aroused by the impressions we make.[24] Thus the "right" to give impressions which arouse certain expectations comes from having the ability to follow through and the intent to do so. In the absence of either of these, we are insincere or irresponsible. If a sincere person finds that he has inadvertently "given off" a signal that was not his intent, he will correct the misunderstanding by sending another, more accurate message.

One of the most important tools for repairing breakdowns in communication is communication about communication, or, what Bateson calls, *metacommunication.*[25] We not only send and receive messages, but we simultaneously pay attention to other signs which serve as checks on the communication process. When we sense that all is not going right, we take more direct action to clear up the communication. If anxiety of any kind makes us unable to take steps toward clarification, communication begins to break down, and the relationship begins to deteriorate.

In one sense things are what they are, and no words can or should change them. In another sense, however, things are what they are *said* to be. Words take the ill-formulated, the chaotic, and create meaning. It *does* make a difference how things are described, whether it be the feeling someone is trying to verbalize in psychotherapy or the description of a nation trying to find its way. John Ciardi said in the election year of 1968:

> This year, as in every year, the issue is language. The power of every great Administration has been precisely the power to describe us to ourselves in a way that could unite and enlarge us within our most spacious image of our best possibilities. . . The issue remains our need to re-create the language in which we can know ourselves and our purposes. Only in that tongue, could we find it, lies our hope of speaking the problems to ourselves and of forming ourselves equal to the problems we have found our own best terms for.[26]

To anyone who says that this is simply a literary problem, we must again insist that as psychologists we are concerned with interpersonal behavior. If Ciardi is right, the most fulfilling interpersonal behavior will partly be the creation of a language that reflects a sensitive perception of unfulfilled possibilities.

Secrets

One of the thorniest problems in interpersonal relationships involves the matter of secrets. What is best kept secret and what is best divulged? There is no easy answer, and behavioral scientists are not in agreement among themselves. Becker and Goffman see a real need for secrets in conventional relationships, and to some extent in intimate relationships. Jung takes a rather complicated position, saying that ". . . every personal secret has the effect of a sin or of guilt," but that ". . . self-restraint is healthful and beneficial; it is even a virtue." Then he adds, . . ."if self-restraint is only a private matter, and perhaps devoid of any religious aspect, then it may be as harmful as the personal secret." He seems to say that secrets are bad and reserve is good, but even reserve should break down in some kind of holy fellowship. He is definite in his rejection of a simplistic confession of secrets: "It would be hard to go too far in condemning the bad taste of a common, mutual confession of sins."[27]

O. H. Mowrer is unequivocally opposed to keeping "sins" secret and bases his whole therapeutic approach on the healing power of "confessing." Even Mowrer, however, would have us limit these confessions to intimate relationships, at least initially, and only gradually expand the circle of people who know us as we really are. But Mowrer does advocate secrets. Taking his start from the idea in Lloyd C. Douglas' novels, *Magnificent Obsession* and *Doctor Hudson's Secret Journal*, Mower develops the thesis that we should keep our virtues secret, at least some of them, because what we keep back is what we really are. In this connection he quotes approvingly the words, "You are your secrets."[28]

We must conclude that the place of secrets in interpersonal relationships is not clear. It might help to distinguish between "then secrets" and "now secrets," and to suggest that "then secrets" could be kept while, in intimacy, there should be very few "now secrets." But this is a complicated problem and we need more evidence. The various kinds of therapeutic group work being done (group therapy, sensitivity training, basic encounter groups) should give us some facts that will point toward a more dependable answer.

True Mutuality

Interpersonal relationships at their best are essentially mutual even when there are great differences in age, strength, or other forms of power. Rudolf Dreikurs, in *Psychology for the Classroom*, insists that even relationships between adults and children should be equal.[29] Szasz puts it this way:

> In order for one person to benefit (grow), the interactions must be beneficial for both.

Narcissism and masochism are similar in being defensive maneuvers designed to avoid the impact of a full and spontaneous relationsiph with another person.[30]

Bernard Steinzor points out that both submitting to and dominating another person show a lack of respect for him.[31]

These writers do not imply that every person in a relationship, regardless of age or any other factor, is equally responsible or should have an equal voice in decision making. They do insist on mutual respect. Each must be seen as having equal worth and importance if the relationship is to be growth-producing for both. True mutuality is a difficult goal to reach; but those who are interested in personal growth will want to move in this direction.

SUMMARY

It is not enough to study the individual and society. The interpersonal relationship deserves to be considered as a phenomenon of equal importance. It is from interpersonal relationships that the self emerges, and nothing is more important for an understanding of the individual than a knowledge of the "self-system."

There are several kinds of interpersonal relationships. In a "symbiotic" relationship neither person is a truly independent self. In a manipulative relationship one person uses or exploits the other. In a transactional relationship both parties are giving and getting something. In an intimate relationship there is real sharing between two people.

Several aspects of interpersonal relationships were noted, including the function of roles, the place of commitments, the meanings of the love relationship, the problems of communication, the question of secrets, and the importance of true mutuality.

QUESTIONS FOR STUDY AND CLASS DISCUSSION

1. What are some important differences between an "I-It" and an "I-Thou" relationship?

2. In what sense is an interpersonal relationship more than adding two individuals together?

3. How does language function in the "self-system"?

4. How does the "self-system" act as a buffer for the individual?

5. Do you know any relationship which illustrates the type called "symbiotic"? Describe it.

6. Do you think it is possible to get along without manipulating people?

7. Do you think that some intimacy goes beyond what Berne calls a "transaction"? Or is there always some element of trying to get something?

8. What are some of the roles you are called upon to play? Which role do you like best? Which role do you like least?

9. Do you think that love can be cultivated, on the basis of a decision to do so, or is it always a "happening"?

10. If two people are to be very close, can they keep secrets from one another? What has your experience been?

SUGGESTIONS FOR FURTHER READING

Becker, Ernest. *The Birth and Death of Meaning.* New York: Free Press of Glencoe, 1962.

Berne, Eric. *Games People Play.* New York: Grove Press, 1964.

Buber, Martin. *I and Thou.* New York: Scribner, 1958.

Goffman, Erving. *The Presentation of Self in Everyday Life.* Garden City: Doubleday & Co., 1959.

Mowrer, O. H. *The New Group Therapy*, New York: D. Van Nostrand Co., 1964.

5

REACTIONS TO FRUSTRATION

Although experimental studies have certainly added to our knowledge of the effects of frustration, this chapter is in Part II, Philosophical Psychology, because the major ideas we shall discuss are speculative and have not yet attained the precision we expect of scientific formulations.

BEHAVIOR: ITS CAUSES AND GOALS

The Contribution of Functionalism

In Chapter 1 we met the functionalists and noted the far–reaching consequences of their plea that man be viewed as an organism seeking to adjust to his environment. From this point of view, all behavior may be understood as the organism's effort to adapt. It would be impossible to exaggerate the importance of this assumption. Once it is adopted, our whole approach to the explanation of behavior is affected. Behavior is seen as *need–based* and *goal–directed*.

Behavior is Need–Based

An organism maintains itself by acting to meet its needs. This organismic activity includes physiological processes within the organism and the behavior of the organism within its environment. If there is a shortage of water in the system, internal processes redistribute and conserve the available water. At the same time, the organism will be most responsive to water in its environment. If none is immediately available, he will probably manifest water–seeking behavior. This tendency to maintain a balance or equilibrium in the system is called *homeostasis,* and, while it is primarily a biological term, it applies equally well to behavior initiated by needs. An organism in motion is in a *drive state*, and this drive state is assumed to be need-based.

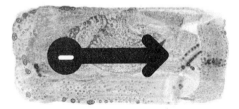

In this diagram, the O stands for organism, the arrow indicates a drive state, and the minus sign indicates a lack or a need.

Behavior is Goal-Directed

If behavior is to meet needs, it must lead to that which will meet the need. By definition, that which meets a need is the *goal* of the behavior. Here we shall not try to settle the controversy between those who see behavior as purposive (teleological) and those who view it as random until conditioned (determined) through reinforcement (see Chapters 8 and 9). Whatever the dynamics may be, it looks as though a thirsty animal searches for water, a hungry animal seeks food, and an animal in heat looks for a mate. The above diagram can be changed to:

The plus sign indicates the goal that will meet the need. Thus behavior is need-based and goal-directed.

Human Behavior

To illustrate the functionalist view of behavior, we have used relatively simple situations applicable to most animals. It is not always so easy to understand human behavior. Nevertheless, it is important to see how far we can go in our understanding of human behavior without going beyond the assumptions that all behavior is need-based and goal-directed.

FRUSTRATION

Blocking an organism from reaching a goal is *frustration*, which can be diagramed as follows:

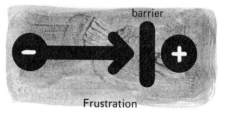

Frustration

To some degree, all organisms experience difficulties in meeting their needs. In the higher animals, and especially in man, these difficulties take on a crucial significance in determining behavior.

In man we can distinguish three kinds of frustration.

Environmental Frustration

The most obvious kind of frustration occurs when something in the environment gets in our way. I am late for an important appointment and a long, slow freight train blocks my route. I try to open a door, but it is stuck. I want someone to do something for me, but he refuses. In each case I am frustrated. Note that we are using the term to describe the event of being blocked, not the feeling. When I *am* frustrated, I may well *feel* frustrated, but here we are using the term to mean *the blocking of a motivated organism.*

Environmental frustration is usually the least painful because the barrier is outside of us and we feel free to vent our feelings against it. In fact, we may at times create barriers outside ourselves that we can hate and blame in order to avoid the more painful experience of admitting that the barriers are within ourselves.

Barriers within Ourselves: Conflict

Many times we are blocked by something within us. We can diagram this as shown:

Conflict

This situation is called *conflict.* In psychology, conflict refers to strife within ourselves—the conflict of motives, values, impulses or ideas. Three kinds of conflict are commonly recognized.

Approach-approach conflict. We want to do two things which are incompatible or go in two different directions at the same time. The story about the donkey immobilized half-way between two equally appetizing stacks of hay illustrates this type of conflict. We have all seen a child in a candy store trying to decide which candy bar to buy when he wants them all. His mother presses for a decision, but he is at an impasse. To choose one is to give up the others. Approach-approach conflict, symbolically represented as (++), tends to paralyze us by preventing decision and action.

Avoidance-avoidance conflict. In this case the choices are the devil and the deep blue sea. We must choose between two equally unhappy courses. Should I risk the dangerous operation or should I run the risk that the tumor might be malignant? Should I accept being drafted or go to jail? Should I mow the lawn or face my father's wrath? Avoidance-avoidance conflicts can be most painful and sometimes lead to what is called "leaving the field." In other words, a person may escape from both alternatives. Someone who has been threatened with punishment in order to make him do something unpleasant may simply leave the field.

Approach-avoidance conflict. This one is perhaps the most painful of the conflicts and is likely to be the most prolonged. Temptation typifies this kind of conflict. We want to do something forbidden, but we are afraid of being caught. Another example is the man who has always worked for someone else while saying that "one of these days" he will go into business for himself. He wants to, but he dreads giving up his security. In this type of conflict a person is both attracted and repelled by the goal. If he moves closer, the negative aspects of the goal create an unbearable anxiety, so he backs up. But when he backs up enough to stop being afraid, the positive aspects of the goal begin to attract him again. Therefore he tends to oscillate at some distance from the goal.

Stress and Frustration

Stress may be of two kinds. Psychological pressure may be too intense or too prolonged. An example of the first is the harried executive whose many phones are all ringing at once while he dictates a letter to his secretary and shouts instructions to several assistants. An example of the second might be a family with an aged relative living with them. A few weeks each year might be bearable, but having him year–round is too much. Stress leads to frustration when we reach our limits. We can't do or take anymore. These internal limits act as barriers, and we experience frustration.

FRUSTRATION AND AGGRESSION

One of the most general principles found in the behavior of animals, from the single-celled amoeba to man, is that when it is frustrated, it increases and varies its behavior. The reason for this seems to be that the increase and variation in behavior may lead over, under, through, or around the barrier to the goal.

This principle is the basis of psychology's famous "frustration–aggression hypo-thesis."[1] Proposed by Dollard and Miller, this theory postulates that frustration often leads to aggressive behavior, and that aggressive behavior almost always is preceded by frustration. There are many practical applications of this theory. If you are around someone who is being badly frustrated, be careful because he is likely to become angry very easily and he may blame you. When someone is angry, it helps to find out what is frustrating him. This is especially helpful in understanding children. The next time you are angry and don't know why, ask yourself, "What do I want that I'm not getting?"

FRUSTRATION AND ANXIETY

Frustration also leads to *anxiety*, and these words open the door to one of the most important chapters in psychology. No problem is greater for man than is anxiety. Anxiety is a pervasive feeling of insecurity. It is the opposite of the feeling of well–being. It is always uncomfortable and in its extreme forms may completely disorganize and paralyze behavior. It may be a general feeling of uneasiness, or it may be a stark, raw fear that blots out everything else. Human beings cannot stand very much anxiety and are usually willing to pay a high price to avoid it. A large proportion of human behavior can be understood as primarily anxiety–reducing.

Anxiety has two sources in frustration. It results when a need is not being met because some goal is being blocked. If the need is pressing, the anxiety will be immediate and intense. If someone's mouth and nose are covered so that he cannot breathe, he will become extremely anxious. Most of us feel anxious at the thought of being lost, especially in a dark cave or in the desert. The other source of anxiety in frustration is quite different and it has to do with the ego. The ego has a stake in our goal–seeking behavior because not reaching the goal means *failure*, and the ego does not like to fail. Since the ego's chief need is to be adequate, it constantly strives to maintain an image of adequacy for others and for itself. Loss of self–esteem is always a threat to the ego. When we are frustrated, anxiety related to the unmet need and anxiety related to loss of self–esteem are aroused.

The ego considerably complicates the problem of frustration. Without ego–involvement the organism may put all of its energies into repeated efforts to get past the barrier to the goal. This is called *adaptive behavior*, which can be diagramed as follows:

Adaptive Behavior

However, if the ego feels threatened, then we will increase and vary the behavior which is aimed at protecting the ego's image of adequacy:

ego

Ego Defense

The more energy we use protecting the ego, the less energy we have to find a way to the goal. The mature, confident person continues to seek a way past the barrier even though he may suffer some loss of self–esteem. He knows that in the long run only real achievements keep self–esteem high. By contrast, the immature, insecure person finds it hard to continue adaptive behavior when his self–image is threatened, and he engages in ego–defensive or ego–inflating behavior. This behavior does not solve the problem and leads to greater frustration, more anxiety, and more threats to the ego which acts to protect itself even more. This vicious circle is the neurotic's style of life.

Our most important choice in life is between being primarily adaptive and problem–solving and being primarily security–oriented and ego–defensive.

Security-oriented Ego Defense

Adaptation or Problem Solving

ego

The Choice: To Adapt or To Defend

A rather "corny" illustration may make this choice more clear. Imagine a stage-coach in the days of the old west. There is one passenger and the driver is whip-ping his horses along. They come to a muddy place and the coach is soon stuck in the mud up to the axles. The passenger leans out the window and asks, "What's wrong?" The driver answer, "We're stuck." "Then *do something*," the passenger frantically shrieks. "I intend to," says the driver. "I thought I'd put some straw under the horses' feet so they can get a better hold, and I'll cut a limb off that tree and see if I can't get some leverage to lift the coach." "I don't mean that," the passenger cries, "Do something so it won't look like we're stuck. Put some leaves over the mud. I'll get out with my picnic basket and if anybody comes along we'll tell them we're having a picnic." A corny story! Yes, but no sillier than some of us are when we get in trouble. Instead of doing what we can, and getting help if we need it, we put up a facade of well–being, pretend things are great, and stay stuck in the mud.

THE EGO–DEFENSE MECHANISMS

No material in psychology is better known to the general public than the various "defense mechanisms."[2] Since they are used to defend the ego rather than the total organism, we shall call them the *ego–defense mechanisms*. Various authors have invented the terms used for these mechanisms, but Anna Freud, the daughter of Sigmund Freud, is usually credited with first systematically assem-bling and describing these patterns of defense behavior.

As we describe some of the ego-defense mechanisms, several points should be kept in mind. Remember that the function of these defensive patterns is the resolution of painful conflicts and the dulling of anxiety. It will also be noticed that all of the mechanisms involve some degree of *denial of reality* and a certain amount of *goal substitution.* In other words, they do not really solve problems and we pay the price of getting out of touch with the way things are.

Rationalization (and other forms of intellectualization)

The most commonly used ego–defense mechanism is *rationalization.* To rationalize is to make up good reasons for our behavior, usually after we've done it. The most famous is the *sour grapes* form of rationalization in which we play down what we can't get or do. "Who wants that?" we say. The opposite form is called *sweet lemon.* In this case we play up what we have, especially if we have invested a lot in it. The car we bought may be a lemon, but we say, "Isn't she a honey!" There are numerous other forms, always involving verbal games by which we try to control people's reactions with the words we use to describe what we do. Those with great verbal skills are particularly good at rationalization, and one of the results of a college education is an increase in this skill. Psychologists are most proficient of all! I was once in a group therapy marathon with some psychologists, and it was both amusing and sad to see how good we were at hiding behind the most plausible of rationalizations.

Displaced Aggression

Another frequently seen ego–defense is *displaced aggression.* A man is called on the carpet by his boss and doesn't dare tell him off. His ego takes a strong beating; he feels weak and inadequate. On the way home he blows his horn at every car that gets in his way. As he walks into his house, the dog gets in his way and gets kicked. Inside, the children greet him, only to be told to get out of the way. Dinner isn't ready and his wife gets scolded. As he storms about he mutters, "Nobody pushes me around!" It is clear that he is displacing a great deal of aggression onto those who are not the cause of it. Unfortunately, this is often seen in the larger context of society where frustrated people displace their aggression onto minority groups.

Compensation

If we fail at something we want very much to do, we are likely to try to make up for this by being good at something else. This process is called *compensation.* If we do this consciously, it may be a wise form of adaptation; but when we do it unconsciously, we call it ego–defense. The two kinds of behavior are very different and the difference can be seen in the attitude toward the activity at which we failed. Suppose I wanted to play football but was not strong enough. If I accept this failure and put my efforts into music or drama, I will still like football and will gladly admit that I would have liked to have made the team. If I refuse to face this failure, I will put my efforts into something else but will now be critical of football players and deride the idea that I would like to be on the team. Sometimes a person is good at something, but because he feels inferior and inadequate in other ways, he will make too much of what he is good at, asserting that nothing else is so importnat. This is a case of *overcompensation*.

Identification

Identification means to look up to someone, to engage in hero–worship. Freud pointed out some hidden meanings in this apparently innocent practice. Freud said that a boy identifies with his father and that it is through this identification that the boy resolves his Oedipus complex. The Oedipus theory, which says that a boy loves his mother and hates his father, is one of Freud's most controversial theories. However, we need not completely accept this theory to see the validity of his explanation of identification. The boy competes with his father for his mother's love, but if the father has a good relationship with his wife, the son realizes that there is no chance of winning her so he identifies with his father. Freud calls this "identifying with the aggressor" and maintains that there is always some hostility involved in this process. When the smallest boy on the block becomes the ally of the biggest boy, he says, "If you can't lick 'em, join 'em." Again, this may be a wise form of adaptation or it may be a form of unconscious ego–defense. When our self–esteem stems largely from those with whom we identify, we may be hollow and vulnerable ourselves. The hostility in this kind of identification can be seen in how we treat heroes who fall. We love the Dodgers when they are winning, but how we hate them when they lose!

Regression

An important psychological principle can be seen in our tendency to return to earlier, less mature patterns of behavior when we are under pressure and feel insecure. This kind of behavior is called *regression*. A child of three who can walk, go to the toilet, and knows several words may lose all these abilities when a baby brother arrives and deprives him of attention. Similar reverses in maturation may be seen at any age. In adults the most common forms of regression are crying, pouting, and fits of temper. A middle–aged woman may try to look and act as young as her daughter. A man in his early forties ("the dangerous years") may try to prove himself by falling in love with a young woman or by competing at sports with younger men. The dynamic involved in all forms of regression is the escape from the responsibilities that go with a certain stage of maturity (see developmental tasks in Chap. 7).

Reaction Formation

When we are confronted with an approach-avoidance conflict, one of the commonest defenses is to deny the attraction and emphasize the avoidance. This exaggerated rejection of what attracts us is called *reaction formation.* A preadolescent girl accused of liking a boy may reply, "Him! I hate him!!" We laughingly say, "Aha! You do like him. I can tell by how strongly you deny it." Shakespeare says, "me thinks the lady dost protest too much." Sometimes a sermon against sin may be far more exciting than sin itself. Whenever anyone talks about something a great deal, even if he is opposed to it, it is likely that underneath the opposition there is a strong attraction. Notice how this resolves the approach-avoidance conflict. I am attracted to pornography, but I feel guilty about this attraction. I take a strong stand against it, which saves me from feeling guilty, and then spend much of my time studying pornographic materials as part of my opposition and thus satisfy my attraction. Although the extremes of any dimension may appear to be opposites, underneath they are often very close. Communism and Fascism, for example, are opposites; but how alike they are! The far left and the far right have an incurable attraction for each other.

Sublimation and Substitution

Here are two patterns which have similar dynamics but dissimilar results. Both *sublimation* and *substitution* involve the indirect expression of a drive. In sublimation the drive finds indirect expression in a socially acceptable way. In substitution the indirect expression is not socially acceptable. The sexual drive may be sublimated into art, poetry, music, and religion. The sexual drive may also be indirectly expressed in a wide variety of deviate behaviors such as homosexuality, voyeurism ("peeping Toms"), exhibitionism (exposing oneself in public), and fetishism (being aroused by an article of clothing or one part of the anatomy). The line is hard to draw, and it changes as mores change. Certain forms of exhibitionism, for example, are at least condoned if not approved; and most American men are fetishistic about women's breasts.

Aggression may be sublimated into fighting injustice, into competing in sports, or into making a living. We would call it substitution if it is expressed indirectly as police brutality or as overly severe parental discipline.

The next three ego-defense mechanisms are relatively harmless in mild form; but when they play too large a part in one's life style, they cause serious damage. In fact, when we look at the neuroses and psychoses, the reader may note how often one or more of these three mechanisms constitute the core of the problem behavior.

Fantasy

Seen most commonly as day–dreaming, *fantasy* plays an important part in everyone's life. Especially in childhood, it is through fantasy that the world is enlarged and new possibilities envisioned. Even as adults our world would be greatly impoverished without the fictional characters from novels and the fantastic personalities from the comics. Yet it is this same ability to fantasize which may cause some of the most serious personal problems.

In the most familiar fantasies we are *conquering heroes* or *suffering heroes.* The boy who is unable to make the team pictures himself as a marvelous player who saves the game. The girl who feels she is not beautiful pictures herself as the belle of the ball, another Cinderella. We vent our anger in fantasy or we construct a make–believe world where all is well. The reason fantasy can be such a problem, is that it is strongly satisfying. Hungry people sometimes spend the money they need for food on a movie, as shown by the high rate of movie attendance in India.

Consider the amount of time spent in fantasy even by people we call normal. Many hours are spent watching television, reading novels, and reading movie magazines. Most of us loudly proclaim our love of truth and our disdain for dishonesty; but when "the chips are down," we are reluctant to give up our own fantastic ideas. There are times when reality is a most unattractive alternative to things as we imagine them to be. Some people, either because they see real life as hopelessly miserable or because they have not developed strength and skill for adaptive living, spend the greater part of their lives in fantasy. They achieve a kind of happiness and pay the price of being largely out of touch with significant areas of reality.

Repression

Repression is very much like forgetting, but it has a different purpose. In normal forgetting we forget what is finished and no longer important. In this way we keep our minds free to attend to what is unfinished and important. In repression we forget what is unfinished and important because remembering brings anxiety and pain.

Repression differs from suppression in that it is unconscious, while suppression is conscious. In suppression we know what we are turning our attention away from but in repression we have put it out of mind so completely that we can't recall it even if we want to.

It is obvious how repression serves to resolve conflicts of all kinds. One of the conflicting elements is simply removed so that no conflict remains. What does remain is an inexplicable uneasiness, rigidity, and the appearance of the most unexpected behavior. This will be clear in the neurotic reactions we shall describe later in this chapter.

Projection

Projection is in many ways the most lethal ego–defense. In projection, rather than learning what is happening by receiving input from the world around us, we color our perception according to our psychological needs. In other words, we "project" pictures from within ourselves onto the environmental screen rather than seeing the pictures which are actually there. This process leads to distortions and ways of behaving that are completely unrelated to reality. In its extreme form this defense is labelled *paranoia,* but to a lesser degree this tendency can be seen in all of us.

We are most likely to project when we feel afraid, inferior, or guilty. When a person spends the night alone in a large, old house he is likely to hear many strange noises. If he has heard that the house is haunted, he will hear the voices, moans, or dragging chains that have been reported by others. Fear contributes to projection as does feeling inferior. When someone goes to a party where very "proper" people have gathered and he is not sure if he is properly dressed, he will probably believe that "everyone" is looking at him, talking about him, and laughing at him. The same thing happens when we feel great guilt. Everyone seems to know what we have done. We think there are insinuations in things people say. Others seem to look at us in a knowing way, while we are sure some people stop talking when we walk up.

Knowing what is back of these projections can help us deal more effectively with people who are completely misperceiving a situation. However, it is difficult to relate to people who are paranoid, and we often find that the only way we can get along with them is to avoid mentioning topics included in their "delusional system." Real help must involve dealing with the feelings of fear, guilt and inferiority and the causes of these feelings.

FRUSTRATION AND PROBLEM BEHAVIOR

The best way to learn about a person is to see how he reacts to frustration. Some people undergo the most amazing transformations! One moment they are sweet, loving and kind; the next moment, vicious—all because they were "crossed." Problems can cause frustrated people, and frustrated people can cause even greater problems.

Nothing is more urgent than doing something about problem behavior. That "something" may be to remove the sources of frustration, as is being attempted in the attacks on poverty, injustice, and inequality. But there is also something that can and must be done for people who cause problems or become problems when they are frustrated. This conflict between the social dimension and the personal dimension is an old issue and maintaining a balanced perspective is not easy. Due to the purpose of this book, we shall focus our attention on the problem behavior which, in itself, deserves our attention. This one-sided view should

not be interpreted as meaning that we do not recognize the need for social re-
forms. Concerned people will work where they can be effective with the reali-
zation that there are many facets to the problems.

There are three major types of problem behavior: neurotic reactions, character disorders, and psychotic reactions. These distinctions are arbitrary and there
are many borderline or mixed types. Nevertheless, there is some value in making
the distinctions.

By *neurotic reactions* we mean behavior which is more ego–defensive than
problem–oriented or growth–oriented. All of us are neurotic at times, and
strictly speaking, there are no neurotic people, only neurotic behavior. As an
oversimplification we might say that people who manifest neurotic reactions are
largely problems to themselves. They tend to be unhappy, ineffective people.

By *character disorders* we mean patterns of behavior that suggest a failure in
the development of a mature, social person. Again as an oversimplification we
may say that people with character disorders cause more problems for others
than for themselves. They "act out" their conflicts rather than suffering inter-
nally.

By *psychotic reactions* we mean the unusually disorganized behavior which
reveals a more complete break with reality. Most commonly accompanied by
hallucinations and delusions, psychotic reactions tend to seem "strange" and
"irrational." The people who manifest such behavior are often called "sick,"
"crazy," or "insane," and are sent to mental hospitals. It is easy to become discouraged with such people and to feel like giving up on them.

A WORD ABOUT LABELS

Before we discuss the various patterns of behavior which have been labelled
by psychiatrists, we should say a word about labelling. In the first place, should
we classify and label at all? In the second place, what is the meaning of the kinds
of labels now in use?

Should We Classify and Label?

People do not like to be typed or "pigeonholed." Nor do most people like to
have their behavior labelled. By the very act of labelling we may alter the person
or the behavior. A person may not be "sick" until we say he is, or a boy may
not be "bad" until we say so.

On the other hand, science demands classification. We cannot gain general
knowledge unless we group phenomena on the basis of similarities. And sometimes people take comfort from labels. The patient will say to his doctor,
"What is it; what have I got? And he may be more relieved to hear that he has
some known disease than that the doctor doesn't know what the trouble is.

The Meaning of Psychiatric Labels

Perhaps the question of whether problem behavior should be labelled depends on what we use the labels to mean. Here the medical model, used by psychiatrists, is confusing. In medicine disease names usually point to a definite cause, such as some bacteria, or to a dysfunction of some specific organ. In psychiatry there are some organically based psychological disturbances, and for these conditions the diagnostic labels have clear referents; but in most of the so-called "abnormal" psychological states no true disease exists. We cannot say that a specific foreign substance has invaded the system or that some well-defined organic function is failing. Most psychiatric diagnostic labels refer only to patterns of behavior, called symptom syndromes, and add nothing to understanding. For example, if a person is suspicious of nearly everybody, and believes that a plot is being organized against him, we say that the person is paranoid which means that he is suspicious of nearly everybody and believes that a plot is being organized against him. It is as though some student comes late to my class every day and someone asks me, "What's wrong with him?" I answer, "Why, he's afflicted with chronic tardiness." The questioner replies, "Really! I didn't realize he was sick." What is it to be afflicted with chronic tardiness? To be late most of the time. So the labels, in most cases, do not tell us anything that we have not already observed. They are simply designations for commonly recurring patterns of behavior. As such they are convenient, much like shorthand, and they provide some basis for grouping phenomena which can then be studied.

NEUROTIC REACTIONS

Neurotic disorders have been classified in many different ways. We shall, in general, follow the designations accepted by the American Psychiatric Association.[3] We should note, however, that most so-called neurotics do not fall into any one of these classes, but tend to show several symptom patterns in their behavior.

Anxiety Reactions

The anxiety reaction is the most common disorder. The subject manifests "free-floating anxiety," which means that he cannot focus on any cause for his anxiety. He is afraid of "nothing," but he is more frightened than if he did have something definite to fear. The symptoms range from vague, persistent feelings of uneasiness to an obsessive dread, accompanied by palpitations of the heart, constriction in the throat and chest, and a cold sweat. Sleeplessness and loss of appetite are common, and often the person is so debilitated that he cannot work or carry on simple functions. According to current theories, this anxiety is usually related to unresolved conflicts which have been put out of awareness.

Dissociative Reactions

Here we include non-organic amnesia (loss of memory), partial or total; fugue states (amnesia plus flight); and multiple personality (made famous several years ago in the story, *The Three Faces of Eve*). In its simplest form, dissociation is seen in somnambulism (sleepwalking). In the dissociative reactions it is as if the personality has split. Some people are so different from one time to another that we hardly recognize them. Perhaps each of us on occasion has surprised himself by his behavior and explained, "I wasn't myself." These are mild examples of dissociation.

Conversion Reactions

Previously called *hysteria*, conversion reactions refer to physical disabilities which have no physical cause. Most common are paralysis, anesthesia, blindness, deafness, and loss of voice. Conversion reactions should be distinguished from malingering (a pretended disability, called "goldbricking" in the armed forces), and from the psychosomatic illnesses (where there is real physical damage). In Chapter 1 we noted that Freud did his first major work with this disorder. Charcot had shown that under hypnosis the hysterical symptoms disappeared, thus demonstrating that they were psychologically rather than physically caused. Sometimes these illnesses are cured through suggestion. No doubt many of the dramatic cures of religious "healers" are examples of hysterics giving up their crutches.

Phobic Reactions

A phobia is most simply defined as an irrational fear—a fear out of proportion to the real danger involved. Most common are acrophobia (fear of high places), agoraphobia (fear of wide open places), claustrophobia (fear of closed places), nyctophobia (fear of darkness), and zoophobia (fear of animals). The most common explanation for a phobia is that it is the result of some early traumatic experience. In Chapter 8 we shall study Watson's famous experiment in which after a baby was conditioned to fear a white rat, he was phobic with all white and furry animals. On the other hand, many phobias seem to be more than conditioned fears. Some seem to continue because they have been rewarded by attention or relief from responsibility. Some phobias seem to protect a person from something he fears even more. An example is the mother who develops a phobia of picking up her new-born baby. The phobia protects her from an even more frightening anger which she is afraid she could not control if she were to pick him up. Many people's fear of heights is apparently not due solely to some childhood trauma. Rather, high places have symbolic meaning— they are afraid of failing to "stay up there," or of wanting to jump to escape the constant struggle to get to the top.

Obsessive-Compulsive Reactions

An obsession is an idea that one cannot get out of his thoughts, like a song that keeps running through the mind no matter how hard we try to stop it. A compulsion is an act that we feel compelled to perform, for example straightening a picture because we "just can't stay in the room with it that way." Since these two kinds of behavior usually go together, we use the term obsessive-compulsive reaction to refer to any behavior, overt or covert, which occurs persistently and repetitiously "on its own," as it were. Common obsessions have to do with sex, death, cleanliness, and religion. Common compulsions have to do with cleanliness rituals, superstitious rites which supposedly ward off bad luck, checking and re-checking locked doors and windows, and avoiding the cracks in the sidewalk. As with some of the phobias, many obsessions and compulsions seem to reduce anxiety, and although they are irritating, they protect us from becoming aware of something that would make us even more uncomfortable.

Kleptomania (compulsive stealing) and pyromania (compulsive setting of fires) are examples of obsessive-compulsive behavior; but because of the sexual meanings often associated with these acts, they are usually classified as fetishistic sexual deviations.

Depressive Reactions

Neurotic depression is very similar to psychotic depression, but it is less severe, usually of shorter duration, and tends to be "used" by the subject rather than overpowering him. This condition is also called reactive depression and is usually related either to loss of self-esteem or to unexpressed anger. Most of us feel depressed when we fail or make fools of ourselves, and we also feel depressed if we are angry at somebody to whom we are afraid to show the anger. This unexpressed anger also leads to a loss of self-esteem if we hate ourselves for being so dependent that we do not dare show our anger.

Other Psychoneurotic Disorders

Traditionally, *neurasthenia* and *hypochondriasis* have been classified as neurotic disorders. Neurasthenia, characterized by chronic fatigue, is now commonly called "asthenic reaction" and is classified as a psychosomatic disorder. Hypochondriasis, characterized by an obsession with one's health, is usually classified as an obsessive–compulsive reaction. Some authorities list *evasion of growth* as a neurotic pattern, but we shall consider it as a personality disorder. Actually, the neurotic reactions and the ego–defense mechanisms may all be thought of as ways to avoid growing. The best way to prevent neurosis is to keep growing, and the best cure for any neurosis is to get on with one's growth.

PERSONALITY OR CHARACTER DISORDERS

At no point do the psychiatric labels seem more inadequate than when we confront the personality or character disorders. Here, more than with the abnormal patterns so far described, we are involved with disturbances that are difficult to define and which inescapably involve values and social norms. Nevertheless, it is in this area that we confront some of the most pressing issues of our society: delinquency, violence, sexual deviation, alcoholism, and drug addiction.

Disorders of personality and character are the concern not only of psychiatrists and psychologists but of social workers, teachers, ministers, judges, and parents. The survival of our nation, as well as that of western civilization, may well depend on whether we can find ways to heal these disorders.

Disturbances of Personality Pattern

These include *inadequate personality, schizoid personality, cyclothymic personality,* and *paranoid personality* and refer to "personality types that can rarely be basically altered by therapy and tend to decompensate to psychosis under stress."[4] These personality patterns may usefully be considered as lesser manifestations of patterns we see in psychotic behavior.

Disturbances of Personality Traits

This group of disturbances relates to "emotional immaturity with inability to maintain emotional equilibrium and independence under even minor stress."[5] Again, at the risk of oversimplification, we may think of these personality traits as related to neurotic symptoms. They include *emotionally unstable personality, passive–aggressive personality, compulsive personality,* as well as certain other trait disturbances. Rather than taking these diagnostic labels very seriously, or considering them as exhaustive, we can consider them to be illustrations of some of the many kinds of personality traits that cause problems for people in our society.

Sociopathic Personality

This type is characterized by "the inability to conform to prevailing social standards and lack of social responsibility,"[6] and includes all who act illegally, immorally, or in ways that offend the prevailing ideas of decency, good manners, or values of a society. A careful analysis of problems related to sociopathy takes the psychologist into sociology, penology, law, ethics, politics, medicine, and religion. In the category of the sociopathic personality we include *antisocial reaction* (sometimes called "psychopathic"), *dyssocial reaction* (the result of being raised in deviant subcultures), *sexual deviation, alcoholism,* and *drug addiction.*

William Glasser, whose therapeutic approach is called *Reality Therapy,* suggests that antisocial people are deficient in the three R's of *right, responsibility,* and *reality.* He believes that these people have not learned what is right, have not accepted responsibility, or have not faced reality.

PSYCHOTIC DISORDERS

The psychotic disorders are usually divided into two groups, the *organic psychoses* and the *functional psychoses.* Organic psychoses are severe psychological disturbances resulting from brain damage or some organic dysfunction. They are the concern of neurologists, psychiatrists, and other medical doctors. Functional psychoses are severe psychological disturbances for which organic causes have not been found. By law they are treated by medical doctors, usually psychiatrists, and many authorities are convinced that they do have physical causes. There are equally eminent authorities, however, who are convinced that these disorders are truly functional, meaning that they reflect failures in the adaptive processes of the person.

Because treatment of the psychoses has been delegated to the medical profession, psychologists have dealt with them mainly by attempting to develop a theory of psychotic behavior and by devising psychological tests to help in diagnosis. Some psychologists have, however, worked with psychiatrists in an attempt to help psychotics by means of psychotherapy.

Traditionally, the psychotic disorders are classified into four main groups:

1. Schizophrenic reactions: simple, hebephrenic, catatonic, paranoid, and childhood schizophrenia or autism.
2. Affective reactions: manic–depressive, and psychotic depressive reaction.
3. Involutional psychotic reaction.
4. Paranoid reactions.

Great strides have been made in the study of psychotic reactions in the past 25 years, but today we are not much closer to fully understanding them. Research has not supported any one theory but has led in at least four directions. One is the chemical basis of some of the psychotic reactions. A second direction is the social meaning of psychotic behavior. A third points to learning as the way in which psychotic behavior is acquired. The fourth direction is existential, taking us into the area of the self and the will.

The most dramatic changes have occurred in the treatment of psychotic reactions. First, and most influential, has been the use of newly discovered drugs. Psychopharmacology now makes it possible to alleviate many of the most troublesome symptoms and to send people home from mental hospitals far sooner than ever before, though we are not sure this is really a cure. The second big change is in the increasing use of techniques of behavior modification. This approach is still very new and firm conclusions are not warranted, but some of the reported results are very promising. (*See* chapter 13.)

THE ETIOLOGY OR CAUSES OF PROBLEM BEHAVIOR

It is difficult to get agreement on how the troublesome behavioral patterns are to be classified. When we ask what *causes* these conditions, we get such a variety of answers that it is clear we do not yet have an explanation that we can call "scientific." We shall review the possible causes and consider the evidence for some of the most fruitful theories.

A Checklist of Possible Problem Areas

Physiological Factors

> Genetic factors—defective genes due to heredity, mutation, or chromosome damage
> Congenital factors—defects present at birth due to intra–uterine damage or birth injuries

General health—its effects on mood, tolerance for tension, level of energy,
   sensitivity to stimuli, etc.
Specific conditions—presence of disease, glandular imbalance, or chemicals
   introduced into the system
Fatigue—disequilibrium due to exhaustion.

The Life Situation

Sociological factors—socioeconomic status, cultural conflict, role confusion, etc.
Interpersonal situation—family conflict, difficulties in loving and being
   loved, and rejection by significant others
Specific pressures—crises, tragedies, and stresses

Learned Responses

The effects that experiences have had on us—conditioning in the Pavlovian
   sense
Habitual ways of adaptation—conditioning according to Skinner's model
The "reality" which has been learned—how we have learned to "see" our
   world, other people, and ourselves

The Human Situation (Existential Factors)

The problem of "meaning"
The problem of self-actualization
The problem of human limits, especially death

Major Approaches to Etiology and Supporting Evidence

Physicochemical theories. One approach to problem behavior assumes that it
has an organic basis. Indeed, some notable discoveries have encouraged such a
view. Most frequently cited, perhaps, is the discovery that the psychotic state of
"general paresis," once thought to be psychologically caused, is due to advanced
syphilitic infection. Interesting evidence also links the B-complex vitamins with
alcoholism. Other studies suggest that anxiety is related, in some people, to a
calcium deficiency which makes sugar an anxiety-creating agent.
   In recent years it has been found that many children who have behavior problems at school are neurologically damaged.[7] Inconclusive studies linking chronic
criminality with certain chromosomal anomalies have also appeared.[8]
   The most concerted effort has gone into the search for a physical basis for
schizophrenia. Several very promising leads are being followed, especially those

linking serotonin and adrenolutin with schizophrenic symptoms, but as yet this question has not been settled.[9] Some authorities still are convinced that a hereditary factor is involved in schizophrenia, and they cite reports that if one identical twin is schizophrenic the likelihood that the other will be also may be as high as 90 percent.[10]

At this point, we can summarize the evidence for physicochemical causation of problem behavior as follows. There is clear evidence for genetic causation of mental retardation and other conditions, such as cretinism. There is clear evidence linking syphilis and arteriosclerosis with abnormal brain function, even though psychological factors seem to determine some of the effects. There is strong, but not conclusive, evidence linking several forms of antisocial behavior with neurological damage, vitamin deficiency, and chromosomal factors. There is important, but far from conclusive, evidence linking schizophrenia with chemical and genetic factors. Finally, there is some evidence that suggests a connection between anxiety and nutritional factors.

Environmental theories. At the opposite extreme from a physicochemical explanation of problem behavior is the view that, except for disturbances clearly resulting from genetic and disease factors, environmental influences play the most crucial role.

One sociological theory sees abnormal behavior as social maladjustment. Even much of the bizarre behavior of the psychotic, it is contended, might be considered normal in another society. Neurotic behavior and personality defects are explained as problems of inadequate socialization and culture conflict.

Interesting evidence supports this sociological approach. Socioeconomic factors are clearly related to the incidence of crime and delinquency and are somewhat related to the incidence of neurosis and psychosis. We know that laws made by the dominant social group often define as illegal the behavior of other groups within the society. Fruitful studies also exist relating changing role definitions and confused role expectations with personality and behavioral difficulties. Some of the strongest evidence relates the breakdown in certain social institutions, especially the family, with many patterns of problem behavior.[11]

The learning theory approach to problem behavior stresses environmental influence. In its simplest form, this theory suggests that people who have bad experiences as a result of their environment will turn out badly. To dramatize the principle, proponents might say, "If we find a dog that bites or is easily frightened, we can only assume that he has been treated badly or that he has been poorly trained. By the same token, if we find a person whose behavior is a problem or shows unusual symptoms, we can only assume that he has been treated badly or that he has been poorly trained."

Certainly much evidence supports such an assertion.[12] That the way a person is treated affects what he becomes hardly needs documentation. Countless studies have been made of the relationship between child–rearing practices and personality and behavioral traits.[13] As might be expected, many correlations have been found. Most influential have been patterns of parental rejection, over-protection, over-permissiveness, and harsh, inconsistent discipline.

Both sociological and learning theories leave many unanswered questions. Too many exceptions still exist: some children from what appear to be "good" homes become problems; some children from what appear to be "bad" homes turn out well. While we intuitively accept the importance of the environment as a molder of personality and determiner of behavior, and while some highly suggestive evidence has been reported, much more research must be done before we fully understand the environmental basis of behavior.

The nature of an open or free society may make it impossible to establish sufficient controls so that environmental influences can be brought under scientific control. The value we place on freedom may demand that we pay the price of unpredictability in this area. *Walden Two*, by B. F. Skinner gives a highly stimulating picture of a carefully controlled social environment. Skinner is one who believes that the environment determines behavior.

Interaction theories. The most influential psychological explanations of problem behavior have come from theorists who look at the *interaction* between physical and environmental factors. Some, like Sigmund Freud, believe that this interaction has rigidly determined effects; while others, like Carl Rogers, see the process as very much affected by a self which may develop important freedom of action. Freud understood all problem behavior, except the organic psychoses, as resulting from conflicts between the instinctive urges, mainly the sexual urge, and restrictions on these urges internalized in the superego.[14]

Adler, a contemporary of Freud, saw the individual as actively striving within the environment, as he experienced it, to overcome feelings of inferiority. This personal striving leads each individual to choose a "style of life" that seems to work best for him.[15]

H. S. Sullivan, who somewhat modified Freudian theory, insisted that problem behavior is primarily the result of the anxiety which stems from poor interpersonal relationships.[16]

Becker[17] and Jackson[18] see communication difficulties as the important causative factors.

Rogers, who sees the self as an active participant in its own destiny, suggests that the main cause of problem behavior is an incongruence between what the self really is and the way it sees itself (self-concept).[19]

A vast amount of research has been generated by these theories, especially those of Freud. As yet, however, we do not have the kind of data which will conclusively establish any of them. Most of the support for a particular theory comes either from clinicians who take a therapeutic approach reflecting one of the theories or from biases based on a personal philosophy or system of values.

Most psychologists would undoubtedly subscribe to a pluralistic view of the causes of problem behavior. Differences between them would tend to be a matter of different emphases. All would agree that we still have much to learn about the causes of disturbed people. Psychology is a young science and has a frontier which beckons to the bold and the imaginative.

SUMMARY

Functionalism assumes that behavior is need-based and goal-directed. We shall try to understand the various reactions to frustration in these terms. Frustration occurs when an organism is blocked in its efforts to reach a goal which is perceived as capable of satisfying a need. This blocking may be due to environmental barriers, inner conflict, or stress. Conflicts may be of three kinds: approach-approach, avoidance-avoidance, or approach-avoidance. The first response of a frustrated organism is to increase and to vary its activity, and this often leads to aggression.

Frustration also results in anxiety about reaching the goal and about the adequacy of the ego. Extreme anxiety is a disturbing experience which tends to interfere with adaptive efforts and to stimulate defensive maneuvers aimed at lessening the anxiety. Some of these maneuvers have been called ego-defense mechanisms. They include rationalization, displaced aggression, compensation, identification, regression, reaction formation, sublimation and substitution, fantasy, repression, and projection.

When a person's reactions to frustration are primarily defensive, his behavior tends to become a problem for himself and for others. This problem behavior can be a neurotic reaction, a character disorder, or a psychotic disorder.

Psychiatric labels are a problem. If they are assumed to stand for real diseases, they can be harmful and misleading. Used as designations for commonly recurring patterns of behavior, they are convenient and may serve the interests of scientific study.

Neurotic reactions include anxiety reactions, dissociative reactions, conversion reactions, phobic reactions, obsessive-compulsive reactions, and depressive reactions.

Personality or character disorders include disturbances of personality pattern, such as inadequate personality, schizoid personality, cyclothymic personality, and paranoid personality; disturbances of personality traits, such as emotionally unstable personality, passive-aggressive personality, and compulsive personality; and sociopathic personality, a term which includes antisocial reaction, dyssocial reaction, sexual deviation, alcoholism, and drug addiction.

Psychotic disorders are divided into organic psychoses and functional psychoses. The functional psychoses include schizophrenic reactions, affective reactions, involutional psychotic reactions, and paranoid reactions.

Great strides have been made in the study of psychotic reactions, but a real understanding of them still eludes us. The most dramatic progress has been made in the area of treatment, due mainly to the use of new drugs and techniques of behavior modification.

The effort to understand the causes of problem behavior has led to physico-chemical explanations, environmental explanations, and to theories about the self in interaction. None of the explanations is adequate and the search for fuller understanding continues.

QUESTIONS FOR STUDY AND CLASS DISCUSSION

1. Do you think that modern city dwellers face more or less environmental frustrations than people who lived on the frontier?

2. Can you identify the major conflicts in your own life?

3. Apply the frustration–aggression hypothesis to problems we see in international relations.

4. Try to describe the physical reactions you experience when you are very anxious. Do you ever have these reactions without being able to point to a cause?

5. How is it possible to use defense mechanisms without being aware that we are?

6. Would it be better to use no defense mechanisms at all? If the use of some is justified, what principle would you suggest for determining how much?

7. Take one of the neurotic reactions and identify the defense mechanisms involved.

8. Are some neurotic people happier than healthy people? If so, why not be neurotic?

9. Why do you suppose some people become neurotic while others develop character disorders?

10. What distinguishes a schizophrenic from an eccentric artist? a "true believer" from a paranoiac?

SUGGESTIONS FOR FURTHER READING

Green, Hannah. *I Never Promised You a Rose Garden.* New York: Signet Books, 1964.
Freud, Sigmund. *The Psychopathology of Everyday Life.* Edited by James Strachey. New York: W. W. Norton & Co., 1961.

McCord, William and McCord, Joan. *The Psychopath.* New York: D. Van
    Nostrand Co., 1964.
Sapirstein, Milton R. *Paradoxes of Everyday Life.* Greenwich, Conn.: A Faw-
    cett Premier Book, 1955.
Yates, Aubrey J., ed. *Frustration and Conflict.* New York: D. Van Nostrand
    Co., 1965.

PART III
SCIENTIFIC PSYCHOLOGY

In Part II we dealt with some of the most important issues in psychology as accurately as we could, but our over-all treatment was more philosophical than scientific. In Part III we change the focus and limit ourselves more to the kind of evidence that we call objective or scientific. While these data both rest on philosophical assumptions and have philosophical implications, our presentation in this section will be largely factual, with a minimum of speculation.

The student will notice a marked difference as he moves from Part II to Part III. If Part II was like a land of luxuriant growth, exciting but easy to get lost in, then Part III will be more like a desert where the ravines and the mountains stand out in clear relief. For some this change will be refreshing; for others it will seem arid.

Whatever our feelings or our biases, we owe it to ourselves, and to a field, to understand it in its own terms. Our brief excursion into the land of philosophical psychology is over; we now embark on a scientific safari.

Chapter 6, *Individual Differences*, explains how individuals differ in terms of factors common to all. Chapter 7, *Growth and Development,* is a study of some of the factors which may account for individual differences. Chapter 8, *Studies of Behavior,* gives a review of the methods and results of behavioral analysis. Chapter 9, *Correlates of Behavior*, is a study of factors in other aresa which are correlated with observed behavior.

6

INDIVIDUAL DIFFERENCES

OVERVIEW

Individuals Differ

In order to describe people, we point to the similarities and differences between them. I am taller than my father; I look like my mother; I can run faster than my sister; I have my grandfather's brown eyes. We also describe people in erms of averages and types. She is smarter than average; that whole family is unusually musical; she is the artistic type; he is a typical Irishman. Some descriptions are quantitative: he is six feet tall; he has an I.Q. of 120. Other descriptions are qualitative: she has blue eyes; she is beautiful.

The description of individual differences becomes scientific when we more carefully define our terms, use more exact methods of measurement, and analyze our data systematically. The science of individual differences had its beginning in a field quite unrelated to psychology, that of astronomy.

Historical Background

In 1796 the Astronomer Royal at the Greenwich Observatory found that his assistant's observations of the movements of stars differed from his own by as much as one second, so he dismissed him. Such errors had serious consequences when observatory clocks were being calibrated.[1] In 1823, at an observatory in Germany, Friedrich Wilhelm Bessel noticed similar discrepancies and decided to study them. He found that even well trained astronomers differed widely in the time it took them to make an observation, and he referred to this factor as a "personal equation." Bessel studied many "instrumental errors," and became the first student of what we now call "reaction time."[2]

However, it was Francis Galton (1822–1911) who laid the groundwork for the study of individual differences. Galton was a counsin of the famous Charles Darwin, whose momumental *Origin of Species* was published in 1859, and he was fascinated with the problem of differences among people. In his *Hereditary Genius* of 1869, he noted that both idiots and men of genius appear with comparative rarity, whereas men of average ability are quite common. Earlier, in 1835, Quetelet had measured the chest girths of Scottish soldiers and the heights of French conscripts and had found a systematic variation, which he called "the normal law of error," in the distribution of his measurements. Boring explains this phenomenon by saying it is "as if Nature were shooting at a target and missed the bull's eye, often a little to one side or the other, but only seldom by a great amount."[3] Galton assumed that this same principle would hold for genius, too. In 1883, he published *Inquiries into Human Faculty and Its Development,* which contained measurements of every conceivable kind, including tests of mental ability. It was these tests, by the way, that Cattell used as the basis for his testing in America, and to which he first gave the name "mental tests."

In 1889, in *Natural Inheritance,* Galton presented in crude form two principles which have been basic to the study of individual differences. One was the idea that it is often necessary to measure the "co-relation" between two variables, as between the statures of fathers and sons. It is this principle, refined by Carl Pearson, and named "coefficient of correlation," that we often meet in statistical studies. Galton's other principle was that the "co–relation" he observed involved two "regressions toward mediocrity." Fathers of unusually tall or short sons tend to be closer to the average height than their sons, and sons of unusually tall or short fathers tend to be closer to the average than their fathers. Today this principle is called "regression to the mean," and can be understood in terms of the pull toward the middle or average that chance factors exert.

The other name that must be noted in this brief historical sketch is that of Alfred Binet (1857–1911). While Cattell's modifications of Galton's tests were called "mental tests," they were actually little more than simple tests of sensory and motor ability. It remained for Binet to develop the first real tests of complex mental ability. His first test, which he developed with Simon, was published in France in 1903. Even today the name of Binet is synonymous with mental tests.

Assumptions Underlying the Study of Individual Differences

The most basic assumption underlying the study of individual differences is that people differ with respect to *traits* which they have in *common.* Only if this is true could there be any point in comparing individuals with one another.

One assumption goes to the heart of the scientific method. A scientific philosophy assumes that whatever exists must exit in some quantity. Even qualities have quantity—and we say that one individual has more of a certain quality than someone else has. Thus, a science of individual differences must rest on the assumption that the traits in terms of which we compare individuals can be measured in quantitative terms.

A third assumption necessary for a science of individual differences is that observed differences show an orderliness and are the result of discoverable causes. Even random or chance variations fall within predictable limits and are regulated by discoverable principles.

THE TRAIT THEORY

The trait theory grew out of the common–sense observation that our language provides us with words for the description of persons and their behavior. Allport and Odbert found that the unabridged dictionary has some 18,000 adjectives that are used to describe how people act, think, perceive and feel, and another 4,000 words that might be accepted as trait names—such as humility, sociability, honesty, and forthrightness.[4] Through careful editing, the list was reduced to 170 words which might be called human traits. Cattell took these 170 trait names and by using a statistical method called *factor analysis*, found that they could be reduced to the twelve clusters or factors shown in the next table.

CATTELL'S TWELVE TRAITS

1. Emotionally expressive, frank, placid	vs.	Reserved, closemouthed, anxious
2. Intelligent, smart, assertive	vs.	Unintelligent, dull, submissive
3. Free of neurotic symptoms, realistic about life	vs.	Variety of neurotic symptoms, evasive, immature
4. Self-assertive, confident, aggressive	vs.	Submissive, unsure, compliant
5. Cheerful, joyous, humorous, witty	vs.	Depressed, pessimistic, dull, phlegmatic
6. Persevering, attentive to people	vs.	Fickle, neglectful of social chores
7. Likes meeting people, strong interest in opposite sex	vs.	Shy, little interest in opposite sex
8. Dependent, immature, gregarious, attention-seeking	vs.	Independent-minded, self-sufficient
9. Polished, poised, composed, introspective, sensitive	vs.	Awkward, socially clumsy, crude
10. Trustful, understanding	vs.	Suspicious, jealous
11. Unconventional, eccentric, fitful hysterical upsets	vs.	Conventional, unemotional
12. Logical mind, cool, aloof	vs.	Sentimental mind, attentive to people

(From Cattell, 1946, adapted from Morgan and King, 1966, p. 464)

When using trait names, it is important to realize that people cannot be characterized as one type or another. We shall note, when we discuss the principles of measurement, that traits tend to be distributed among people in a way that produces a normal distribution curve. Thus for each trait, more people will be in the middle than on either end, and a person who is extreme on one trait may not be extreme on another.

It is most useful to plot a *personality profile* for an individual using a list of several traits. For example, on a personality test for teenagers, adapted from Cattell's list of traits, profiles were obtained from three 16-17 year old girls in a home for delinquent adolescents. (See table above.) All three were on probation for infractions of the law, but notice how different the profiles are. Mary is reserved, stable, phlegmatic, sober, placid, self-sufficient, and relaxed; Jane is also reserved, but she is expedient while Mary is self-sufficient. Ruth is just as relaxed as Mary but is outgoing while Mary is reserved, and is group-oriented while Mary is self-sufficient. The differences between those delinquent girls imply that there is no single "delinquent type."

Jr.-Sr. HSPQ TEST PROFILE

Name: _____ Age: ____ Sex: ____ Grade in School: ____ Date: ____

FACTOR	RAW SCORE			Sten Score	LOW SCORE DESCRIPTION	STANDARD TEN SCORE (STEN) → Average	HIGH SCORE DESCRIPTION
	Form A	Form B	Total			1 2 3 4 5 6 7 8 9 10	
A					RESERVED, DETACHED, CRITICAL, COOL, (Sizothymia)		OUTGOING, WARMHEARTED, EASY-GOING, PARTICIPATING (Affectothymia, formerly cyclothymia)
B					LESS INTELLIGENT, CONCRETE-THINKING (Lower scholastic mental capacity)		MORE INTELLIGENT, ABSTRACT-THINKING, BRIGHT (Higher scholastic mental capacity)
C					AFFECTED BY FEELINGS, EMOTIONAL-LY LESS STABLE, EASILY UPSET, CHANGEABLE (Lower ego strength)		EMOTIONALLY STABLE, FACES REALITY, CALM (Higher ego strength)
D					PHLEGMATIC, DELIBERATE, INACTIVE, STODGY (Phlegmatic temperament)		EXCITABLE, IMPATIENT, DEMANDING, OVERACTIVE (Excitability)
E					OBEDIENT, MILD, CONFORMING (Submissiveness)		ASSERTIVE, INDEPENDENT, AGGRESSIVE, STUBBORN (Dominance)
F					SOBER, PRUDENT, SERIOUS, TACITURN (Desurgency)		HAPPY-GO-LUCKY, IMPULSIVELY LIVELY, GAY, ENTHUSIASTIC (Surgency)
G					EXPEDIENT, EVADES RULES, FEELS FEW OBLIGATIONS (Weaker superego strength)		CONSCIENTIOUS, PERSEVERING, STAID, RULE-BOUND (Stronger superego strength)
H					SHY, RESTRAINED, DIFFIDENT, TIMID (Threctia)		VENTURESOME, SOCIALLY BOLD, UNINHIBITED, SPONTANEOUS (Parmia)
I					TOUGH-MINDED, SELF-RELIANT, REALISTIC, NO-NONSENSE (Harria)		TENDER-MINDED, DEPENDENT, OVER-PROTECTED, SENSITIVE (Premsia)
J					VIGOROUS, GOES READILY WITH GROUP, ZESTFUL, GIVEN TO ACTION (Zeppia)		DOUBTING, OBSTRUCTIVE, INDIVIDUALISTIC, INTERNALLY RESTRAINED, REFLECTIVE (Coasthenia) TIVE, UNWILLING TO ACT
O					PLACID, SELF-ASSURED, CONFIDENT, SERENE (Untroubled adequacy)		APPREHENSIVE, WORRYING, DEPRESSIVE, TROUBLED (Guilt proneness)
Q₂					GROUP-DEPENDENT, A "JOINER" AND SOUND FOLLOWER (Group adherence)		SELF-SUFFICIENT, PREFERS OWN DECISIONS, RESOURCEFUL (Self-sufficiency)
Q₃					UNDISCIPLINED SELF-CONFLICT, FOLLOWS OWN URGES, CARELESS OF PROTOCOL (Low integration)		CONTROLLED, SOCIALLY-PRECISE, SELF-DISCIPLINED, COMPULSIVE (High self concept control)
Q₄					RELAXED, TRANQUIL, TORPID, UNFRUSTRATED (Low ergic tension)		TENSE, FRUSTRATED, DRIVEN, OVERWROUGHT (High ergic tension)

A sten of about | 2.3% | 4.4% | 9.2% | 15.0% | 19.1% | 19.1% | 15.0% | 9.2% | 4.4% | 2.3% of teenagers is obtained by about

SECOND-ORDER AND DERIVED SCORES

Second	Exvia	Anxiety
Stratum	Cortertia	Independence

Neuroticism ____ Achievement ____

Comments: _____

Mary ....
Jane ———
Ruth ------

104

In addition to personality traits, individuals may be characterized by ability traits, such as artistic, musical, athletic, and mathematical abilities. These traits are actually composites of simpler traits. Intellectual ability can also be subdivided into the traits of linguistic, numerical, and spatial relations abilities, and so on. In fact, Guilford thinks that there may be as many as 120 different intellectual traits or factors.

Still other traits have been measured. These include needs (Murray), interests (Strong, Kuder), tendencies toward mental illness (MMPI), vocational aptitude (DAT), and various physical characteristics (physical fitness tests, for example). Actually there is an almost limitless number of characteristics on the basis of which people can be compared. The traits we select will reflect our particular interests and purposes.

PRINCIPLES OF MEASUREMENT

The beginning student of psychology does not need a complete knowledge of the principles of measurement; but a grasp of the main ideas is important in order to understand scientific psychology.

The Minimum Requirements for Measurement

To measure something is to describe it in quantitative terms. The simplest form of quantification is counting, technically called the *nominal system.* In answer to the question "how much?" or "how many?" we simply count, one, two, three, and so on. The next step in quantification is comparison. We say that John is taller than Joe, which is to say that John has more height than Joe. In the same way, to say that Bill is smarter than Harry is to say that Bill has more of the quality of smartness than Harry has. When we have a group of subjects that we want to compare, we rank them from greatest to least using the *ordinal system.* Then we can answer the question "how does he rank in the group?" by saying, first or third or tenth, and so on.

We have not achieved an adequate system of quantification, however, until we can assign numerical equivalents for all of our measurements. In order to do this we need a measuring instrument that approaches three conditions:

1. It must provide numerical values over the full range of the phenomenon to be measured
2. It must be capable of being divided into units of equal value
3. It must have a true zero.

In measuring distance, for example, we have "measuring rods" which can reach from one end to the other of nearly anything we want to measure. They are divided into units of equal value, such as miles, feet, inches, etc., and they have a true zero. It is much more difficult, however, to devise instruments for measuring psychological traits. The problem of getting equal units is particularly thorny, and finding a true zero has been impossible.

Criteria for a Measuring Instrument

Four questions must be answered when evaluating any measuring instrument including a psychological test.

Is it valid? Does it measure what we claim it measures? This question has to do with the *use* to which a test is put. A test might be a fine measuring instrument for something other than what we are using it for and still be completely invalid for our purpose. For example, a thermometer is an excellent way to measure temperature; but as a measure of blood pressure, it is invalid. Thus, when speaking of validity, we should always ask, "Valid *for what*?" With respect to psychological tests, the most important factor may be the *naming* of the test, for it is the name that makes the claim for what the test is supposed to measure. This is the major issue with respect to "intelligence" tests. Do they test intelligence or scholastic aptitude or, maybe, training in home and school?

Is it reliable? Does it measure consistently and precisely? A test may be valid in principle but invalid in practice because of unreliability. No unreliable test is valid, while an invalid test may be highly reliable. The thermometer we mentioned, for example, may be very reliable, but still be an invalid measure of blood pressure.

To be reliable, we said, a test must be *consistent* and *precise*. If I stand on my bathroom scales and get a reading of 165 in the morning, 150 at noon, and 170 at night, I would suspect that they are not reliable. They are not consistent. If I want to see if a letter needs more postage, I do not weigh it on my bathroom scales, even if they are consistent. They do not have the precision to reliably distinguish between a letter just under one ounce and another just over one ounce.

Is it objective? Are the scoring procedures well-defined? A measuring instrument lacks objectivity if different people get different readings from it. An objective test can be scored by anyone who has the scoring key and the score will be the same no matter who does the scoring. If a test is not objective it is neither reliable nor valid.

Is it standardized? A raw score has no meaning. This point is underlined because many people, including some teachers, believe that raw scores do have meaning. A score of 70 or 100 is reported as if it meant something, but it does not. A raw score can be interpreted only if *norms* for the test have been established. By means of norms we can compare someone's score with the scores of people of similar age, schooling, or whatever is being used as the basis for grouping.

The Normal Curve and Interpretations of Test Scores

In our brief historical survey of the study of individual differences, we noted Galton's principle called "the normal law of error." This principle says that when traits are randomly distributed throughout a population, there will be a piling up in the middle and a thinning out on each end. When this is pictured as a *distribution curve* it resembles a bell and is called a "bell–shaped curve" or the normal distribution curve.

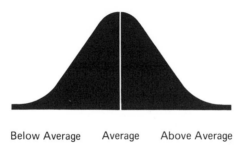

Below Average   Average   Above Average

In order to interpret an individual's score, we need to know two things about the distribution of which it is a part. What is the central tendency (average) of the distribution? What is the variability (spread) of the distribution?

Central tendency. There are three measures of central tendency: *mean, median,* and *mode.* For purposes of illustration, let us take a very simple distribution of ten scores (see Table 4).

Table 4

A SAMPLE DISTRIBUTION OF TEN SCORES

Student	Score	Student	Score
a	5	f	5
b	9	g	7
c	6	h	3
d	7	i	5
e	2	j	4

The *mean* is the arithmetic average and can be calculated by adding all of the scores and then dividing the sum by the number of scores. If we add our ten scores we get 53. If this sum is divided by 10 (the number of scores), the quotient is 5.3 which is the mean.

The *median* is the score which divides the distribution into an upper half and a lower half. It is the middle person's score. If the ten scores above are ranked in descending order we get: 9, 7, 7, 6, 5, 5, 5, 4, 3, 2. Since there are ten scores we count down to the fifth score, which is a 5, and up to the fifth score, which is also a 5. The midpoint of the distribution is half-way between these two scores, or 5. This score is the median.

The *mode* is the score which occurs most frequently. It is thus the most typical score. In the ten scores above, there are three 5's and no other score occurs this many times. Thus the mode is 5.

In our distribution, then, the mean is 5.3, the median is 5, and the mode is 5. The fact that the mean, median, and mode are so close together indicates that the distribution is fairly well balanced; it approaches being *symmetrical.* If these measures of central tendency differed significantly it would mean that the distribution was *skewed* or over-balanced in one direction.

Remember, the mean, median, and mode are all *averages.* Each is a different kind of average, and the one we choose will depend on our purposes. In a symmetrical distribution it will not matter which measure of central tendency we use because all three fall at the same point in the distribution. But if the distribution is skewed, the mean does not provide an accurate picture of the middle of a group of people and we would generally prefer to use the median, which is less affected by extreme scores. If we are interested in the most typical performance the mode is the preferred measure.

Variability. The simplest measure of variability is the *range*, which is determined by the highest and the lowest scores. In the distribution we have been using, 9 is the highest score and 2 is the lowest. Thus the range is 9 minus 2, or 7 points. The range is a very crude measure and very much affected by extreme scores. For these reasons, it is used only for rough approximations of variability.

The most stable, and the most frequently used, measure of variability is the *standard deviation*, abbreviated SD. The SD is always computed from the *mean* and it gives us a measure of how much the scores deviate from the mean. Since most students using this book will have no need to compute standard deviations, we shall not give detailed instructions for doing so. However, the principle behind the SD is basic to an understanding of almost all test interpretations.

Essentially, the standard deviation is a measure of how much, on the average, the scores in a particular distribution deviate from the mean. To visualize how this works, we must recognize that every raw score can be converted into a score that tells us how far it deviates from the mean. Let us suppose we have a distribution with a mean of 50. A score of 60 would then deviate +10; a score of 40 would deviate –10; and a score of 50 would deviate 0 from the mean. Can you see that every raw score can be converted in this way to a deviation score with respect to the mean? Then can you see that all of the deviations can be added and divided by the number of them in order to determine the average deviation? It is this concept which lies behind the standard deviation. To understand how the mean and standard deviation are used in interpreting the meaning of a score, we must know some of the facts about normal curves.

Let us examine Figure 8. First, notice that along the base of the normal curve the standard deviations have been marked off, from –3 SD to +3 SD. The curve has been divided into sections corresponding to the standard deviations marked on the base line, and percentage figures have been put in each section under the curve. These percentages represent the proportion of the scores that will be found in each section. For example, 34.13 percent of the population lies between the mean and –1 SD. Thus a total of 68.26 percent lies in the large middle area under the curve between –1 SD and +1 SD. We typically say that 68% of a population will fall in the area ± 1 SD from the mean.

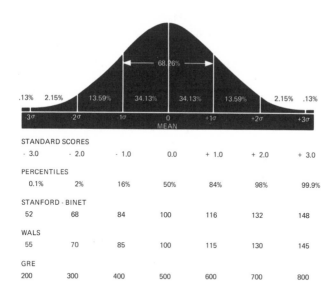

Figure 8. Area Under the Normal Curve

Now let us apply this information to the interpretation of scores. Suppose someone tells us he got a score of 70 on a test. What does this mean? What can we say about this score? If the raw score is all that we have, we do not know the meaning of it. *A raw score by itself means nothing.* Let us suppose we learn that the *mean* on this test was 50. Now what can we say? Only that a score of

70 is above the mean or above average. Then we are told that the lowest score was 20 and the highest was 90, or that the *range* was from 20 to 90. This gives us a little better basis for interpreting, but we still do not have a clear picture. The score of 70 may be the next to the best score or it may be the next one above the middle. We must have a better picture of the spread or variability. We finally learn that the *standard deviation* was 10. Now we can interpret the score. A score of 70 is two standard deviations above the mean (70 minus the mean of 50 equals 20, which is divided by the standard deviation of 10, giving us two SD's). By checking Figure 8 again we can see that a score that is two standard deviations above the mean corresponds to the 98th percentile. How good is the score of 70? Very close to the top.

By continuing to work with the data in Figure 8, let us do some more interpreting of scores. Note that the Stanford–Binet intelligence test has a mean of approximately 100 and a standard deviation of approximately 16. What would an IQ of 132 mean? It would be two SD's above the mean, and the percentile would be the 98th. So only two per cent of the population would be expected to do better than 132. What does an IQ of 116 mean? It is one SD above the mean and corresponds to the 84th percentile. The same procedure may be followed for the Wechsler Adult Intelligence Scale (WAIS) with a mean of 100 and an SD of 15, the Graduate Record Exam (GRE) with a mean of 500 and an SD of 100, or any other test where we know the *mean* and the *standard deviation.*

In statistical terminology, the *range* of the *average* is usually considered to be from –1 SD to +1 SD since no one in this area deviates from the mean more than the average amount of deviation shown by the whole population. Thus, the range of average IQ's would be 84 to 116 on the Stanford–Binet. Unfortunately, many people are not aware of this fact and tend to think of an IQ of 84 as below average or even a sign of retardation, while they tend to think of an IQ of 116 as above average or even superior. The principles underlying these tests, and the facts about normal distributions, require that we say of both the 84 and the 116 that they are *average.* They are both a part of the big middle group of 68 percent of the population. Above them will be found the 16 percent of the population which is above average, and below them will be found the 16 percent of the population which is below average.

Correlations

In the opening historical sketch, we noted that Galton presented a principle of the "co-relation between two variables," and that Karl Pearson refined this into "the coefficient of correlation."

We shall not present here the mathematics for computing correlation coefficients, but we shall try to make the concept meaningful. If two factors are related in such a way that the action of one can be predicted to some extent from the action of the other, the two factors are said to be *correlated.* If there is no such relationship, we say that the coefficient of correlation is .00, while if the relationship is such that we can perfectly predict the one from the other, we say that the coefficient of correlation is ± 1.00. If the two factors operate in the same direction, the correlation is positive. If the two factors operate in opposite directions, the correlation is negative.

Let us note some examples of correlation. A person's height and weight are positively correlated, but not at all perfectly. In other words, there is a tendency for weight to increase as height does, but the relationship is not close enough to perfectly predict one from the other. A person's IQ and his school grades are positively correlated. The higher the IQ, the higher school grades are likely to be, but the correlation is not perfect because many factors other than IQ determine school grades.

The significance of correlations. While many technical problems are related to determining the meaning of a specific correlation coefficient, some general agreement has been reached which we may state as follows:

From .00 to ± .20 denotes an indifferent or negligible relationship
From ± .20 to ± .40 denotes a low correlation—present but slight
From ± .40 to ± .70 denotes a substantial or marked relationship
From ± .70 to ± 1.00 denotes a high to very high relationship

(from Henry E. Garrett, *Statistics in Psychology and Education,*
New York: Longmans and Green and Co., 1958, p. 176.)

With a basic understanding of the principles of measurement and the meaning of measures of central tendency, variability, and correlation we can now consider some common tests of individual differences.

SOME BETTER KNOWN TESTS OF INDIVIDUAL DIFFERENCES

Intelligence Tests

The first complex trait whose individual differences were studied was intelligence. That some people are smarter and some duller than average had been noticed by almost everyone.

Galton had thought that intelligence might be related to such factors as sensory discrimination and reaction time. Cattell followed him and added tests of motor and simple perceptual processes. These men thought that tests aimed at getting at intelligence more directly would not yield results of any precision, while quite exact measurements could be made of the sensory and motor processes.

Alfred Binet, of Paris, was critical of the Galton–Cattell approach and advocated the direct approach on the grounds that less precise measurements of intelligence itself were to be preferred to exact measurements of processes of doubtful relationship to intelligence. Binet's intuition proved to be sound, and, in 1904 he had his chance to prove it.

The Minister of Public Instruction appointed a commission to study procedures for the education of subnormal children attending Paris schools. Binet, in collaboration with Simon, developed his first tests in 1905 to meet this practical need. The first Binet–Simon Scale contained 30 short tests arranged in ascending order of difficulty. These 30 tests had been selected empirically by administering a wide variety of tests to 50 normal children, aged 3 to 11, and to a few subnormal and feeble-minded children. The tests were gradually refined and in the 1908 Scale the test items were tied to an age scale by means of which the *mental age* of a child might be determined. By the time of the 1911 Scale, the age range extended from 3 years to the adult level.

In America, Terman of Stanford University, adapted the Binet Scale to American usage. The first Stanford–Binet appeared in 1916, with the innovation of the IQ. The IQ, or intelligence quotient, had first been proposed by William Stern in Germany. It provides a numerical statement of the relationship between a child's mental age (MA) and his chronological age (CA). If the mental age, as determined by the Binet test, is the same as the chronological age, the IQ is average and is set at 100. Thus, the formula is: $IQ = MA/CA \times 100$. (Since 1960, Binet scores are not really IQ's but are deviation scores, but we continue to speak of IQ's.)

The Binet test is an excellent example of test construction, and a study of it provides an ideal occasion for discussing the problem of measuring intelligence.

Binet's basic assumption was that if children have spent the same amount of time in a similar environment, then differences in their ability reflect differences in their capacity to learn, and this capacity is intelligence. Notice that even Binet was not getting at intelligence directly. He was inferring it from the amount of learning that had occurred in comparison with other children of the same age. Actually, there is a two-step inference from test score to intelligence. Ability is inferred from test performance; and intelligence is inferred from ability. Important assumptions are involved at each step in this sequence. We are justified in inferring ability from test scores only if the test is valid, reliable, objective, and standardized. Furthermore, such an inference is justified only if we have good reason to assume that the subject who took the test was motivated to do his best. Then we are justified in inferring intelligence from the inferred ability only if we can assume that the subject had an equal opportunity for learning as did the group used to standardize the test (an assumption seldom justified). Finally, we are justified in inferring intelligence only if we have good reasons for asserting that the ability we are measuring is an adequate indicator of intelligence. It should be clear from this discussion that we must be cautious when we interpret scores on a so-called intelligence test.

Criticisms of traditional intelligence tests have generally focused on the fact that they have favored one or two abilities, usually verbal and numerical facility. Two efforts to get away from this weakness deserve to be noted.

Factored tests. The Binet, as well as most other intelligence tests, is constructed on the assumption that there is one general capacity underlying intelligence. Factored tests assume that intelligence consists of more than one factor. The Wechsler tests, for example, have a verbal part and a performance part. This division enables us to distinguish between two kinds of intelligence. For example, two children may have an IQ of 100, but be quite different:

Child A: verbal score 43, performance score 36 = 119 or IQ of 114
Child B: verbal score 61, performance score 58 = 119 or IQ of 114

It was Thurstone who pioneered the factored test with his Primary Mental Abilities (PMA) Test. He included five factors in his test: word fluency (W), verbal comprehension (V), numerical fluency (N), reasoning (R), and spatial relations (S). Currently, Guilford is developing batteries of tests on the assumption that intelligence may involve as many as 120 different factors.[5]

Creativity tests. Among the factors which Guilford is investigating are several which he believes are related to what is called creativity. This capacity is a kind of intelligence, but it differs from the kind usually measured. The kind of intelligence usually measured involves what Guilford calls "convergent factors," while creativity involves "divergent factors." *Convergent factors* refer to such abilities as memory, manipulating words and numbers quickly, and following instructions to get "correct" answers. *Divergent factors* refer to such abilities as sensitivity to problems, fluency and flexibility in dealing with figures, words, and symbols, and the spontaneous elaboration of detail. As yet, tests of creativity are only in the experimental stage, but we may soon have a creativity test that is reasonably valid and reliable. Such a test should help us to identify a much wider variety of intellectual abilities than we are now measuring.[6]

Aptitude Tests

The most widely used aptitude tests are very similar to intelligence tests and are called scholastic aptitude tests. They measure essentially the same factors measured by intelligence tests, but they are based on the straightforward claim that they are measuring school-related abilities. Rather than yielding IQ's, they give us scores from which a child's ability to do school work may be predicted. Probably the best known of the scholastic aptitude tests is the School and College Ability Tests (SCAT), which correlates in the .80's with standardized achievement test scores, and in the .50's and .60's with school grades for high school students.

An example of a general aptitude test is the Differential Aptitude Test (DAT), which yields eight scores: Verbal Reasoning, Numerical Ability, Abstract Reasoning, Space Relations, Mechanical Reasoning, Clerical Speed and Accuracy, Language Usage I (spelling), and Language Usage II (sentences).

Besides the more general aptitude tests, a wide variety of special abilities tests are used. These include tests of sensory capacities, motor functions, mechanical aptitude, clerical aptitude, artistic aptitude, musical aptitude, and literary aptitude.

The sensory capacities most widely tested are hearing and vision. The importance of these capacities for school children is obvious, and children are now routinely tested for deficiencies in both. Since many jobs require special capacities in hearing and vision, tests for job placement often include the testing of these sensory capacities. An increasing number of psychological clinics are checking sensory capacities both as a means of discovering possible irritations and tensions resulting from deficiencies in these areas, and as a means of locating possible neurological damage.

The motor function most often tested is that of manual dexterity, and the major use for such tests is in personnel selection. Both in industry and in the armed forces, applicants for jobs requiring a special amount of motor coordination are screened by means of a wide variety of motor tests. Motor tests tend to be highly specific, resembling very closely the actual job for which the applicant is being considered.

Personality Tests

In a sense, any test is a personality test; but we generally use this term to describe self-report inventories, measures of interests and attitudes, and projective techniques for assessing personality traits.

Self-report inventories. A self-report inventory is a type of questionnaire that asks people to provide information about themselves. Some inventories are used to describe temperament, some claim to measure the level of social adjustment, and others are designed to identify pathological traits.

One of the most respected inventories is the Minnesota Multiphasic Personality Inventory (MMPI), and we shall use it as an example. The MMPI is probably used most frequently for diagnostic purposes. It is designed to distinguish between "normal" people and those who show "traits that are commonly characteristic

f disabling psychological abnormality." Answers to 550 questions yield scores
n nine scales:

1. hypochondriasis
2. depression
3. hysteria
4. psychopathic deviate
5. masculinity–femininity
6. paranoia
7. psychasthenia
8. schizophrenia
9. hypomania

The norms were empirically derived by comparing the responses of people
ho were hospitalized for mental illness with the responses of a normal control
oup consisting of 700 visitors to University of Minnesota hospitals.[7]

As with all personality tests, the MMPI should be used only by trained clini-
ans and, even then, with great caution. It has been most difficult to construct
ersonality tests of dependable validity and reliability. No test, by itself, should
e used to decide someone's future. Personality tests do not answer questions;
ey raise questions and uncover leads that must be pursued by other means.

Measures of interests and attitudes. Measures of interests and attitudes have a
ore modest goal than do the self–report inventories. Rather than aiming at a
omprehensive description of an individual's personality, the goal of interest and
titude inventories is to find out how a person feels about certain specific mat-
rs so that a prediction can be made as to how he will react in situations where
ese feelings are present.

By far the best known of these measures is the Vocational Interest Blank
IB) developed by Strong. Widely used in vocational counseling, the VIB has
oved more useful in identifying prospects for jobs in the upper ranges of the
ccupational hierarchy than in the lower ranges.[8]

As is true of the MMPI, the norms for the Vocational Interest Blank have been
eveloped empirically. When a person marks his VIB, his responses are compared
ith those of people who are successful in various occupations. He is told that
s interests are most similar to successful people in such–and–such an occupa-
on. A person's VIB score does not tell us how successful he will be in a particu-
r occupation, or even that he will like it. All we can say is that his responses are
milar to those of others whose occupational success we know. On this basis we
ust make inferences about the likelihood of our subject's occupational success.

Projective techniques. The most interesting, and the most problematical,
rsonality tests are those employing projective techniques. The principle

underlying these tests is the assumption that if the stimulus presented to the sub ject is ambiguous, then his response will tell us a great deal about him, In other words, if there is not very much "out there" to which the subject may respond, we will get more of what is "inside" him in his response. This kind of reading into things or putting oneself into things is what is meant by the term *projection*

The best known projective test is the Rorshach Inkblots. Consisting of a seri of ten cards on each of which is printed a bilaterally symmetrical inkblot, the Rorshach has been a standard clinical tool for inferring a wide variety of person ality traits as well as for diagnosing mental illnesses. The subject is asked to respond to each inkblot by stating what he sees or what the blot might represent. The tester must keep very careful notes on the verbal responses, emotional reactions, and incidental behavior of the subject. Scoring procedures are very complicated, and the skill of the tester is a most important factor in the reliability o the test.

All efforts to validate the Rorshach Inkblots have so far failed to demonstrat that the test is a dependably valid tool. For this reason, "it would seem best at this stage to regard the Rorshach as an interview aid for the skilled clinician, rather than as a test."[9]

SUMMARY

Science demands quantification, and the field of individual differences has been particularly susceptible to the methods of scientific measurement. Startin with Bessel's observations of differences in reaction time in the early nineteenth century and continuing with Galton's studies of genius in the latter part of that century, the study of individual differences came of age in the early twentieth century in the work of Binet.

The basic assumption in the study of individual differences is that people hav common traits in terms of which they can be compared. It is further assumed that these traits can be measured and that the reasons for the differences can be discovered. Rather than trying to classify individuals in terms of types, it is mo fruitful to describe how individuals differ with respect to traits. This is done by means of the personality profile.

In order to describe individual differences in quantitative terms, we must be able to assign numerical equivalents to observed characteristics. A measuring instrument must be valid, reliable, objective, and standardized. The data obtained from measuring traits of a group of people can be put into the form of a frequen cy distribution. Most frequency distributions approach the shape of a bell-shaped curve when plotted on a graph. The bell-shaped curve, or normal distribution curve, provides a convenient framework for the statistical treatment of group data. In order to compare one score with others in a sample, we must kno the central tendency and the variability of the distribution. Another important

ool for expressing relationships between various measurements is the coefficient
f correlation.

Better known tests of individual differences include intelligence, aptitude, and
ersonality tests. The best known intelligence test is the Binet, which in America
s the Stanford–Binet. An example of a factored intelligence test is Thurstone's
rimary Mental Abilities Test. Efforts are also being made to construct tests
vhich will measure creativity factors in intelligence. The best known aptitude
est is the School and College Abilities Test. Personality tests include self–report
nventories, like the Minnesota Multiphasic Personality Inventory; measures of
nterests and attitudes, like the Strong Vocational Interest Blank; and projective
ests, such as the Rorshach Inkblots.

QUESTIONS FOR STUDY AND CLASS DISCUSSION

1. What are some practical reasons for measuring certain traits or characteristics of people?

2. Can you think of any problems or undesirable consequences resulting
   from measuring people's traits and assigning numerical values to them?

3. How would you go about proving that a test measures (a) school ability, (b) mechanical ability, (c) social adjustment?

4. What do you think of the following statement? "We must not be content with an educational system that produces a majority of students
   with only average ability."

5. A student achieves a score of 80 on a history test, a score of 50 on a
   math test, and a score of 90 on an English test. What can you say of
   the student's ability in English compared to his ability in history and
   math?

6. If you are an average student in a relatively small class where there are
   two or three students who always score very high, which measure of
   "average" (central tendency) would you wish the teacher to use: mean,
   median, or mode?

7. You are a teacher in a school district in which there is a large percentage of children who come from homes where English is spoken little,
   if at all. You want to know how your students compare with students
   of previous years in your district. Would you use national norms or
   local norms in interpreting the results of a scholastic aptitude test?
   Explain.

8. How dependable is the picture of your personality you are likely to

get by taking a personality test which might appear in a magazine or newspaper? Why?

9. What is the main difference between a scholastic aptitude test and an intelligence test?

10. How much do you think you can tell about a person by looking at a photograph of him? by studying his handwriting? by the sound of his voice?

SUGGESTIONS FOR FURTHER READING

Barron, Frank. *Creativity and Personal Freedom.* New York: D. Van Nostrand Co., 1968.

Eysenck, H. J. *Uses and Abuses of Psychology.* Baltimore: Penguin Books, 1953.

Franzblau, Abraham N. *A Primer of Statistics for Non-Statisticians.* New York Harcourt Brace Jovanovich, 1958.

Huff, Darrell. *How to Lie With Statistics.* New York: W. W. Norton, 1954.

Tyler, Leona E. *Intelligence: Some Recurring Issues.* New York: D. Van Nostrand Co., 1969.

7

DEVELOPMENT AND GROWTH

HE GENETIC APPROACH

The genetic approach focuses on the *origins* and the *development* of life. his emphasis assumes that we can understand something better if we watch it egin and then follow it as it changes through time.

Genetic studies by psychologists reflect four major influences:

1. The emphasis on a developmental approach which was spurred by Darwin evolutionary hypothesis
2. The new knowledge of the mechanisms of heredity that accompanied the re-discovery of Mendel's work
3. The interest in early childhood generated by psychoanalysis
4. The need for better studies of children that grew out of a commitment to universal education

Few approaches to the study of man have proved so fruitful as the genetic approach. The result has been nothing less than a major revolution in our attitude toward the child. Child study centers can now be found in every advanced nation, and a solid body of facts is accumulating. Immense problems remain, and many gains are offset by new problems, such as over-population; but the value of the approach is beyond question.

We do not want to stress the early stages of development to the neglect of the mature person. Just as children should be studied as children, and not as miniature adults, so adults should be studied as adults, and not as oversized children. A full use of the genetic approach would utilize developmental principles in the study of every stage of life, from conception to old age. In fact, as the life expectancy has increased, old age has received more attention as an area of study.

THE PROCESS OF REPRODUCTION

Every individual human life has its origin in the process of reproduction. The most complex form of life that we know, a mature man, develops from a single-celled creature called a *zygote.* The zygote begins its life in one of the Fallopian tubes of a woman when one of the eggs (ova) released from her ovaries is fertilized by a male sperm which has been injected into her vaginal tract. The ovum and the sperm are special cells, called *gametes* or germ cells, which carry half the number of chromosomes present in the usual body cells.

It has long been known that the transmission of characteristics from parent to child is accomplished by something in the chromosomes, which are found in the nucleus of the cell. These unknown "somethings" are called *genes.* In the last 25 years biologists and biochemists have made exciting progress toward understanding the makeup of genes. It has been found that the chromosomes carry two long strands of molecules called deoxyribonucleic acid, or DNA. Along with the DNA molecules in the cell nucleus are other molecules which work with them and are called ribonucleic acid (RNA). These are forbidding words; but if they are broken down, they are not so difficult. First, both DNA and RNA are acids similar to the amino acids of which proteins are made. Second, they are both ucleic acids, acids found in the nucleus of the cell. Hence the designation NA. ut the RNA contains a sugar called ribose while the DNA contains a sugar with ne less oxygen atom called deoxyribose. So RNA is ribonucleic acid and DNA deoxyribonucleic acid.[1]

According to present DNA theory, the DNA molecules constitute a detailed ode of instruction which determines the kind of human being the zygote will evelop into. It is truly amazing when we consider that, while all the DNA in a zygote weighs only about two ten-trillionths of an ounce, billions of bits of information are carried in these molecules. Someone has suggested that if this information were written in English, it would fill three 24-volume sets of the *ncyclopedia Brittannica.*

For approximately two weeks after conception, during what we call the *germinal period,* the zygote multiplies by repeatedly dividing. In this way millions f duplicates of the original zygote are made, each one carrying the same genetic ode in its nucleus. If, during the germinal period, one of the cells is moved from ne part of the mass to another part, it will later develop into the kind of organ emanded by its position in the mass. In other words, at this stage any cell can ecome anything in the body. But at the end of this two week period an amazg thing happens. Cells begin the process of differentiation, and we call this the eginning of the embryonic stage.

During the embryonic stage, the mass of cells begins the process of shaping itlf into the complex organism it is destined to be by the genetic code. Once is process of cell differentiation gets under way, a cell moved from one part to other part will not develop according to the needs of the new location, but will ntinue to develop into what its previous location had determined that it would e. It is for this reason that some serious deformities may appear at birth.

At about the end of the eighth week after conception, the embryo is recognibly human, although only 1-1/4 inches long, and we now refer to it as a fetus. or about seven more months the fetus continues to develop in the womb; then is born and begins to breathe.

The newborn infant is by no means a finished product. In fact, nothing is so aracteristic of man as this unfinished condition at time of birth. Thus man is e of the most helpless of creatures. At the same time, it is because of this cononis that he can be shaped so radically by his environment.

EVELOPMENT

hysiological Principles

Among the principles that have been noted in studies of physiological development, three have far-reaching implications for the study of behavior.

Undifferentiated to differentiated. Development proceeds from the undiffer
entiated to the differentiated and finally to the integrated. As we have noted,
during the first stage after conception, by a process called *mitosis,* the fertilized
egg divides into two identical cells which, in turn, divide into two identical cells
and so on, until a small mass of millions of identical cells is formed. Then, as if
someone blew a whistle, the amazing process of cell differentiation begins. The
first differentiation is into three kinds of tissue, called *ectoderm, mesoderm,* an
endoderm. Then the differentiation continues as all the cells, tissues, and organ
develop from these. Finally, organs and systems which have been developing
separately become integrated into one organized whole. This principle of undif
ferentiated mass to differentiated part to integrated whole reappears in other as
pects of development and organismic function. For example, in motor develop
ment we first see mass action (as when an embryo is stimulated), then specific
movement, and finally integrated action. In perception, also, we see this s
quence: first we see an undifferentiated mass, then we begin to make out parts
and finally we integrate the whole picture. Even in a process as complex as mer
orizing a poem we find it: mass practice, special work on parts, and final integration. So it would seem that this principle is one of great generality and wide
applicability.

Table 1

ECTODERM
Skin, hair, nails
Entire nervous system, including receptor cells
Adrenal medulla

MESODERM
Muscles
Blood and blood vessels
Connective tissue, including bone
Kidneys, ureters
Testes, ovaries, oviducts, uterus
Mesenteries
Lymphatic system

ENDODERM
Lining of alimentary canal
Lining of trachea, bronchi, and lungs
Lining of urethra and bladder
Liver
Pancreas

(from J. W. Kimball, *Biology,* Addison–Wesley, 1968)

The physiological gradient. A second principle is called the *physiological g*
dient which states that development has a directional quality proceeding from

head to tail (cephalocaudal) and from the spinal column outward (proximo–distal). This directional quality can be seen in many characteristics of the organism. The newborn baby's head is far more developed than any other part, increasing only twofold from birth to adulthood, while the legs increase sixfold. Nerve development also follows the physiological gradient with the greatest sensitivity at birth found in the face and much less in the extremities. Motor development, too, proceeds along this gradient with the ability to use the extremities coming last. Abnormal growth patterns, associated with pituitary disorders further illustrate this principle. An overactive pituitary from birth causes giantism, where the abnormal growth is seen most in the lengthened arms and legs, while an underactive pituitary produces dwarfism in which the lack of growth is seen mainly in the arms and legs.

Motor primacy. A third principle important in the study of behavior is that of *motor primacy.* This principle states that the development of structure must precede the ability to function. We are most accustomed to see this principle in children learning to walk. There is no point in trying to teach a six–month–old baby to walk. His bones and muscles have not developed sufficiently for this function. Many other kinds of behavior must wait for sufficient maturation before they can be taught. In the field of education this principle is involved in the problem of "readiness." Much research is being done to determine when a child is most ready to be taught various activities such as reading, writing, and calculating.

Psycho–Social Principles

The psycho–social principles of development are not so easy to identify as the physiological principles. Furthermore, they are complicated by the fact that they are thoroughly mixed with the process of learning, a process that will be described in Chapter 8.

Coleman lists seven characteristics of psycho–social development which he calls "trends toward maturity."

1. dependence to self-direction
2. pleasure to reality
3. ignorance to knowledge
4. incompetence to competence
5. diffuse sexuality to heterosexuality
6. amorality to morality
7. self- to other-centeredness

All of these might be summed up in one word—*socialization.*

Sigmund Freud suggested that to be a healthy adult means to be able *to work* and *to love,* while the Neo-Freudian, Harry Stack Sullivan, simplified maturity to one thing: to be mature is to be able *to love non-possessively.* Recently, the Overstreets have studied maturity and conclude that it primarily involves *tension capacity.* The following four principles seem to get at the heart of what these writers are suggesting: *the ability to wait; the ability to deal with ambiguity; the ability to control "closure";* and *the ability to love.*

The ability to wait. When the infant wants something, he wants it "right now." As children grow older, they become more capable of waiting, until, by adulthood, people are able to work for very distant goals. This principle is an excellent example of how organic development and learning are related in psychosocial development. There is no point in trying to teach a baby to wait; he has developed neither the neural nor the conceptual basis for it. The same thing can be seen, even more dramatically, in working with animals. They do not have the neural basis for working for rewards delayed very long, although, as might be expected, chimpanzees do better at this than animals with less developed brains. The same kind of problem is seen in working with a neurologically handicapped child. He, too, finds it very difficult to handle the tension of waiting.

The ability to deal with ambiguity. Again we have a principle that combines organic development with learning. The immature human being, in common with animals of lesser brain capacity, cannot respond effectively to ambiguous stimuli. In training children or animals, the instructions must be clear and consistent. Stories for children demand sharply drawn characterizations. When watching a movie, children want to be able to tell who the "bad guy" is and who the "good guy" is. With increased mental growth and increased learning, the ability to deal with ambiguity develops. Under stress even adults are likely to "regress" and lose their ability to handle the tension of ambiguity.

The ability to control "closure." The term "closure" comes from the work of the Gestalt psychologists who use the word to stand for the process, in perception, whereby we come to a conclusion about what something is. If I see someone in the distance but can't make out who it is, this would be an inability to make closure. If the person walks toward me until I can recognize him, I would make closure. In one study, the process of closure was correlated with maturity and with anxiety. Subjects were rated on a maturity and an anxiety scale and then were asked to name a picture "as soon as they were sure what it is." The picture was then projected onto a screen one piece at a time. Immature and anxious subjects tended either to make closure too quickly, thus making more errors, or to make closure too late, thus being unnecessarily slow. The more mature and more secure subjects tended to wait a little longer, then made fewer errors. It seems, therefore, that one of the abilities that comes with age and emotional maturity is the ability to control closure, so that we can tolerate both the tension of waiting until we are reasonably sure and the tension of committing ourselves even though there is still some uncertainty.

The ability to love. We shall risk this ambiguous term because no other word communicates as much. No other ability is so characteristic of maturity as is the ability to love. Perhaps it is the climax of learning to wait, to deal with ambiguity, and to effectively make closure. We are able to love when we have achieved both a reasonable degree of independence and a reasonable ability to be dependent. We are able to love when we have come to terms with the ambiguities in ourselves and in others. We are able to love when we have developed the ability to work for distant goals.

Major Developmental Theories

Many theoretical frameworks have been used in describing development. We shall look at five of them:

1. psychoanalytically based theories
2. the normative–descriptive theory of Arnold Gesell
3. Piaget's study of the origins of intelligence
4. Havighurst's theory of developmental tasks
5. Rogers' theory of the fully functioning person

Psychoanalytically based theories. One of the most interesting and controversial theories is the psychosexual theory advanced by Freud. Freud saw sexual development as the core around which the entire personality is shaped. This view was based partly on his clinical observations and partly on a broad hypothesis. He had observed, in working with hysterical patients, that all had sexual problems going back to the earliest periods of their lives. He hypothesized that sexual energy, which is called *libido*, is the urge to live and to reproduce and is involved in every aspect of development. He further hypothesized that libidinal energy (life–energy or sexual energy) is erotic or pleasure–producing when it is expressed in behavior. Freud called this hypothesis *the pleasure principle.* It is as if Nature, wanting to make sure that what is necessary for life and procreation will occur, has made the basic life processes pleasurable. Freud further noted that each of the basic life processes is associated with some part of the body which is highly sensitive to stimulation and is capable of giving the individual great pleasure. These parts of the body he called *erogenous zones* or pleasure–producing zones; and since these zones and the activities associated with them are each important at different periods of development, he named the stages of development after these erogenous zones. Finally, Freud felt that some people get "hung up" or *fixated* at one of these stages and develop a character or personality type which he named for the erogenous zone involved (*See* table 2).

Table 2

FREUD'S PSYCHOSEXUAL THEORY

Erogenous Zone	Stage of Development	Character Type
Oral (mouth)	Oral: the stage when the predomiant activity is using the mouth to take in nourishment and to get oral satisfaction.	Oral: the infantile type, who demands immediate gratification of his wants or he will pout.
Anal (anus)	Anal: the stage when the predominant activity is developing control of bowel movement and the satisfaction of controlling the muscular process of holding back and letting go.	Anal: the childish type who makes a "big thing" of every thing he does and is rigid and compulsive in process of giving and taking.
Phallic (genital)	Phallic: the stage when the genitals are discovered as objects of pleasure and interest.	Phallic: the childish type who gets pleasure out of watching or showing off rather than in participative doing.
Latency	Latency: the stage when the child forgets his body and moves out into the world to learn and adapt.	
Genital	Genital: the stage of sexual maturity characterized by sexual intercourse with a member of the opposite sex.	Genital: Healthy maturity

The major revision of Frued's psychosexual theory is that of Erik Erikson; and because it modifies the parts of Freud's theory which have been most controversial, it has found much wider acceptance. We shall discuss it in greater detail. Erikson begins with Freud's five stages, but treats them in a broader way, adding interpersonal and social aspects to the picture. Then he adds three more stages to cover the entirety of an individual's life.[2]

Erikson, along with Freud, noted that various zones of the body are important in development, but he observed that body experiences are part of an interpersonal context that is even more important. Thus, while he follows much of Freud's terminology, he concentrates on the interpersonal crisis a person encounters as he grows and attempts to meet his changing needs.

The crisis the infant faces is one of *trust*. Will he be cared for, or will he not? Is his world dependable or undependable? To appreciate how crucial this problem is for the infant, we must remember his almost complete helplessness. There are two things he can do: he can suck and he can cry. If his cries consistently bring a loving mother who satisfies his need for food, for oral gratification, for warmth, and for comfort, then he can relax, sleep, and feel secure. If his cries bring inconsistent responses, harsh responses, or no response, then he experiences anxiety or deep mistrust. Much evidence has accumulated indicating that severe anxiety may result in serious organic difficulties and even death for the infant.[3] It is clear, then, that the crisis of trust is a most real problem in the early months of life; and, as the chart (Table 3) suggests, the way this crisis is resolved will affect the individual's ability to meet the crises which follow.

Table 3

ERIKSON'S EIGHT STAGES OF MAN

Oral Sensory	Trust vs. Mistrust
Muscular– Anal	Autonomy vs. Shame and Doubt
Loco- motor Genital	Initiative vs. Guilt
Latency	Industry vs. Inferiority
Puberty and Adolescence	Identity vs. Role Diffusion
Young Adulthood	Intimacy vs. Isolation
Adulthood	Generativity vs. Stagnation
Maturity	Integrity vs. Disgust and Despair

(From Erikson, 1950)

Around age two the child faces the crisis of *autonomy*. He is beginning to do things for himself. He is learning to feed himself, he is being toilet trained, and he is beginning to assert his will. His favorite words are "No!" and "Mine!!"— both with definite exclamation points. Many frustrated parents have called this stage "the terrible two's." Parents may either delight in this emerging autonomy or they may be threatened by it and feel that they must "break the child's will." If the child finds that it is fun to do things for himself, that his self-will is appreciated and loved, then he will develop self-confidence and be ready to take the initiative in exploring the world which he finds so interesting. However, if he loses parental love when he asserts himself, if he is told that he is bad when he tries to do what he wants to do, then he will be confused and feel shame and doubt.

Erikson says the next crisis is that of *initiative*. Around age three, when the child has learned to get about freely and is rapidly adding to his vocabulary, he enters a period of exploration. He gets into everything imaginable and asks every conceivable question. One of the most interesting things he has noticed is that human beings come in two varieties, boys and girls; and he wants to know more about this. So he is likely to play "doctor" with the little girl next door, each giving the other a thorough physical examination. This initiative which is shown during this pre-school period may be an exciting, rewarding experience, leaving the child ready to forget the pleasures of mother, his own body, and his toys so that he can move confidently on to the challenge of play groups and school. Or, this initiative may be met with irritated commands to "stay out of that," or "quit asking so many questions and get out," or "don't ever let me catch you doing that again, you nasty, bad boy," and he will turn in upon himself with fear and guilt.

The crisis of the elementary schoool years is that of *industry*. Going to school means being on one's own, having to do what someone else says, and working and having one's work judged. For the confident child, nothing could be more exciting. For the insecure child, nothing could be more terrifying. For the child who has found his environment warm and trustworthy, who has experienced autonomy and initiative as pleasurable and rewarding, being asked to be industrious is challenging. For the child who has found his environment harsh and untrustworthy, who has experienced autonomy and initiative as occasions for shame and guilt, being asked to be industrious is threatening. But even for the healthy mature child, the school years present crises of a new kind. The child quickly observes that his work is being compared with the work of others. There are tremendous individual differences in both ability and readiness for school. The school system makes these differences painfully obvious. Within a few years it becomes a clearly competitive situation both on the playground and in the classroom. Much more research needs to be done on the effects of competition during these early school years. It would seem that some children respond to competition by becoming more industrious while others respond by becoming less industrious.

Then comes puberty and the crisis of *identity*. Even during the elementary school years the child is forming his self-concept. He is discovering his skills, how well he is liked, what it means to be a boy or a girl. With puberty and adolescence this search for identity becomes intense. He is no longer a child, but he is not yet an adult. It is a time of testing, of experimentation, of trying out ways of dressing, talking, and acting. Who am I? What am I going to be? Whom do I want to be like? What do I believe? How am I going to act? What do people think of me? Will somebody love me? Am I going to be successful? These are the questions that the adolescent asks, and the answers do not come easily.

The late teens and sometimes the early twenties are a time for learning to be *intimate.* Called by Erikson the period of young adulthood, this is a time for learning to be close to others. It is especially a time for courtship and the working out of a good relationship with some member of the opposite sex. Here again we can see how one stage of development succeeds another and how the later stage is dependent on the earlier. If a person has not resolved the identity crisis of adolescence, healthy intimacy with another person is difficult. He is likely either to be afraid of intimacy or to enter into a dependent relationship in which, rather than expressing his identity, he seeks his identity.

The crisis of adulthood is *generativity* or productivity. Freud, as we noted earlier, suggested that the healthy adult is able to work and to love. Both of these activities reflect a responsible participation in the ongoing processes of the species. By choosing the term "generativity," Erikson points to parenthood as the central crisis for the adult. It is as if he is saying, "When a person is ready to have children, he is an adult." He is not saying that all persons who have children are adults, nor is he saying that all who do not have children are not adults. But he is saying that there is something about the way in which we accept the responsibilities of parenthood that is central to adulthood. Few things force us to grow up as does parenthood, and few things bring to light our lack of growth as does the effort to rear children.

Then comes maturity with the final, and probably most crucial crisis. Erikson calls it the crisis of *integrity.* Sometime between 35 and 45 we realize that we are the person we have spent our lives trying to become. When we were children we said, "When I grow up I will be such and such." As adolescents we talked about what we would do after graduation or after we married. But then comes the time when we know that the future is not going to change things very much. We have to face ourselves and our limitations. This is what Erikson means by integrity. When we have become what we will be, we will either like ourselves or we will feel disgust and despair. Happy is the person who finds, at maturity, that he really likes himself; how tragic is the person who spends his life becoming someone that he cannot stand!

The normative-descriptive theory of Arnold Gesell. In Gesell's work we see an approach to development that is radically different from the psychoanalytic. From 1943 to 1956 he and his associates at the Clinic of Child Development at Yale University published three books[4] describing development from infancy to age sixteen. This description was based on detailed observations of hundreds of children, and the aim was to provide profiles of the *typical* child at any age. This is why his approach is called "normative–descriptive." It might also be called a cross–sectional approach.

Table 4

EXAMPLES OF TYPICAL BEHAVIOR CITED BY GESELL

Prehensory Behavior

1)	12 weeks	—	Looks at cube
2)	20 weeks	—	Looks and approaches
3)	24 weeks	—	Looks and crudely grasps with whole hand
4)	36 weeks	—	Looks and deftly grasps with fingers
5)	52 weeks	—	Looks, grasps with forefinger and thumb and deftly releases
6)	15 months	—	Looks, grasps, and releases to build a tower of two dubes

Reading Behavior

1)	15 months	—	Pats identified picture in book
2)	18 months	—	Points to an identified picture in book
3)	2 years	—	Names three pictures in book
4)	3 years	—	Identifies 4 printed geometric forms
5)	4 years	—	Recognizes salient capital letters
6)	5–6 years	—	Recognizes salient printed words

Acquisitive Behavior

1)	5 years	—	Takes pride in certain personal possessions (e.g. hat or a drawing of his own).
2)	6 years	—	Collects odds and ends rather sporadically (e.g. Christmas cards)
3)	7 years	—	Collects with purpose and specific, sustained interest (e.g. postal cards).
4)	8 years	—	Collects with zeal and strong interest in size of collection (e.g. comics, paper dolls)
5)	10 years	—	Collects more formally with specialized, intellectual interest (e.g. stamps)
6)	15 years	—	Saves money with discriminating thrift and interest in money values

(From Gesell and Ilg — 1946, pp. 21, 23, 24 by permission of Harper & Row, Publishers.)

Unusually complete descriptions are given of the infant at birth, and then at four weeks, 16 weeks, 28 weeks, 40 weeks, and one year. During the second year, descriptions are available for each three-month step; during the third year, for each six-month step; and after that, at intervals of one year. The descriptions cover such areas as sleep, eating, elimination, bath and dressing, self-activity, and sociality. By referring to Gesell's books, any parent or teacher can find a description of what is typical for a child at any particular age (see examples of typical behavior cited by Gesell, p. 130).

While Gesell's work reflects a maximum of careful description and a minimum of theorizing, there are theoretical underpinnings to his system. Much like the father of developmental psychology, G. Stanley Hall, Gesell accepts a "biologically oriented theory of predetermined maturation."[5] In other words, he sees development as largely determined by inherited characteristics of the human species. Over and over again he reminds readers that a particular kind of behavior is related to maturational factors. To quote Gesell:

> . . . no one taught the baby this progressive series of eye-hand behavior. He scarcely taught himself. He comes into his increasing powers primarily through intrinsic growth. . . Environmental factors support, inflect and modify; they do not generate the progressions of development. The sequences, the progressions come from within the organism.[6]

Gesell sees *organization* as the crucial principle in growth, and this organization is laid down in the inherited nervous system.

> This nervous system . . . is so constructed that it reacts in a patterned and patterning manner to the world of things. It reacts in the same patterning manner to the world of persons,—which is equivalent to saying that personality is subject to the very mechanisms and the laws which govern the growth of perceptions and of intelligence.[7]

While Gesell's studies were done some time ago, his work stands as a classic. The three volumes which report his findings are as good an introduction to the description of development as can be found today.

Piaget's study of the origins of intelligence. The Swiss psychologist, Jean Piaget, has studied development with one primary question in mind: How does intelligence emerge and what are the processes by which it develops? Like Gesell, he stresses the inherited characteristics of the species; but he places more emphasis on the way that these inherited characteristics interact with the environment in the shaping of intelligence.

Piaget sees intelligence as developing in three major periods: the sensorimotor period (first two years), the concrete operations period (2-11 yrs.), and the formal operations period (11-15 yrs.). His most detailed description is of the sensorimotor period, and a rather full summary of the six stages of this period is given in order to indicate the flavor of Piaget's work (see p. 132).

Piaget stubbornly refuses to side with either the environmentalist or the geneticist. He insists on an interactionist position which gives primary emphasis to the activity of the child, but which sees this activity as constantly being influenced by the environment in which the child acts.

> Piaget postulated that each organism is an open, active, self–regulating system. Mental development would then be characterized by progressive changes in the process of active adaptation.[8]

Piaget's theory of intellectual development is firmly rooted in biology, and he sees two biological functions as the basis for three basic intellectual functions. One is the biological principle of *organization* (note, also, Gesell's emphasis on organization, p. 131), and the other is the biological principle of *adaptation* (which we discuss further in Chapter 9).

Table 5

THE SENSORIMOTOR PERIOD OF INTELLECTUAL DEVELOPMENT

First Stage: The use of reflexes; sucking and grasping, crying and vocalization, movement and positions of the arms, the head or the trunk.

Second Stage: The first acquired adaptation. For example, when the child systematically sucks his thumb, no longer due to chance contacts but through coordination between hand and mouth.

Third Stage: Secondary circular reactions: the repetition of an action which brings satisfaction and is, thus, the core around which intentional behavior develops.

Fourth Stage: The application of known means to new situations. Occurs about the eighth or ninth month and is illustrated in the baby's searching for an object which has disappeared from view.

Fifth Stage: The discovery of new means through active experimentation. Called the tertiary circular reaction, an example would be a child learning to put a watch chain into a narrow opening.

Sixth Stage: The invention of new means. Appearing around sixteen months of age, an example would be a child discovering that he can use a stick to get something he cannot reach by hand.

Adapted from Jean Piaget, *The Origins of Intelligence in Children,* New York: International Universities Press, Inc., 1952.

From the principle of organization, Piaget derives the intellectual function which he calls the "regulating function." Essentially, he is referring to the tendency of the organism to act as a whole, in which all parts are related to all other parts. This tendency he sees permeating every aspect of mental life.

From the principle of adaptation, Piaget derives the intellectual functions of *assimilation* and *accommodation.* By assimilation he means the way in which the organism takes the data from the environment into itself. By accommodation he means the way in which the organism changes in response to the environment. This process of adaptation, involving a constant interaction between assimilation and accommodation, is the organism's way of "progressing from a less to a more complete equilibrium and manifests therein the organism's steady tendency toward a dynamic integration."

For Piaget, then, intelligence is best understood as an extension of the most basic organismic processes. This, it will be noted, is very similar to what Gesell said of personality (see p. 131).

Havighurst's theory of developmental tasks. Robert Havighurst approaches development in still another way. He observes that as a child grows physically, his social environment imposes certain "tasks" upon him. The child is told, "You are now big enough to do such and such," or "You are now too big to be doing such and such." Thus Havighurst combines in an ingenious way the biological and social aspects of development. He has listed the "developmental tasks" for each period of development (see below).[10]

Thus, according to Havighurst, the problems of development are associated with difficulties a person may have in mastering the tasks that people of his age are expected to master.

Table 6

HAVIGHURST'S DEVELOPMENTAL TASKS

Early Childhood 0–6 years	Acquiring a sense of trust in self and others. Developing a healthy concept of self. Learning to give and receive affection. Identifying with own sex. Achieving skills in motor coordination. Learning to be member of family group. Beginning to learn physical and social realities. Beginning to distinguish right and wrong and to respect rules and authority. Learning to understand and use language. Learning personal care.
Middle Childhood 6–12 years	Gaining wider knowledge and understanding of physical and social world. Building wholesome attitudes toward self. Learning appropriate masculine or feminine social role. Developing conscience, morality, a scale of values. Learning to read, write, calculate, other intellectual skills. Learning physical skills. Learning to win and maintain place among age-mates. Learning to give and take, and to share responsibility.
Adolescence 12–18 years	Developing a clear sense of identity and self-confidence. Adjusting to body changes. Developing new, more mature relations with age-mates. Achieving emotional independence from parents. Selecting and preparing for an occupation. Achieving mature values and social responsibility. Preparing for marriage and family life. Developing concern beyond self.
Early Adulthood 18–35 years	Seeing meaning in one's life. Getting started in an occupation. Selecting and learning to live with a mate. Starting a family and supplying children's material and psychological needs. Managing a home. Finding a congenial social group. Taking on civic responsibility.

Table 6 (Continued)

Middle *Age* *35–60 years*	Achieving full civic and social responsibility. Relating oneself to one's spouse as a person. Establishing adequate financial security for remaining years. Developing adult leisure–time activities, extending interests. Helping teen–age children become responsible and happy adults. Adjusting to aging parents. Adjusting to physiological changes of middle age.
Later *Life*	Adjusting to decreasing physical strength. Adjusting to retirement and reduced income. Adjusting to death of spouse and friends. Meeting social and civic obligations within one's ability. Establishing an explicit affiliation with age group. Maintaining interests, concern beyond self.

Rogers' Theory of the Fully Functioning Person.   Another theory of development focuses on psychological health or personal maturity. For the psychotherapist, Carl Rogers, the most important kind of development involves the processes by which persons come to function freely and fully. Here the emphasis is not on passing through normative growth stages, nor is it on learning to live up to social expectations. The kind of development Rogers is interested in is not even necessarily associated with "growing up," for it is quite possible for an infant to be a much more fully functioning person than an adult. The fully functioning person manifests three characteristics:

1. he is open to his experience
2. he lives in an existential fashion
3. he finds his organism to be a trustworthy means of arriving at the most satisfying behavior in each existential situation[10]

It is Rogers' observation that people move in the direction of these characteristics when they are in a relationship in which they experience warm, unconditional acceptance, empathic understanding, and genuineness in the other person. It is Rogers' theory that most people move away from these characteristics because of interpersonal relationships in which they are loved and valued for their conformity to values imposed from outside themselves.

The following is Rogers' picture of the fully functioning person:

> He is able to live fully in and with each and all of his feelings and reactions. He is making use of all his organic equipment to sense, as accurately as possible, the existential situation within and without. He is using all of the data his nervous system can thus supply, using it in awareness, but recognizing that his total organism may be, and often is, wiser than his awareness. He is able to permit his total organism to function in all its complexity in selecting, from the multitude of possibilities, that behavior which in this moment of time will be most generally and genuinely satisfying. He is able to trust his or-

ganism in this functioning, not because it is infallible, but because he can be fully open to the consequences of each of his actions and correct them if they prove to be less than satisfying.

He is able to experience all of his feelings, and is afraid of none of his feelings; he is his own sifter of evidence, but is open to evidence from all sources; he is completely engaged in the process of being and becoming himself, and thus discovers that he is soundly and realistically social; he lives completely in the moment, but learns that this is the soundest living for all time. He is a fully functioning organism, and because of the awareness of himself which flows freely in and through his experiences, he is fully a functioning person.[11]

Such a view of development has obvious implications for child–rearing, education, religion, and social theory.

SUMMARY

One of the most fruitful approaches to the study of persons is the genetic approach, which focuses on origins and development.

The process of reproduction, in which each individual human life originates, is a cellular process. Special cells, called gametes or germ cells, with half the number of chromosomes found in other body cells, are united at conception to form a zygote. Especially important for understanding hereditary processes is the expanding knowledge of DNA and RNA molecules.

The concept of development may be understood in several different ways, and these differences in meaning are reflected in the developmental theories advanced.

Physiological principles in development include the change from relatively undifferentiated to more differentiated, growth along a physiological gradient, and the principle of motor primacy.

Among psycho–social principles of development, outstanding are: development of the ability to wait, the ability to deal with ambiguity, the ability to control "closure," and the ability to love.

Major developmental theories include psychoanalytically based theories, the normative–descriptive theory of Gesell, Piaget's study of the origins of intelligence, Havighurst's theory of developmental tasks, and Rogers' theory of the fully functioning person.

QUESTIONS FOR STUDY AND CLASS DISCUSSION

1. What are some of the values of studying persons by means of the genetic approach?

2. In what ways is the human being most "finished" at birth and in what ways is he most "unfinished"?

3. Show how the differences in the proportionate sizes of various body parts in the infant and the adult illustrate the physiological gradient in development.

4. What are some of the factors involved in developing the ability to wait?

5. Give some illustrations of ways in which children find difficulty with ambiguity.

6. What are some differences between "childish" love and mature love?

7. What is the major difference between Freud's psycho-sexual theory and Erikson's description of developmental crises?

8. What is the main value of Gesell's normative-descriptive theory? What is the main drawback?

9. Can you make a list of the developmental tasks facing freshmen in college? Newlyweds? A person just starting on a new job?

10. Do you know someone that might fit Rogers' description of the fully functioning person?

SUGGESTIONS FOR FURTHER READING

Bruner, Jerome. *The Process of Education.* Cambridge, Mass.: Harvard University Press, 1961.
Erikson, Erik. *Childhood and Soceity.* New York: W. W. Norton, 1950.
Friedenberg, Edgar Z. *Coming of Age in America.* New York: Vintage Books, 1965.
Furth, Hans G. *Piaget and Knowledge.* Englewood Cliffs, N.J.: Prentice-Hall, 1969.
Muus, Rolf E. *Theories of Adolescence.* New York: Random House, 1962.

8

STUDIES OF BEHAVIOR

In Chapter 1 we noted how psychology moved from the study of the mind to the study of behavior, from structuralism to functionalism. For the functionalist, this shift was not so much an abandonment of the study of mind as it was a change in the way that mind would be approached. Instead of studying the structure of the mind, the functionalists studied its function.[1] *Following Darwin's clue,*

> *... they reasoned that if there was physical continuity between the bodily structures of men and other animals, there may also be continuity of mental activities as well. Following yet another Darwinian hypothesis, the functionalists argued that the mind could also be regarded as helping the organism to adapt to its environment just as the physical structures did. These changes in theoretical orientation eliminated the ancient distinction between animal behavior as merely instinctive, and human behavior as rational.*

The vast majority of American psychologists in the twentieth century have thought of themselves as students of behavior.

STUDIES BASED ON THE S–R MODEL

Classical Conditioning: Pavlov's Studies of Respondent Behavior

While they were not the first studies in point of time, Pavlov's conditioning experiments deserve first mention because of the simplicity of the behavior studied.

Ivan Pavlov was a Russian physiologist who, in the early years of this century, was studying digestive problems. As part of this study, he had developed a technique for measuring the salivary response of experimental dogs. The dog's cheek was cut with a scalpel, one of the salivary ducts was pulled outside the cheek, the cut was sewn up, and then a tube was attached to the salivary duct so that saliva could be collected and precisely measured. Meat powder was put into the dog's mouth to induce salivation, but Pavlov noticed that many times the dog salivated before the meat powder was presented. Pavlov was not the first to notice that animals may drool before being fed, but he was disturbed by what others took for granted, and this, as we noted in Chapter 1, is the first step toward new knowledge. For over 20 years, Pavlov and his associates conducted thousands of experiments in search of exact information about this salivary response in dogs.

In the classical experiment, a dog was systematically conditioned to make the salivary response to a neutral stimulus such as the sound of a bell. The neutral stimulus was regularly paired with meat powder. At first the dog did not salivate when the bell was rung; but as the combination of bell and meat powder was repeatedly presented, the dog gradually came to salivate at the sound of the bell (see Table 1).

Table 1

Start of Experiment	Experimental Procedure	End of Experiment
	Bell (Neutral Stim.)	Bell (CS)
Meat Powder (UcS)	Meat Powder (UcS)	Salivation (CR)
Salivation (UcR)	Salivation (UcR)	Meat Powder (UcS)
		Salivation (UcR)
UcS = Unconditioned Stimulus		CS = Conditoned Stimulus
UcR = Unconditioned Response		CR = Conditioned Response

Note that the bell, originally a neutral stimulus as far as the salivary response was concerned, became the conditioned stimulus capable of eliciting the salivary response, which is called a conditioned response when it occurs following the bell.

Three aspects of classical conditioning should be noted. First, it always involves the *pairing of two stimuli*, a neutral stimulus (such as the bell) and an unconditioned stimulus (such as meat powder). Second, conditioning occurs only when there is *reinforcement*, which is the name given to the influence of the unconditioned stimulus. Third, classical conditioning has to do with *reflexive behavior*.

A reflex is a specific response consistently elicited by a specific stimulus. Thus the reflex is called "stimulus dependent" or a "respondent." Some examples, other than the salivary reflex studied by Pavlov, include the eliciting of tears by onion juice, of sneezing by pepper, and of the knee jerk by tapping on the patellar tendon. Some reflexes involve skeletal muscles (sneezes, knee jerks, shivering), some involve cardiac muscles (heart-rate changes), some involve glands (salivation, tears), and some involve smooth muscles (blanching of skin, pupillary changes.) Some of these reflexes (the knee jerk, for example) have not been successfully conditioned. "CR's seem most convincingly formed in respondents which depend on the function of the autonomic nervous system."[2]

Pavlov noted several other consistent relationships between stimuli and responses in the conditioning process. *Extinction:* When a conditioned stimulus is repeatedly presented without being followed by the unconditioned stimulus (reinforcement), the conditioned response progressively weakens until it ceases to occur. *Spontaneous recovery:* If, after a conditioned response has been extinguished, a certain period of time is permitted to intervene, the conditioned response will reappear when the conditioned stimulus is presented again. *Stimulus generalization:* Once a conditioned response has been established, there is a tendency for it to occur in response to other stimuli closely resembling or closely associated with the original conditioned stimulus. The dog which has been conditioned to salivate to the bell will also salivate to other similar sounds. *Respons generalization:* There is a tendency for the response to the conditioned stimulus to show some variability. Besides salivating to the bell, the dog will make other movements in anticipation of food.

Before we leave Pavlov, we should look at one other kind of classical conditioning. *Higher order conditioning:* Once a conditioned response has been well established, the conditioned stimulus can be paired with another neutral stimulu and function as the reinforcement. The neutral stimulus will become a second conditioned stimulus for the conditioned response. The bell which has become the conditioned stimulus for the salivary response can be paired with a light which will then come to elicit the salivary response. This use of a conditioned stimulus as a reinforcer is called "secondary reinforcement."

Instrumental Conditioning: Thorndike's Studies of Trial and Error Learning

In 1898, eight years before Pavlov published his first results, Edward L. Thor dike reported his first studies of what he called "instrumental behavior." Working at Columbia University, Thorndike experimented mainly with cats in puzzle boxes. In the typical experiment, a hungry cat was put into a box with a concealed mechanism operated by a latch. When the cat correctly manipulated the latch, the door opened, and the cat gained access to food on the outside. The behavior of the cat in the box was typical of that commonly called "trial and error" learning. Progress over repeated trials was measured in terms of the time that elapsed from the moment the cat was put into the box until he escaped. A the cat was repeatedly put into the box, he gradually took less and less time unt he would manipulate the latch immediately. Since the latch manipulation was *instrumental* to obtaining food, Thorndike called this kind of learning *instrumen tal learning.*

In current psychology, the kind of behavior Thorndike studied is called *operant,* in contrast to the kind studied by Pavlov which is called *respondent.* As we noted above, the respondent is stimulus–dependent, which means that it is *elicited* by the stimulus. An operant, on the other hand, is *emitted* by the organism and is followed by the unconditioned stimulus (see Table 2).

Table 2

Start of Experiment	Experimental Procedure	End of Experiment
Cat in box	Cat in box	Cat in box
Random movements	Random movements	Latch manipulated (CR)
	Latch manipulated	Open door leads to food (UcS
	Open door leads to food	

Note that manipulating the latch is only one of many responses that the cat makes to the experimental situation and that none of these is elicited by any specific stimulus. Manipulating the latch, however, is the only response followed by reinforcement. Instead of having two stimuli paired, as in classical conditioning, we have a response and a stimulus paired in instrumental conditioning.

In his early work, Thorndike stated three fundamental principles involved in this kind of learning: *readiness, exercise,* and *effect.* By readiness Thorndike meant preparation for action, and the law of exercise refers to the increase in learning with practice. Neither of these two principles held up very well in further research, and Thorndike first modified them and then used them less in his later work. However, the law of effect, which referred to the strengthening or weakening of a learned response as a result of its consequences, has proved to be one of the most fruitful principles in the field of behavioral studies and survives today as a fundamental principle.

Popularly stated, the law of effect has to do with *reward* and *punishment.* When a particular act is followed by reward, it is likely to be repeated in similar circumstances; when an act is followed by punishment (or no reward), it is less likely to be repeated. Thorndike was an "associationist" and thought in terms of the neural connections between stimuli and responses being strengthened or weakened. In the technical language of associationism the law of effect would be stated as follows:

> When a modifiable connection is made and is accompanied by or followed by a satisfying state of affairs, the strength of the connection is increased; if the connection is made and followed by an annoying state of affairs, its strength is decreased.[3]

For half a century some of the most pressing theoretical and practical questions faced by psychologists have been discussed in the form in which Thorndike posed them. Theoretical questions include:

1. Does an organism have to be motivated in order to learn?
2. Does learning require repetition or can learning occur in one trial?
3. Are reward and punishment equally effective in learning?

Among practical questions are:

1. Of what use is drill in the teaching process?
2. How effective is punishment in preventing undesirable behavior?
3. How much of what is learned in school can be used in other situations outside of school?

Watson's Behaviorism: Generalizations from Pavlov

As we have noted, it was functionalism that led the way as the field of psychology began to focus on behavior, and it was John B. Watson who first attempted to explain all psychological processes in terms of the simplest behavioral concepts. Watson found in Pavlov's principles of classical conditioning a basis for explaining all behavior. To him the most complex behavior is simply a series of reflexes modified by a long chain of conditioning. One of his most famous statements boldly claimed,

> Give me a dozen healthy infants, well formed, and my own specified world to bring them up in and I'll guarantee to take any one at random and train him to become any type of specialist I might select—a doctor, lawyer, artist, merchant-chief, and yes, even beggar-man and thief, regardless of his talents, penchants, tendencies, abilities, vocations, and race of his ancestors.[4]

Two experiments illustrate Watson's approach. In the first, he conditioned an eleven-month-old infant to fear a white rat by making a very loud sound every time the infant touched the rat. After only seven pairings of the rat and the noise, the baby was terribly frightened of even the sight of the rat. Furthermore the fear of the rat spread (stimulus generalization) to other white furry objects: a rabbit, a dog, a fur coat, etc. For the second experiment, conducted three years after the one just described, Watson used a three-year-old boy who showed strong fear reactions to white rats, rabbits, fur coats and the like. This was a different child from the infant Watson had previously conditioned to fear such things, but he wanted to see if this child's fears could be "unconditioned." The procedure involved bringing a rabbit into a large room where the child was eating crackers and milk. The rabbit was brought as close as possible without disturbing the child's eating, but no closer. This process was repeated each day. The child permitted the rabbit to get closer and closer until, finally, he was playing with the rabbit with one hand while he was eating with the other. Just as the conditioned fear of the infant spread to other objects similar to the white rat, so did this child's loss of fear spread to other objects similar to the white rabbit.

Watson saw two principles in conditioning: *frequency* and *recency*. These, he asserted, more accurately explained learning than did Thorndike's law of effect.

> He believed that animal learning, as in the maze or problem-solving box, could be explained according to what the animal had most often been led to do in the situation, with the most recent act favored in recall. Because the successful act was both most frequent and most recent, its occurrence could be explained without recourse to an added principle of effect.[5]

Watson's position on learning has not been accepted by later students of behavior, but his insistence on a purely objective methodology has been followed by a whole generation of experimental psychologists, some of whom call themselves behaviorists, some neo-behaviorists, and still others operationists. No one typifies today's objectivism in psychology so well as does B. F. Skinner, who is classified as an operationist.

Skinner's Studies of Operant Behavior

Just as Watson's work represents an extension of Pavlov's classical conditioning, so Skinner's work represents an extension of Thorndike's instrumental conditioning. Skinner is best known for his work with rats and pigeons, although in his forty years of research he has encompassed a wide range of animal and human behavior. His approach can best be portrayed through a description of his prototype experiment with the "Skinner box."

A rat which has been deprived of food is put into a box with a food cup and a bar just above it. In the course of random movements about the box, the rat inevitably presses the bar above the food cup and this action releases a pellet of food into the cup. Gradually the rat presses the bar more often, until within a relatively short period of time, the bar-pressing reaches a maximum frequency where it levels off. This behavior is clearly of the instrumental type studied by Thorndike, but Skinner prefers the term *operant*. He distinguishes operant from respondent conditioning, calling the former Type R, because the response is crucial, and the latter Type S, because the stimulus is crucial. It is Skinner's opinion that there are very few examples of pure Type S behavior, while Type R behavior is seen in the everyday behavior of all animals and men.

Skinner differs from the other researchers we have studied in that while they are interested in theoretical formulations, he has stubbornly refused to construct a general theory. In other words, Skinner is well satisfied with scientific descriptions which specify how changes in stimuli are related to changes in responses.

Skinner's method of operant conditioning is extremely simple to state: *somehow get a response to occur, then reinforce it.* On the issue of reward vs. punishment, Skinner is unequivocally on the side of reward. It is his view that doing the "right" thing and having it reinforced is at the heart of learning, while making "mistakes" for which we are punished does not lead to learning.

> Punishment, according to Skinner and his associates, is defined as an experimental arrangement whose effects remain to be investigated empirically.[6]

This view of learning has influenced the development of "teaching machines" where the learning increments are so small that students make very few errors. Instead, they are encouraged to make "right" responses which are reinforced through positive feedback.

In the shaping of complex behavior, Skinner uses a technique called the *method of approximation.* Since the response must occur before it can be reinforced, and since a complex response is not likely to occur, Skinner reinforces any movement in the direction of the desired response. Then, gradually, he reinforces only behavior that gets closer and closer to the desired response until, in the end, he reinforces only the exact behavior desired.

In his emphasis on reinforcement, Skinner avoids theorizing about motivation or drive. For him, "any stimulus is a reinforcer if it increases the probability of a response."[7] He notes that under certain circumstances, such as deprivation of food, animals are more likely to be active and thus to make responses which can be reinforced. For Skinner it is enough to note these facts without theorizing that the animal learns because he is hungry.

In this connection, Skinner has extensively studied the influence of various reinforcement schedules. How, for example, is learning affected if a rat gets a food pellet every fifth time he presses the bar (ratio reinforcement)? There are two aspects to this question: How is rate of learning affected? How is strength of learning affected? With respect to rate, 100% reinforcement leads to the most rapid learning. But strength of learning, as measured by resistance to extinction, is another matter. With 100 percent reinforcement, extinction is rapid, while with a variable–interval schedule (reinforcing at irregular intervals) the behavior is extremely resistant to extinction. For example, "A pigeon has given as many as 10,000 unreinforced responses in extinction following such variable–interval reinforcement."[8] This principle can be seen in human behavior—you deposit very few quarters in a vending machine from which nothing comes out while a very great quantity of quarters will be put into a slot machine which is only intermittently returning anything. This principle also raises important questions with respect to training in the home and school. If a child is reinforced every time he makes a desired response, he might acquire behavior which can very easily be extinguished, while rewarding him intermittently might lead to the acquisition of behavior very difficult to extinguish.

An intriguing side effect that can occur with certain kinds of intermittent reinforcement was noted by Skinner in 1948. He described it in a paper called, " 'Superstition' in the Pigeon," and we quote from it at length.

> A pigeon is brought to a stable state of hunger by reducing it to 75 percent of its weight when well fed. It is put into an experimental cage for a few minutes each day. A food hopper attached to the cage may be swung into place so that the pigeon can eat from it. A solenoid and a timing relay hold the hopper in place for five sec. at each reinforcement.

> If a clock is now arranged to present the food hopper at regular intervals *with no reference whatsoever to the bird's behavior,* operant conditioning usually takes place. In six out of eight cases the resulting responses were so clearly defined that two observers could agree perfectly in counting instances. One bird was conditioned (spontaneously learned) to turn counter–clockwise about the cage, making two or three turns between reinforcements. Another repeatedly thrust its head into one of the upper corners of the cage. A third bird developed a "tossing" response. . .

> The conditioning process is usually obvious. The bird happens to be executing some response as the hopper appears; as a result it tends to

repeat this response. If the interval before the next presentation is not so great that extinction takes place, a second "contingency" is probable. This strengthens the response still further and subsequent reinforcement becomes more probable. It is true that some responses go unreinforced and some reinforcements appear when the response has not just been made, but the net result is the development of a considerable state of strength.[9]

uperstitions in human beings are probably not acquired in this way, but rather mple behavioral principles may explain even complex human behavior. Think, or example, of the stereotyped mannerisms of baseball players as they prepare ɔ hit a pitched ball, or basketball players preparing to throw a foul shot.

Under the heading of S–R theorists we have considered two men who worked rimarily with stimulus–dependent or respondent behavior (Pavlov and Watson), ıd two men who worked primarily with emitted behavior, called instrumental r operant behavior (Thorndike and Skinner). We shall leave for later considera-on the question of whether respondent behavior and operant behavior are really vo different kinds of behavior or whether they can both be understood in terms f common principles.

TUDIES BASED ON A COGNITIVE MODEL

olman's Purposive Behaviorism: Sign Learning

Of the three men whose work we shall study as examples of a cognitive model, ɔlman published most recently, yet we shall look at his work first because it ovides a better transition from the stimulus–response studies we have dealt ith.

Hilgard points up the difference between S–R and cognitive theories:

> Stimulus–response theories, while stated with different degrees of sophistication, imply that the organism is goaded along a path by internal and external stimuli, learning the correct movement sequences so that they are released under appropriate conditions of drive and environmental stimulation. The alternative possibility is that the learner is following signs to a goal, is learning his way about, is following a sort of map—in other words, is learning not movement but meanings. This is the contention of Tolman's theory of sign learning.[10]

Tolman and his associates experimented mainly with three kinds of behavior: tent learning, place learning, and reward expectancy. We shall look at one ex-eriment of each kind.

Latent learning. Three groups of rats were put in a maze leading to a food box. Group One was rewarded with food each time the food box was successfully reached. Group Two was never rewarded. These two groups constituted control groups for Group Three which was not rewarded for the first ten days, but was rewarded regularly beginning with the eleventh. As the figure below shows, Group Three performed in the same manner as Group Two through the first ten days; but, once it began to be rewarded, its behavior became superior even to Group One. Tolman concluded from this evidence that the rats did learn the maze when there was no reward even though this learning was not shown in performance. In other words, the rats were learning about the maze but did not use the knowledge they were gaining because there was no use for it. This kind of learning was called *latent learning.* It led Tolman to believe that learning takes place even when it is not reinforced and that what is learned is not a series of movements but some kind of "cognitive map."

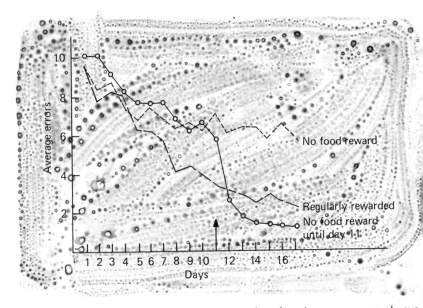

Place learning. Eight rats, designated the *place-learning group,* were always rewarded with food at the same place (F_1) even though they were required to start in random alternation from different places, (S_1 and S_2). Thus the rats had to make a right turn or a left turn at (C), depending on the place from which they were started. Eight rats, designated the *response-learning group,* were started in random alternation from either S_1 or S_2 and always found food by turning to the right at F_1 and F_2. Thus one group was rewarded for always going to the same place, while the other was rewarded for always making the same response. The place-learning group was much more successful.

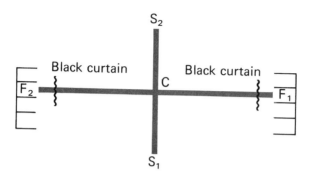

The eight rats of the place–learning group all learned within 8 trials, so that the next 10 trials were without error. None of the eight rats of the response–learning group learned this quickly, and five of them did not reach the criterion in 72 trials.[11]

To Tolman this was clear evidence that it is not a response that is being learned but knowledge about a place.

Reward expectancy. A banana was placed under one of two containers while a monkey who was watching was prevented from immediately going to get it. When the monkey was released, he chose the correct container. Then after a banana had been hidden, it was exchanged for a piece of lettuce, a food less preferred by the monkey. When the monkey was released, he chose the container under which he had seen the banana placed; but when he found the lettuce, he rejected it and continued to search. Thus a definite reward expectancy had been learned rather than either a response or even a place.[12]

These experiments led Tolman to postulate two principles which he offered as alternatives to the principles formulated by others: Expectancy vs. Habit, and Confirmation vs. Reinforcement. What others called habits Tolman called expectancies or "sign significates," and what others called reinforcement he called confirmation.

In Tolman, then we see a true *behaviorism* dedicated to the most stringent objectivity, but a behaviorism that is *molar* rather than *molecular*. Furthermore, Tolman saw behavior as purposive in the sense that it is goal-seeking.

Köhler's Studies of Insightful Behavior

The Gestalt psychologist Köhler regarded learning not as the formation of S–R connections, but rather as requiring the ability to perceive the materials to be learned in a new and different way. He called this important component of learning "insight."

Two experiments with an intelligent ape named Sultan illustrate what Köhler means by "insight." In the first one a banana was attached to the top of Sultan' cage beyond his reach. His repeated efforts to get it by jumping proved fruitless. There were two boxes in his cage and later while Sultan was playing with them, he "happened" to put one on top of the other, whereupon he "saw" that he could use them to reach the banana. He immediately placed them under the banana, climbed up, and got it.

In the second experiment a banana was put outside the cage beyond Sultan's reach. Again, after repeated efforts failed, he stopped and began to play. There were two sticks in his cage and Sultan tried first with one and then with the othe to reach the banana, but again he failed to reach it. Sultan went back to his play during which he "happened" to fit the two sticks together, making one long stick. At this point he "saw" that he could reach the banana and, without any delay, he raked it in.

In both of these experiments the main features are the same. Sultan tried to reach the banana: his behavior was goal-seeking. Sultan was unable to get the banana: he was frustrated in his direct efforts. He played in a seemingly aimless way: this play did not constitute direct goal-seeking behavior. Sultan "happened" to put the boxes or the sticks together: a new stimulus suddenly confronted him. He "saw" that he could reach the banana: he perceived a relationship between the new stimulus and the unsolved problem. This perception is what Köhler means by "insight."

While these experiments illustrating insight were conducted with an intelliger ape, it should not be assumed that Köhler and other Gestalt psychologists woulc limit the use of the term to such examples of higher order behavior. In commor with Tolman, Köhler would suggest that even the simpler kinds of behavior calle *respondent* and *operant* may be more adequately explained in terms of the "mei ing" of the situation to the animal. For example, the reason the dog salivates when the bell sounds is that the bell has come to "mean" that food is coming. So, also, with the rat in the Skinner box: although at first the rat is not able to "see" that pressing the bar will bring food, gradually he does come to see this.

It should be noted that Köhler does not use such terms as "insight" and "me ing" to stand for mysterious "mental faculties." He is using them in a strictly c scriptive sense and they are cognitive only in the sense that they refer to princip of organization centered in the brain.

It is significant, however, that it is in experiments with chimpanzees and human beings that insightful behavior finds its strongest support. It is in these sar experiments that the principles of respondent and operant conditioning have proved least adequate as explanatory principles. For this reason the kind of be havioral principles enunciated by Köhler have been especially attractive to educ tors seeking light on problems of human learning.

Wertheimer's Studies of Perceptual Behavior

Nowhere has the Gestalt approach proved so useful as in the area of perceptual studies. In Chapter 1 we noted that it was Wertheimer's report in 1912 on the "phi phenomenon" (apparent movement) that launched the Gestalt movement. Wertheimer, along with Köhler and Koffka, proceeded to attack molecular views and the associationist philosophy on which they were based. Their primary attack was against structuralism and its "additive" concept of perception. As behaviorism grew in influence, it too was attacked for its effort to add up S–R connections into complex behavior.

> The primary attack upon association theory was an attack on the "bundle hypothesis" sensation theory—the theory that a percept is made up of sensation–like elements, bound together by associations. [13]

The study of perception is central in psychology for several reasons. For one thing, in perception so–called "subjective" experience and the physical conditions accompanying it are simultaneously available for study. For another, the same phenomena lend themselves to many different experimental approaches: e.g., the behaviorist may deduce what is being perceived through conditioning experiments, while the cognitive theorist does the same thing through the verbal reports of the subject. Most important, in perception we are dealing with some of the "purest" psychological phenomena: i.e., whatever "mind" may turn out to be, in perception we are forced to come to grips with organismic activity which is qualitatively different from the processes studied by physiologists.

We do not have to join the Gestalt school, nor do we have to abandon behavioral methodology, to recognize that Wertheimer and his associates, by their emphasis on the processes of perception, have helped to get psychology back to the kind of problems which gave the field its reason for existence.

In his classic report on apparent movement ("phi phenomenon"—see Chapter), Wertheimer demonstrated that even when there is no real movement in the physical world a person will sometimes perceive movement. This is an example of an *illusion*, or a misinterpretation of sensory data. The reader is familiar with numerous examples of illusion, from the well–known mirage to the famous Mueller-Lyer illusion (see below).

PSYCHOLOGY AS PHILOSOPHY, SCIENCE, AND ART

Here is another interesting and maddening illusion.

Such examples make it clear that perception is not a passive process in which the outside world is somehow taken in and reproduced by the sensory processes. Rather, perception is an active process in which the organism takes in sensory cues and organizes them into meaningful patterns. Therefore we are subject to illusions, but the same process enables us to maintain a stable perceptual relationship with the environment.

For example, as a friend walks toward us from some distance he will appear to remain the same size, even though his image on the retina of our eye gets larger and larger. The same principle is seen in the way we perceive shapes. The top of a drinking glass appears circular regardless of the angle at which we hold it, even though the shape of the image on the retina of the eye may be elliptical rather than circular. In a similar way, objects seem to remain stable in the environment even though we move our head, thus producing movement on the retina of the eye. It is this organizing tendency in perception that Wertheimer pointed to, and he sought the lawful principles by which it works.

Wertheimer called his most general principle the Law of Pragnanz, meaning that "psychological organization tends to move in one general direction rather than in other directions, always toward the state of Pragnanz, toward the 'good' gestalt."[14] Popularly, we might call this the "law of best fit," meaning that there is an effort to make things fit together in the most economical way.

Four of Wertheimer's more specific laws are easier to understand and they can serve as illustrations of the general law.

The Law of Similarity. In perception, similar items tend to be grouped together.

XXOOXXOOXXOOXXOOXXOO

In the row of X's and O's, we tend to group the X's together and the O's together even though the spaces between letters are constant.

The Law of Proximity. Things which are close together tend to be grouped together.

XO OX XO OX XO OX XO

This grouping is according to nearness, not similarity.

The Law of Closure. In perception there is a tendency to see figures as closed ven when they are open.

n the above figure, we easily read the word from the sketchy markings. This aw is offered by the Gestalt school as an alternative to Thorndike's law of effect. he fact that the organism seems to prefer completed situations is suggested as ne reason that goal-reaching behavior is experienced as rewarding. In Chapter 7 ve pointed out some of the developmental problems associated with tendency oward closure.

The Law of Good Continuation. There is a tendency to see lines, straight or urved, as continuing.

n the above figure we tend to see curves and straight lines rather than other napes.

Wertheimer makes it clear that perception is an active process by which the rganism organizes the stimuli which impinge upon it. He shows that there is a wfulness in this organization and identifies some of the principles to be observed. He also suggests that the principles evident in perception may be equally : work in other kinds of behavior.

> Modern cognitive theorists view learning in terms of the concepts of information storage and retrieval. "Learning is viewed as the process by which information about the environment is acquired, stored, and categorized. This cognitive viewpoint is very different from the view that learning consists of the acquisition of specific responses; in modern cognitive parlance, responses are mediated by the nature of the stored information, which may consist of facts or strategies or programs analogous to the grammar that is acquired in the learning of a language. Thus "what is learned" may be a system for generating responses as a consequence of the specific information that is stored.[15]

TUDIES OF MORE COMPLEX BEHAVIOR

xperimental Studies of Symbolic Processes

So far we have noted studies of behavior that is as characteristic of subhuman animals as it is of man. Now we turn to studies of behavior which, while it may not be completely absent in the lower animals, is most characteristic of man.

As we noted in Chapter 2, man is most different from other animals in the ability to symbolize. The importance of this ability, called "thought," is difficult to exaggerate. With it man has achieved nothing less than a kind of emancipation from bondage to time and place. In perception the organism responds to physical stimuli which are present to the senses, while in thinking the organism responds to stimuli no longer physically present. Therefore some *representation* of the stimuli has been made by the organism, and it is this process that we study under the heading of symbolic processes.

Ebbinghaus. One of the earliest series of psychological experiments dealt with the learning of verbal material. In 1885, Ebbinghaus used nonsense syllables in studies aimed at discovering how words are learned. He used nonsense syllables in an effort to study the process with a minimum of interference from previous experiences of the subjects. In some of the experiments, subjects were required to learn nonsense syllables in pairs, so that when one syllable of the pair was presented the other was to be recalled. In other experiments subjects were asked to learn lists of nonsense syllables in serial order, so that they could start at the beginning of the list and recall all the syllables presented.

Ebbinghaus undoubtedly described some common learning processes. The alphabet is learned in serial order. The multiplication tables and the vocabulary of a foreign language are learned by pairing. However, Ebbinghaus did not concern himself with the representational process by which symbols are originally learned.

Hull. In the 1920s, Hull reported a series of experiments on concept formation. Using Chinese characters with which nonsense syllables were paired, Hull studied the process by which different things come to be called by the same name (concept) on the basis of some common element or elements. For example, how do we learn to call a St. Bernard, a Dachshund, a Great Dane, a Chihauhua, and a Bulldog by the name *dog* when they are so different? From his studies with the Chinese characters, Hull concluded that the essential process in concept formation is *dissociation.* The common element or elements are attended to while other elements are ignored.

Hull's work brings us closer to the actual process of language acquisition, especially some of the more complex processes, but it still misses some of the most basic issues.

A Natural Experiment: Helen Keller. While it does not meet the rigorous requirements of a controlled scientific experiment, the story of Helen Keller's first grasp of language dramatically focuses on some of the most crucial aspects. Without either the ability to see or to hear, Helen had been unable to learn the symbols (language) that would make communication and complex thought possible. For many weeks her teacher, Ann Sullivan, had unsuccessfully tried to get her to associate the tactile stimuli provided by Ann Sullivan's fingers with the objects they were meant to stand for. Then one day it happened! Helen connected the tactile sign with the objective counterpart. The water she was touching could be represented by forming shapes with her fingers. So could the tree, the earth, her doll, and her parents. Everything could be represented (named), and once represented, could be referred to in communication with another person.

In language, then, a written sign, vocal sound, or hand gesture comes to stand for a concrete thing, a class of things, an action, or a relationship. The representation of the thing is repeatedly presented in association with that which it represents, until by attending to the significant stimuli and ignoring the irrelevant stimuli (dissociation), the connection is somehow established. That "somehow" is still not understood.

Studies of Problem-Solving

The adaptive behavior model. It is difficult to distinguish experimental studies of problem-solving from experimental studies of learning. In fact, the instrumental conditioning experiments as well as the insight learning experiments could be formulated as problem-solving experiments. The differences are largely of terminology and frame of reference.

Problem-solving experiments have mainly been formulated in terms of the key concept of the Functionalists—that behavior serves as the means by which the organism adapts to its environment. In this frame of reference, a problem means a situation in which the organism is blocked in its effort to meet some need. Dashiell[16] is credited with the following diagram which illustrates this view of adaptive behavior. An organism is in a drive state related to a need in the organism (1) and to a goal (5) which is perceived as capable of meeting this need. The motivated organism is blocked (2) or frustrated. The organism reacts by increasing and varying its behavior (3). Finally, if a way to the goal is found the organism manifests consummatory or goal-reaching behavior (4). This whole process is called adjustive behavior and forms the frame of reference for studies of problem-solving. (In Chapter 5 this model was used in our discussion of reactions to frustration.)

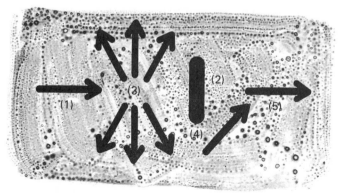

Durkin's experimental study of problem solving. In 1937[17] Durkin performe(
an ingenious study using a series of two-dimensional construction puzzles. The
subjects were assigned the task of putting pieces together to form a square. The(
were five puzzles in the series (see Table 3). After all five had been solved one a
a time, the subjects were given all of the pieces and instructed to form a large
Maltese cross (see below.)

THE SIMPLE SQUARE PUZZLES
as presented

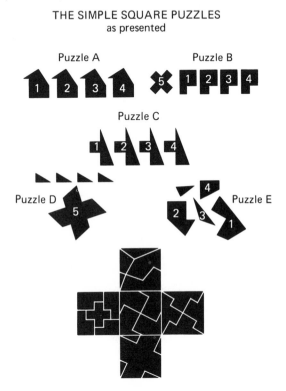

The Completed Total Cross Puzzle

To facilitate an understanding of the problem–solving process, the subjects wer(
asked to think out loud as they worked; and when they had finished, to reflect
on how they had thought. They were also observed and photographed while
they worked.

Durkin found three different approaches to problem solving which she calle(
Trial–and–Error, Sudden Reorganization, and Gradual Analysis. In the table or
the following page are her observations relating to these approaches. Durkin sa(
these different kinds of thinking as being on a continuum rather than as being
mutually exclusive. Underlying all three kinds of thinking she saw the same pr(
cesses. In her words, "These are, observation, recall, seeing relations, and atten(
tion to the goal. To this manipulation can be added, and inferences can be con(
sidered as a high level of seeing relations."[18]

Table 3

Trial–and–Error	Sudden Reorganization	Gradual Analysis
1. "Blind" groping	Groping suddenly	No groping but a gradually developing understanding.
2. Hindsight	Sudden foresight	Foresight
3. Confusion till the last moment	Confusion suddenly cleared	Cleared step by step
4. Hopeless feeling	Excitement, elation, sometimes relief	Satisfaction
5. Aim—to match pieces	To look for wholes or interrelations	To satisfy goal needs
6. Attention to goal distant, diffuse	Attention not centered on goal	Attention concentrated on specific goal needs
7. Attitude not definite, but wandering, haphazard	Passive, receptive	Active, directed search
8. Error curve irregular; transfer poor	Curve irregular, then sudden drop; transfer good	Error curve step–like; transfer good
9. Manner baffled	Baffled, then suddenly well organized, efficient	Calm, well organized

Duncker's experiment on the solution of practical problems. In 1945 Duncker[19] investigated the question: "How does the solution arise from the problem situation? In what ways is the solution of a problem attained?" Using college students as subjects, Duncker assigned such problems as the following: Given a human being with an inoperable stomach tumor, and rays which destroy organic tissue at sufficient intensity, by what procedure can one free him of the tumor by these rays and at the same time avoid destroying the healthy tissue which surrounds it?

As in the Durkin experiment, the students were told to think out loud. They were also assured that this was not a test of knowledge so they might ask the experimenter any question they desired. One student's approach to a solution is reproduced below.

Protocol of Student

1. Send rays through the esophagus.
2. Desensitize the healthy tissues by means of chemical injection.
3. Expose the tumor by operating.
4. One ought to decrease the intensity of the rays on their way; for

example, would this work? Turn the rays on at full strength only after the tumor has been reached. (Experimenter: False analogy; no injection is in question.)

5. One should swallow something inorganic (which would not allow passage of the rays) to protect the healthy stomach walls. (Experimenter: It is not merely the stomach walls which are to be protected.)

6. Either the rays must enter the body or the tumor must come out. Perhaps one could alter the location of the tumor—but how? Through pressure? No.

7. Introduce a cannula. (Experimenter: What in general does one do when, with any agent, one wishes to produce in a specific place an effect which he wishes to avoid on the way to that place?)

8. (Reply:) One neutralizes the effect on the way. But that is what I have been attempting all the time.

9. Move the tumor toward the exterior. (Compare 6.) (The experimenter repeats the problem and emphasizes, ". . . which destroy *at sufficient intensity.*")

10. The intensity ought to be variable. (Compare 4).

11. Adaption of the healthy tissues by previous weak application of the rays. (Experimenter: How can it be brought about that the rays destroy only the region of the tumor?)

12. (Reply:) I see no more than two possibilities: either to protect the body or to make the rays harmless. (Experimenter: How could one decrease the intensity of the rays en route?) (Compare 4.)

13. (Reply) Somehow divert . . . diffuse rays . . . disperse . . . stop! Send a broad and weak bundle of rays through a lens in such a way that the tumor lies at the focal point and thus receives intensive radiation. (Total duration about half an hour.)

From such protocols, Duncker drew several conclusions about the process of problem solving. First, the solution of a problem is simply a more productive way of formulating the problem. Second, the reformulation of the problem is primarily a matter of grasping the principle involved and of making it more and more concrete. Third, the process does not proceed in a straight line but shifts about, often returning to ideas tried earlier.

Studies of Creativity

Of all human behavior, none has more value than that which we call creativity. This behavior is most complex and therefore most resistant to scientific study.

n recent years, however, a heightened interest in creativity has led to important scientific studies and stimulating theories of creativity. Here we shall give only three studies which illustrate the work being done in this area.

Guilford's factor analysis of creativity. For over thirty years, Guilford and his associates at the University of Southern California, have explored the nature of intelligence by means of factor analysis. In this method a large number of tests are administered to subjects and inter-correlations are computed for all the scores. If the scores on two or more tests have high correlations with each other but low correlations with other tests in the battery, these tests are said to represent one *factor*. As many such factors emerged, Guilford developed a general hypothesis, called the Structure of the Intellect, in which he predicted that at least 120 different intellectual factors would be discovered. Research has so far identified over 80 separate factors.[20] Among these the following have been defined as factors in creativity.

Sensitivity to problems
Fluency (word fluency, ideational fluency, expressional fluency, and associational fluency)
Flexibility (adaptive flexibility and spontaneous flexibility)
Originality
Redefinition (figural redefinition, semantic redefinition, and symbolic redefinition)
Elaboration

For Guilford, creativity is measured by tests that put a premium on the ability to produce unique, uncommon answers rather than on the ability to remember "correct" answers. The following tests will serve as examples and as an operational definition of creativity.[21]

A test for sensitivity to problems: The subject is asked to state things that are wrong with common devices such as telephone, refrigerator, and electric toaster.

A test for fluency (in this case word fluency): The subject is asked to list all the words he can think of that begin with one particular letter.

A test for flexibility: The subject is instructed to think of all the possible uses for a brick, and the test is scored for the number of different kinds of uses named.

A test for originality: The subject makes up punchlines for cartoons.

A test for redefinition ability: The subject is shown a picture with hidden figures which he is to identify.

A test of elaboration: The subject draws a picture by adding to a few lines which have already been drawn and the test is scored for the amount of elaboration of detail.

Mednick's remote associations test. This test is based on Mednick's definition of the creative thinking process as "the forming of associative elements into new combinations which either meet specified requirements or are in some way useful."[22] The test items consist of sets of three words selected to represent what Mednick calls "remote associative clusters." The subject is required to find a fourth word which can serve as an associative link between the words in each set.

Example 1:   rat   blue   cottage

The answer is "cheese," as in rat–cheese, blue–cheese, and cottage–cheese.

Example 2:   railroad   girl   class
Example 3:   surprise   line   birthday
Example 4:   wheel   electric   high
Example 5:   out   dog   cat

The answers are: 2. working; 3. party; 4. chair or wire; 5. house.[23]

The following experiment indicates how this test might be used in research.

> The Remote Associations Test was administered to a group of first year psychology graduate students at the University of Michigan whose native language was American English (N = 35). Faculty research supervisors (who had been directing the independent research effort of the students), rated the eight highest and eight lowest RAT scorers either "high" or "low" in research creativity (no middle category allowed). Research creativity was defined as being demonstrated if the student developed new research methods and/or pulled together disparate theory or research areas in useful and original ways. Of the 16 research supervisors, one felt that he had not had enough contact with his student to make the judgment. His student was a low RAT scorer. Of the eight high RAT scorers, six were rated high on research creativity and two were rated low; of the seven low RAT scorers, only one was rated high, the other six being rated low.[24]

Barron's studies of the creative personality. Barron's approach has been to determine the personality characteristics of people who are rated as creative. Barron states two criteria which a response must meet if it is to be considered creative: it must be uncommon, and it must be adaptive to reality.[25] Drawing on years of research with creative people, he proposed five hypotheses which he tested by comparing 15 creative people with 15 non–creative people.

Hypothesis 1:   That original persons prefer complexity and some degree of apparent imbalance in phenomena.

Hypothesis 2:   That original persons are more complex psycho–dynamically and have greater personal scope.

Hypothesis 3:   That original persons are more independent in their judg-
                  ments.
Hypothesis 4:   That original persons are more self-assertive and dominant.
Hypothesis 5:   That original persons reject suppression as a mechanism for
                  the control of impulse.

All five of the hypotheses were supported.[26] Barron interpreted these findings as indications that creativity is an expression of personal freedom.

> We have spoken here of the disposition toward originality, with origi-
> nality being so measured as to be equivalent to the capacity for pro-
> ducing unusual adaptive responses. But unusualness of response may
> be considered a function as well of the objective freedom of an or-
> ganism, where this is defined as the range of possible adaptive respon-
> ses available in all situations.[27]

The creative personality exhibits traits which are valued by society and those
which are viewed as negative.

> The disposition toward originality may thus be seen as a highly orga-
> nized mode of responding to experience, including other persons,
> society, and oneself. The socially disrated traits that may go along
> with it include rebelliousness, disorderliness, and exhibitionism, while
> the socially valued traits which accompany it include independence
> of judgment, freedom of expression, and novelty of construction and
> insight.[28]

SUMMARY

Experimental studies of behavior fall into two large categories: the S-R
model and the cognitive model. Pavlov, Thorndike, Watson, and Skinner are
examples of S-R theorists. Tolman, Kohler, and Wertheimer are examples of
cognitive theorists. S-R theorists tend to be associationists who look for the
laws by which discreet elements are combined. Cognitive theorists are more
wholistic and organismic. They look for the laws by which the organism "makes
sense" of its environment.

Behavior that is elicited by a specific stimulus is called respondent, and behavior that is emitted in the absence of a specific stimulus is called operant.

Three examples of more complex behavior were considered: symbolic processes (thinking), problem solving, and creativity. These more complex forms
of behavior are viewed in the context of the Functionalists' hypothesis that behavior can be viewed as the organism's attempts to meet its needs in an environment where simple behavior is often blocked.

QUESTIONS FOR STUDY AND CLASS DISCUSSION

1. Using Pavlovian principles explain why our mouths water when we think of pickles. What other responses seem to have been acquired in this way?

2. Using Skinner's principles explain how we learned tp speak.

3. Can you explain what causes a habit to persist? Compare nail-biting with shaving.

4. Does Tolman's "place learning" describe how you learn how to get around a town? Do you need to be motivated in order to learn how to get from one place to another?

5. Can you explain Köhler's experiment with the ape by using only Skinner's operant principles?

6. Perls, a Gestalt therapist, spoke of "unfinished business." Which of Wertheimer's principles might be the source of this idea?

7. Try to invent a new concept. Give it a name and define it so that another person can use it.

8. Try to imagine the world Helen Keller experienced—no sights, no sounds.

9. In understanding Durkin's and Duncker's experiments, which theory helps most: Pavlov's, Skinner's, or Köhler's?

10. Do you think that Guilford, Mednick, and Barron are using the word "creativity" in the same sense? What similarities do you see? What differences?

SUGGESTIONS FOR FURTHER READING

Barlow, John A. *Stimulus and Response.* New York: Harper & Row, 1968.

Braun, John R. *Contemporary Research in Learning.* Princeton: Insight Books, 1963.

Evans, Richard I. *B. F. Skinner: The Man and His Ideas.* New York: E. P. Dutton & Co., 1968.

Kohler, Wolfgang. *Gestalt Psychology.* New York: The New American Library (Mentor Books), 1947.

Ray, Wilbert S. *The Experimental Psychology of Original Thinking.* New York: Macmillan Co., 1967.

9

CORRELATES OF BEHAVIOR

By "correlates of behavior" we mean the factors that are associated with it. In the preceding chapter we limited ourselves to objective experimental studies of behavior. Such studies are primarily descriptive, and science must start with accurate description. But science also seeks explanations, and this is a more difficult task.

One of the major approaches to explanation is the careful observation of factors that are consistently correlated with the phenomenon we are seeking to explain. Factors which consistently precede behavior are usually viewed as causes; *other factors which consistently* follow *behavior are called* purposes *by some and* reinforcers *by others. Factors that are* concurrent *with behavior are viewed as part of the behavior itself or as the basis for behavior.*

One warning we must remember is that correlation does not necessarily imply causation. Just because two events consistently appear together or in regular sequence does not prove that they are causally related. Nevertheless, it is true that correlates offer some of the most dependable clues to causal relationships. Here we shall not consider the question of cause and look for necessary conditions *for behavior.*

WE ARE STUDYING THE BEHAVIOR OF AN ORGANISM

Since behavior is a characteristic of animals, behavior must be kept within the context of organismic function. As we noted in Chapter 1, this leads to the view that the formula for behavior is more adequately expressed as S–O–R than as S–R because the response to a given stimulus depends on factors in the organism as well as on the particular stimulus.

Some principles of behavior can be applied to all animal forms. For example, the tendency to display avoidance behavior in the presence of noxious stimuli is seen in animals of every type, from man all the way down to the one–celled amoeba. Other principles of behavior are limited to certain broad groups of animals, such as mammals or birds. Still other principles are derived from what is called species–specific behavior. We shall note an example of this when we look at imprinting in ducks. The general point we are stressing here is that there are always organismic processes which are necessary conditions for behavior.

ALL BEHAVIOR HAS CHEMICAL CORRELATES

The Endocrine Glands

It is known that life processes are chemical processes. In the higher animals the chemical processes are largely the function of endocrine glands (also called "ductless" glands because they secrete their products directly into the blood stream). The endocrine glands produce a wide variety of chemicals called *hormones.*

While all of the endocrine glands are related to the behavior of the organism, four of them are of special interest to psychologists because of their direct relationship to behavior: the *pituitary,* the *thyroid,* the *adrenal,* and the *gonads.*

The pituitary gland. Located in the middle of the head, just under the cerebral cortex, this pea–sized gland is sometimes called the master gland because it secretes "middle-man" hormones which regulate the chemical balance of many of the other endocrine glands. The *anterior lobe* produces at least seven different hormones, the most dramatic of which is the growth hormone. Inadequate secretion of this hormone in infancy leads to dwarfism, and over–secretion leads to giantism. Other hormones from the anterior lobe stimulate activity of the mammary glands, the thyroid gland, the adrenal gland, the ovaries, and the testes. The *posterior lobe* of the pituitary gland is primarily a storehouse for hormones produced in the hypothalamus of the brain. In fact, both lobes have close connections with the hypothalamus (about which we shall speak later) and are thus deeply involved in organismic responses to stress–inducing stimuli.[1]

The thyroid gland. Located in the neck, this double–lobed structure produces several hormones, the most important of which is *thyroxin.* Thyroxin is the chief agent in the regulation of the rate of body metabolism, the rate at which food is turned into energy. When the thyroid gland is overactive (hyperthyroidism) the body reacts as if the "accelerator is being floor–boarded." When the thyroid gland is underactive (hypothyroidism), the system has no "acceleration;" the body becomes overweight and the features coarse. Thyroid deficiency in infancy leads to *cretinism,* a condition in which normal physical and mental development do not occur. The administration of thyroxin to such infants leads to normal development.[2]

The adrenal glands. There are two adrenal glands, one on top of each kidney. Each of these has two parts: an exterior portion called the *adrenal cortex,* and an interior portion called the *adrenal medulla.* The adrenal medulla secretes *adrenaline* and *noradrenaline.* These hormones are released in response to stress and they mobilize the resources of the body. Adrenaline causes the rate and strength of the heartbeat to increase; a redistribution of the blood to the skeletal muscles, coronary arteries, liver, and brain; an increase in blood sugar; dilation of the bronchi; dilation of the pupils of the eyes; erection of body hair; and an increase in blood clotting time. The most characteristic emotion showing this pattern is fear. Noradrenaline causes the contraction of the arterioles and hence the rise in blood pressure characteristic of anger.[3]

The adrenal cortex secretes three groups of hormones. In the first group are cortisone and hydrocortisone which promote the conversion of fat and protein into glucose or sugar. This stored sugar seems to carry the body through prolonged stress, after the initial mobilization for stress triggered by adrenaline has worn off (see discussion of the General Adaptation Syndrome below). The second group of hormones is related to kidney function. The third group is the sex hormones which promote the development of masculine traits. Over–secretion of these hormones in women leads to such traits as facial hair, deep voice, and angular body contours.[4]

The gonads. Gonads are the sex glands, *ovaries* in the female and *testes* in the male. Their prime function is the production of eggs and sperm. The testes also secrete *androgens* (especially *testosterone*) which are primarily responsible for the secondary sexual characteristics which appear in adolescence. The removal of the testes is called *castration.* In some countries boys were castrated so that they could continue to sing soprano in the choir. Animals are often castrated to produce better meat or an easier temperament. Geldings are castrated horses. Capons are castrated fowl. Hogs and cattle are often castrated to fatten them for market. Gonadal androgens have some effect on the masculine temperament, but their influence in humans is complex.

The ovaries secrete *estrogens, progesterone,* and *relaxin.* The estrogens have two major functions: first, they promote the development of secondary sexual characteristics such as mammary development, broadening of the pelvis, genital development, growth of pubic hair and oxillary hair, and more rounded body contours through promoting fat deposits; second, they participate in the body changes associated with the menstrual cycle. Progesterone regulates the preparation of the body for pregnancy and, if it occurs, prevents premature birth. Relaxin is produced just before birth and makes a more flexible passageway for the exit of the baby.[5]

The Functions of Body Chemistry

As we noted earlier, the life processes are chemical processes. Thus, the body chemistry organizes and maintains the life of the organism.

The chemical system works directly on body cells. Chemical substances travel in the blood stream and in the nerves, and they can pass through the cell membranes.

The chemical system is an intricate balance of various chemicals which must be present in proper proportions if life is to be maintained, growth is to occur, and the organism is to behave adaptively in its environment. It is mainly the hormones produced by the endocrine glands that maintain the chemical balance in spite of the changing environment and the changing needs of the organism.

The major channel of chemical action is the bloodstream, which reaches every cell in the body. The coordination of these billions of cells is the work of chemical messengers in the bloodstream, such as hormones, and the chemical messengers in the cell nucleus, such as DNA (see Chapter 7).

Chemical regulation follows the same homeostatic principles observed throughout the organism. It is a system in dynamic equilibrium and every disruption of this equilibrium, whether due to environmental changes or to internal imbalance, sets in motion processes that lead to a restoration of the equilibrium.

What is known of this story of chemical equilibrium is quite fascinating. An example is the way a proper amount of thyroxin (the thyroid hormone) is maintained in the bloodstream so that body metabolism (energy production) can meet the varying needs of an active man. This process involves two glands working together to achieve a balance.

> Now suppose that, as a result of a racing metabolism, inroads are made on the thyroid hormone supply, causing the blood level to drop. As the blood passes through the anterior pituitary, the lower–than–normal level of thyroid hormone stimulates the secretion of additional TSH (thyroid stimulating hormone), and the blood level of TSH rises. When the blood passes through the thyroid carrying its extra load of TSH, the secretion of thyroid hormone is stimulated and the demands of the high metabolic rate are met.

> If the thyroid hormone should now be greater than the body requirements, its blood level will rise. This rising thyroid hormone level will cut off TSH production, which will in turn cut off thyroid hormone production. By the action of the two glands in smooth cooperation, the thyroid hormone level will be maintained at an appropriate blood level despite continued shifts in the body's requirement for the hormone.[7]

Examples of Chemical Correlates of Behavior

There are at least three kinds of experimental evidence linking chemicals in the body with specific behaviors. In the first kind behavior and endocrine activity are compared. In the second kind chemicals are injected and behavior is observed. In the third learned behavior is related to chemical changes in the brain.

Endocrine activity and behavior. In one experiment, increased secretion from the adrenal cortex was found when mice fought.[8] Other experimenters found this increased secretion even when the mice did not fight but were confronted with a dominant animal.[9]

Experiments with birds have shown that gonadal secretions are associated with courting behavior in doves[10] and with the migratory flights of birds.[11] Other experimenters have found that thyroidal secretions are involved in these migratory flights.[12]

One of the most interesting series of experiments involved putting estrogen (the female gonadal hormone) directly into the hypothalamus of female cats whose ovaries had been removed. A high percentage of these cats subsequently developed the full cycle of estrous (mating) behavior in contrast to similar cats which received the estrogen in another part of the brain.[13]

Injected chemicals and behavior. From ancient times the effects of certain chemicals on behavior have been known. Most notable are alcohol, the opiates, and mushroom and cactus derivatives such as peyote and mescaline. More recently, we have learned the effects of the newer tranquilizing drugs and certain psychedelic (mind–changing) drugs like LSD.

One of the best known examples of chemical injection is the use of sodium amytal and sodium pentothal, the so–called "truth serums." Recent evidence suggests that the injection of these drugs does not guarantee access to truth, but they do result in people talking much more freely.[14]

There is a great deal of evidence that chemicals such as chlorpromazine and reserpine can radically change the behavior of hospitalized schizophrenics.[15] And doctors in Canada have found important changes in the behavior of schizophrenics following the administration of a vitamin, niacin.[16]

Experiments with rats and monkeys have shown that animals, too, can become addicted to narcotics and that their behavior closely parallels that of the human addict.[17]

Chemical basis of learning. For some years a variety of experiments have purported to indicate that learning and memory are the result of chemical changes in the brain, perhaps in the RNA molecules of the brain cell nuclei. One of the most dramatic of these experiments involved teaching planaria (flat–worms) an avoidance reaction, then killing the worms and feeding them to other planaria. The avoidance reaction was then observed in these "cannibals."[18] Unfortunately, other experimenters have had difficulties replicating these studies.

More recently, other experimenters have claimed success in even more complex experiments. Ungar first conditioned rats to avoid the dark, which they usually prefer, and to choose a well lighted environment. He then killed the rats, took material from their brains, and injected it into untrained rats which had shown a definite preference for the dark. Thereafter, the recipients showed a tendency to choose the lighted side more often than did a control group.[19] However, as with the McConnell experiments with planaria, efforts to replicate these experiments have led to very inconsistent results. McGaugh sums up the present situation: "At the present time it can only be concluded that these experiments have not as yet shown that memories are stored in macromolecules."[20]

BEHAVIOR HAS NEURAL BASES

The Nervous System: A functional Description

The chemical system is the older, more basic, organizer of bodily activity and the nervous system is a more rapid communication network which enables the organism to make adaptive responses to its environment. While the system functions as a whole, it is useful to divide it into three major functional parts: receptors, connectors, and effectors.

The *receptors* are, as the name implies, the parts of the system which are sensitive to stimulation. They are structures which cause the nerve cells to which they are attached to release a nerve impulse when certain specific changes occur in either the external or internal environment.

Photoreceptors. Some receptors are sensitive to radiant energy, most espe-cially light and heat. The receptors sensitive to light are in the eye, an instru-ment of unbelievable complexity. The human eye consists of an adjustable *lens,* just behind the *pupil,* which is an adjustable opening for letting light in (like the lens opening on a camera). At the back of the eye are *rods* and *cones,* which are the receptors. The rods, of which there are around 100 million in each eye, pro-vide black-and-white vision and are extremely sensitive to light. It is estimated that they are capable of detecting light a billion times less intense than that of a bright, sunny day. The cones, which are much fewer in number, provide color vision. It is assumed that there are three kinds of cones which absorb red, green, and blue light, respectively. The rods operate in groups which activate one nerve impulse while the cones act individually. Thus, it is the cones that, besides mak-ing color vision possible, give vision acuteness and sharp definition.

Two kinds of receptors in the skin are sensitive to temperature changes: heat receptors and cold receptors. There are also warmth and cold receptors in the hypothalamus of the brain that register changes in blood temperature and thus help regulate body heat.

Mechanoreceptors. Some receptors are sensitive to mechanical stimuli, such as pressure or vibrations in the air. Gentle pressures (usually called touch) stimu-late receptors that are found next to the hair follicles in the skin. Stronger pres-sures stimulate Pacinian corpuscles found in the subcutaneous layer, under the epidermis and the dermis. Pacinian corpuscles are also found scattered through-out the interior of the body and provide the brain with information about the movement of internal organs. Other receptors, sensitive to pressure, are found in the walls of the aorta and carotid arteries and record rises in blood pressure.

Sense receptors found in muscles and tendons are called *proprioceptors,* and they respond to the stretching and contraction of muscles thus facilitating mus-cular control.

The sensation of pain is due largely to massive mechanical stimulation of the skin which seems to stimulate a network of nerve fibers that are not attached to specialized stimulus receptors. Excessive heat, cold, and certain chemicals may also result in the sensation of pain.

The most complicated mechanoreceptor is, of course, the ear. Vibrations in air enter the outer ear and travel down the auditory canal and strike the *tympanic membrane* (commonly called the eardrum). Vibrations from the tympanic mem-brane are transmitted by *ossicles* (three tiny linked bones), the last and tiniest of which is called the stirrup, through the *round window* of the *cochlea.* Here the *organ of corti* and the *tectorial membrane* send nerve impulses along the auditory nerve to the brain. The human ear is sensitive to vibrations from 16 to 20,000 cycles per second. The range in volume is even greater, the loudest sound we can hear being one trillion times as loud as the faintest sound we can hear. A trained musician may be able to discriminate about 15,000 separate pitches.

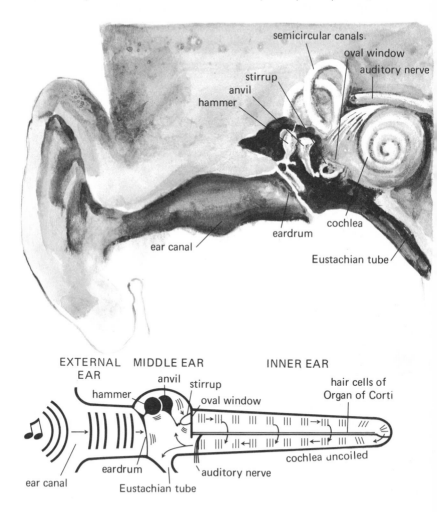

The sense of equilibrium also depends on the inner ear. Receptors in the semicircular canals are sensitive to the motion of the body, and the position of the body with respect to gravity is registered by hair cells in two lymph-filled sacs just above the cochlea.

Chemoreceptors. Some receptors are sensitive to the presence of chemicals. The gustatory sense (taste) depends on receptors in the tongue, of which only four types have been identified. Receptors in the tip of the tongue and along its edges are sensitive to sweet, receptors at the back of the tongue are sensitive to bitter, receptors in the front of the tongue are sensitive to salt, and receptors on the edges of the tongue are sensitive to sour. These taste receptors are sensitive only to substances that are soluble in the moisture of the mouth.

The olefactory sense (smell) depends on receptors high up in the nasal passages that are sensitive to certain molecules carried in the air. While modern man does not depend much on his sense of smell, it is actually extremely sensitive, and may constitute his most intimate contact with his environment since particles of the thing being sensed must actually contact the olfactory receptors. Furthermore, the smell receptors are directly attached to the olfactory lobe of the brain, making it the only one of our senses that does not involve sending impulses to the brain via a nerve. This direct involvement of the brain in smell is what makes such activities as glue sniffing and injection of other chemicals into the nose so dangerous. The olfactory receptors can detect a virtually unlimited variety of odors. One theory attempts to explain this by grouping all odors as varying combinations of four basic types: fragrant, acid, rancid, and burnt.[21] The sensitivity of the nose is truly amazing. For example, as little as 0.0000000002 gm. of vanillin vaporized in 1000 liters of air can be detected.

Throughout the body there are various receptors sensitive to chemical changes. Cells in the carotid arteries are sensitive to carbon–dioxide and help to regulate the rate of breathing. Carbon–dioxide–sensitive receptors in the medulla oblongata of the brain also effect the rate and depth of breathing. As was mentioned earlier, receptors sensitive to various chemical changes are present in the hypothalamus of the brain.[22]

The *connectors* carry impulses from the receptors, process them in nerve centers (either in the spinal cord or the brain), and transmit them to the *effectors* (mainly glands and muscles that make the response to the stimuli).

Technically called *neurons,* the connectors are actually the nerves themselves, and they are of three different kinds: *sensory neurons,* the nerves to which the receptors are attached and that carry impulses toward nerve centers; *association neurons,* found exclusively in the spinal cord and brain, that pick up impulses from sensory neurons, route them in a wide variety of ways through the central nervous system, then pass them on to motor neurons; and *motor neurons,* which carry impulses to the effectors.

The *neuron,* or nerve cell, has three main parts: the cell body, with its nucleus; dendrites which receive impulses; and the axon which transmits impulses from its end brush.

The *nerve impulse* is a reaction that has electrical properties but is essentially chemical and travels much more slowly than electricity. The speed of a nerve impulse varies from 3 or 4 ft. per second to about 300 ft. per second at its fastest.

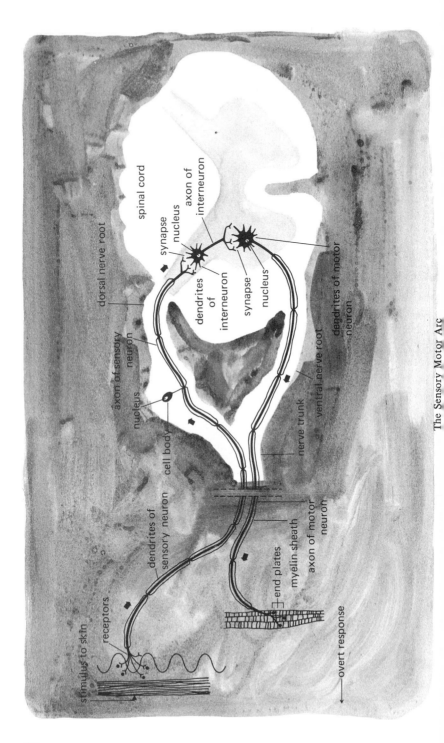

The Sensory Motor Arc

The nerve impulse operates on an all-or-nothing principle, so that all nerve impulses are the same strength. The strength of a stimulus, then, is known not by the strength of the nerve impulse generated but by the frequency and number of these impulses. A strong stimulus will trigger impulses in more rapid succession and it will trigger more neurons to send impulses.

The axon of one neuron is not in direct contact with the dendrite of another neuron. There is a gap, called a *synapse*, which the impulse must cross by causing the end brush of the axon to release a chemical called acetylcholine (ACh). When enough ACh accumulates in the gap, the neuron across the gap fires. Because this chemical is released only by axons, it is possible for nerve impulses to travel in only one direction, axon to dendrite.

Once a neuron fires, it cannot immediately fire again. This delay is called the *refractory period*, and it usually lasts about 1/1000 of a second, which means that a neuron can transmit no more than about 500 to 1,000 impulses per second.

The simplest example of how nerve conduction works is the *reflex arc*, or sensory motor arc.

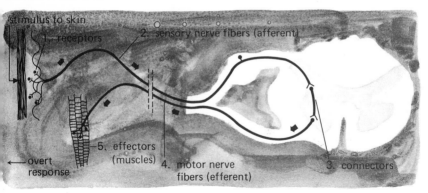

A stimulus is picked up by a receptor and transmitted by sensory neurons to the spinal cord, connected by one or more association neurons to appropriate motor neurons which cause the response. In the simplest reflex arcs, the nerve center involved is in the spinal cord, and the response occurs without the brain being involved (except to receive a message that the event has occurred). The knee jerk is an example of such a simple reflex arc.

The *effectors* carry out the instructions brought from nerve centers by the motor neurons. Primarily, effectors are either *glands* or *muscles.* The glands bring about changes in the internal environment and the muscles bring about effects in both the internal and the external environment.

Glands are of two general types: duct (like the salivary glands), which empty their secretions into ducts, and ductless (like the thyroid glands) which empty their secretions directly into the bloodstream.

Muscles are of three kinds: skeletal or striated muscles, which move the skeleton; cardiac muscle, which moves the heart; and smooth muscles, which line the walls of our hollow organs and regulate their size. Skeletal muscles are under voluntary control and are activated through the motor nerves of the central nervous system. Cardiac muscle, while it normally has connections with both sympathetic and parasympathetic nerves, is activated chemically through the blood (as has been demonstrated in recent heart transplants where nerves to the heart could not be re-attached). Smooth muscles are controlled by the sympathetic and parasympathetic nervous systems and are not under voluntary control.[23]

Major Parts of the Nervous System

The central nervous system consists of the spinal cord and the brain.

The spinal cord. In discussing the reflex arc we noted many facts about the spinal cord. It has a center of gray, consisting of nerve cell bodies, and outer portions of white, consisting of sensory and motor nerve fibers. The spinal cord has two major functions: it transmits impulses to and from the brain, and it serves as the center for many of the simple reflexes.

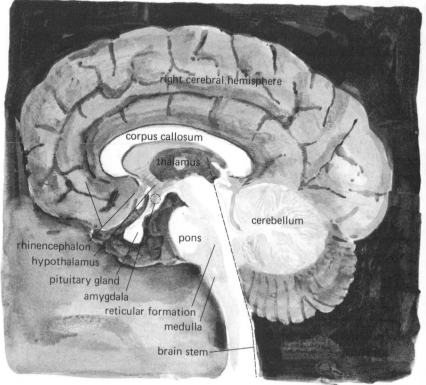

The Brain

The *brain.* The human brain is the most marvelous organ that we know any-thing about, and here we can give only the briefest description of it.

For convenience, the brain is divided into three main parts: the hindbrain, the midbrain, and the forebrain.

The hindbrain includes the medulla oblongata, the cerebellum, and the pons. Probably the oldest part of the brain, it appears to be a thickening of the spinal cord, and is sometimes called the brain stem. The *medulla* contains vital centers for breathing and heart rate and also has centers that relay sensory impulses up-ward to the midbrain and forebrain. The *cerebellum* is one of the main centers for motor coordination, making possible smooth and accurate movements and the maintenance of posture and balance. The *pons* contains fibers connecting the two hemispheres of the cerebellum and includes upward and downward nerve tracts as well as other important nuclei of the central nervous system.

The midbrain is mainly a relay and arousal area. Containing tracts which tra-vel upward and downward, it also has important centers for controlling reflex postural changes of the body in response to visual and auditory stimulation. Most important, however, is the *reticular formation,* or reticular activating system. It is a sensory relay station on the way to the cerebral cortex, and is responsible for arousing the forebrain when certain kinds of stimuli are received from the sensory nerves. It is crucially important in determining whether a person will sleep or be awake.

The forebrain is considered to be the highest part of the brain, and also the newest. The most obvious part is the *cerebrum* or cerebral cortex. Its hemi-spheres are mirror images of each other, and together contain over five billion nerve cells, only 1 percent of which send fibers out. It is, then, clearly a vast center of infinitely complex interconnections. For some purposes, the cerebrum follows the principle of mass action, which means that it acts as a whole and its effectiveness is proportional to the amount of it which is undamaged. For other purposes, it follows the principle of localization of function, with certain func-tions clearly related to specific, fixed areas. Specific areas have been located for muscle movement, body senses, ability to speak, ability to understand speech, and for vision, among others. Beneath the cerebral cortex, in the subcortical area, is the *thalamus.* It is primarily a relay station, shunting incoming sensory impulses to various parts of the cerebrum. Located next to the thalamus is the *limbic system,* another important relay center, containing the *hypothalamus,* septal area, amygdala, and cingulate gyrus. Best known is the hypothalamus, mentioned earlier in connection with the body's chemical system. It is particu-larly closely tied in with the sympathetic and parasympathetic nervous systems, and is therefore importantly involved in emotional experiences.

The peripheral or autonomic nervous system has two branches, the sympa-thetic and the parasympathetic.

The *sympathetic* nervous system consists of a chain of ganglia just outside the spinal cord and is primarily an arousal system for the body, stimulated by the secretion of adrenaline and noradrenaline. The *parasympathetic* nervous system is served mainly by the vagus nerve, or 10th cranial nerve, and is involved in maintaining the normal functioning of the vital organs of the body.

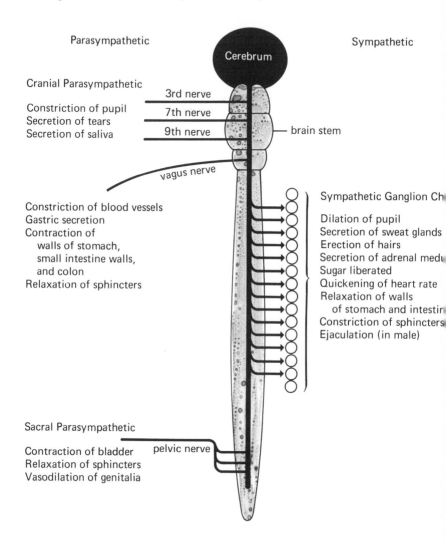

Parasympathetic

Cerebrum

Sympathetic

Cranial Parasympathetic

Constriction of pupil
Secretion of tears
Secretion of saliva

3rd nerve
7th nerve
9th nerve

brain stem

vagus nerve

Constriction of blood vessels
Gastric secretion
Contraction of
   walls of stomach,
   small intestine walls,
   and colon
Relaxation of sphincters

Sympathetic Ganglion Ch

Dilation of pupil
Secretion of sweat glands
Erection of hairs
Secretion of adrenal medu
Sugar liberated
Quickening of heart rate
Relaxation of walls
   of stomach and intestin
Constriction of sphincters
Ejaculation (in male)

Sacral Parasympathetic

Contraction of bladder
Relaxation of sphincters
Vasodilation of genitalia

pelvic nerve

Some Examples of Experiments on Brain Function

Extirpation experiments. In the 1920s K. S. Lashley pioneered one of the most fruitful approaches to determining relationships between the brain and behavior. Called the method of extirpation, it consists in destroying a part of the brain and then noting what changes occur in behavior. It was these early studies by Lashley that led him to formulate his "law of mass action" and "law of equipotentiality," which summarized his findings that learned behavior in rats was not lost by lesions in any specific part of the cerebral cortex, but rather was lost in proportion to the amount of damage ("mass action"), regardless of where the damage was done ("equipotentiality").[24]

Later extirpation experiments have sought to clarify overly simple conclusions drawn from Lashley's work:

> It is probably true that no simple habit can be eliminated by a cortical lesion: on the other hand, some types of behavior are certainly much more affected by lesions in one area than they are by equally large lesions elsewhere, at least in the more advanced mammals.[25]

One group of experimenters found that rats with frontal lobe lesions behaved significantly differently than rats with temporal lobe lesions. The former showed impairment of the ability to inhibit responses, while the latter showed impairment of the ability to discriminate visually.[26]

Another experimenter found that in dogs, too, damage to the frontal lobe results in loss of ability to inhibit responses, and concluded that this is a general result of such damage.[27]

Direct stimulation experiments. Another fruitful approach involves the direct stimulation of parts of the brain, then observation of the resulting behavioral changes.

Some of the most interesting work of this kind has been done on human subjects whose brains were exposed in order to remove brain tumors. Such patients are under local anesthesia and are fully conscious, and so are able to report sensations resulting from the stimulation of various areas of the brain. The experimenter can, of course, also observe any motor responses which may occur.

In 1950, Penfield and Rasmussen carefully mapped the motor area of the brain, and found that it is as if the body were projected upside down along the precentral gyrus at the back of the frontal lobe (see diagram on following page). Note the disproportionate space for the head and the hands.[28] Penfield and Roberts, in 1959, published similar studies for the sensory area, which lies just across the central fissure in the front part of the parietal lobe.[29]

The work of Olds and Delgado illustrates another kind of experimentation with direct stimulation.

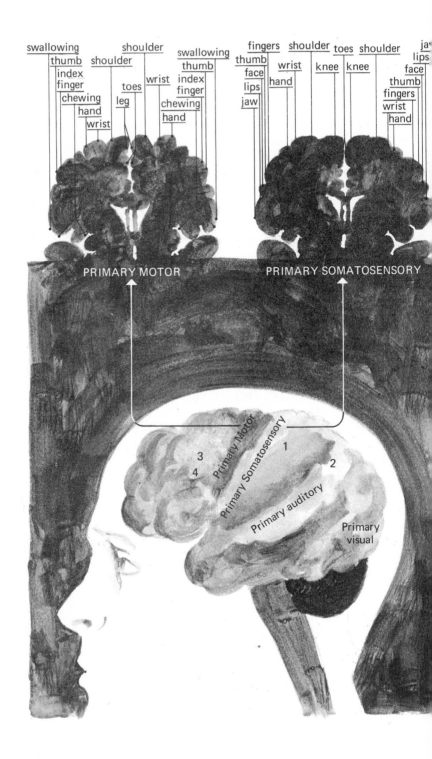

In 1956, Olds reported on experiments in which electrodes planted in certain parts of the brain (the upper part of the midline system) caused the rats to press the lever in the Skinner box apparently for the sake of receiving the shock. This led Olds to conclude that there must be a pleasure center in the brain. Some of the rats pressed the bar and received electrical stimulation as much as 5,000 times an hour and continued for as long as 24 hours without rest.[30]

For some years, Delgado and his associates at Yale have been electrically stimulating the lower part of the midline system in monkeys with the result that they displayed rage and aggression. In one interesting experiment, Delgado trained other monkeys in the same cage to turn off the current. Then, when Delgado turned on the current and the stimulated monkey became enraged and aggressive, another monkey would run and turn off the current and the enraged monkey would immediately be calm again.[31]   (See Chapter 13)

BEHAVIOR HAS MOTIVATIONAL AND EMOTIONAL CORRELATES

To the naive observer, nothing seems more obvious than that people eat because they are hungry, work because they want money, and put on warm clothes because they are cold; or that people cry because they are sad, laugh because they are happy, and run because they are afraid. Yet no problem in psychology has been more elusive than that of motivation and emotion.

As long ago as 1890, William James questioned that emotion was a cause of behavior. He theorized that we actually feel sad because we cry, feel happy because we laugh, and feel afraid because we run. And recently Skinner has challenged motivation as an explanation of the cause of behavior. The problem is elusive because we tend to be circular in our reasoning. How do we know a person is sad? Because he cries. How do we know someone is hungry? Because he eats. Thus we explain behavior by positing a motivation or an emotion, and we demonstrate the existence of motivation and emotion by pointing to behavior.

As we suggested at the beginning of this chapter, we shall bypass the question of whether motivation and emotion *cause* behavior and shall limit ourselves to a presentation of motivational and emotional states as correlates of behavior.

Motivation

We have already noted some organismic, chemical, and neural correlates of behavior. As necessary conditions of behavior, they contribute to any explanation of behavior, including the concept of causality. Whatever we may mean by motivation, we cannot mean something that works separately from these correlates. In fact, some writers would call the chemical and neurological processes we have described motivational states, since they clearly influence behavior. Such usage of the term "motivational state," while understandable, seems unwise. It would avoid semantic confusion to use the term for more wholistic factors, such as deficiency states, organismic tensions, mental states involving goals, and other total organismic processes. These more wholistic states will certainly involve chemical and neural processes, but they are somehow more than just physiological processes. A rat can be made to eat, even when it is sated with food, by electrical stimulation of a part of the brain.[32] But this is not equivalent to that same rat eating after it has been deprived of food. We seek to identify this difference, however it is conceptualized, by using the word *motivation.*

In this survey of motivating states correlated with behavior, we shall present a classification of motives, and a description of how motives are measured.

A classification of motives. Table 1 shows one possible way of classifying motives. Any system must be arbitrary and this one should be used only as a suggestive outline.

Deficiencies or hungers. One of the most consistent correlates of behavior is depriving the organism of something essential to its life. In Chapter 8 we pointed out how the concept of homeostatis was borrowed from biology and used in the adaptation model of behavior by the functionalists. Applying this concept, the deprivation theory of motivation hypothesizes that a deprived animal is likely to be active, and that certain things in the environment will have a greater stimulus value. For example, an animal that has been deprived of water will be active, and water will have a greater attraction for the animal. We call the deficiency a *need,* and the attractive stimulus a *goal.* Deficiency-motivated behavior, then, is need-based and goal-directed. The major deficiency needs are air or oxygen, water, and food.

Tensions. Another implication of the homeostatic theory is that the organism seeks equilibrium through behavior that reduces tension. Actually, deficiencies lead to tensions (hungers), and might be classified as one group of tensions. But there are two other groups of tensions unrelated to deficiencies of any substance necessary for the organism. One group we have called *psycho-physical.* Here we have listed the tension of discomfort, of sexual arousal, of bowel and bladder distension, of fatigue, of inactivity, and of separation from warm softness. Another group we have called *psycho-neurological.* Here we have listed tensions resulting from stimulus patterns too confused to be grasped, loss of equilibrium, lack of stimulation, unresolved uncertainty, and frightening stimuli.

Socially acquired motives. Another kind of motive is that acquired in the process of being socialized. Motives may be learned, and most human learning is social. We learn to satisfy biological and physical needs in approved ways, we learn specific likes and dislikes, we learn to need people and to act in ways that they approve of, and we learn to value objects, feelings, ideas, and ways of behaving characteristic of the people who are important to us.

Table 1

A CLASSIFICATION OF MOTIVES

I. Deficiencies or Hungers

    1. Lack of air or oxygen
    2. Lack of water
    3. Lack of food (specific for carbohydrates, proteins, minerals, vitamins, etc.)

II. Tensions

    A. Psycho–physical tensions
      1. Tension of discomfort—pain, heat, cold, etc.
      2. Tension of sexual arousal
      3. Tensions from bowel and bladder
      4. Tensions of fatigue
      5. Tension from inactivity
      6. Tension of separation from softness (contact comfort)

    B. Psycho–neurological tensions
      1. Tension of an ungraspable stimulus pattern (need for some consistency in environment)
      2. Tension of instability or loss of equilibrium
      3. Tension from lack of stimulation
      4. Tension of unresolved uncertainty (need for closure)
      5. Tension of frightening stimuli (need for safety)

III. Socially Acquired Motives

    1. Learned ways of satisfying biological and physical needs
    2. Specific likes and dislikes
    3. The need for other people and for ways of getting along with them
    4. A system of values

IV. Self-Related Needs

    1. A recognizable self-structure that is reasonably consistent (identity)
    2. A sense of self-worth; being valued by significant others
    3. A sense of belonging; a sense of social security
    4. The experience of being accepted and loved
    5. The experience of loving

V. Self-Actualization Needs

    1. The realization of individual potential
    2. The liberation of creative talents
    3. The widest possible use of abilities and aptitudes

Self-related needs. It is hard to know whether self-related needs are innate or acquired. Whatever their source, one cannot be an effective person unless these needs are met. One must have an identity, a sense of self-worth, a sense of be-longing, the experience of being loved and of loving.

Self-actualization needs. This group of needs, suggested by Maslow,[33] is diffi-cult to define. The basic idea, however, is that once its deficiencies are met, the organism does not settle into inactivity but rather tends to grow and to engage in spontaneous, self-initiated activity. Maslow sees this activity as being the reali-zation of potential, a delight in creativity, and a response to challenge.

The measurement of motives. Careful experimental measurement of motiva-tion has tended to be limited to the biological hungers and tensions. The follow-ing criteria have been used in experimental measurement:

1. gross motor activity
2. rate of responding
3. amount of obstruction required to prevent the animal from reaching the goal
4. preference shown by the animal when given a choice of two or more goals
5. force or amplitude of a response
6. action of the autonomic nervous system
7. speed of learning[34]

Deprivation of necessities, such as air, water, or food, results in an increase in motor activity. A measurement of this activity may serve as an indicator of the strength of the motivation.

Skinner has found the rate of response to be one of the most reliable of behav-ioral measures. The number of times within an hour that a rat will press a bar to get a specific reward may serve as a measure of the strength of the motive in-volved.

Obstructions, such as an electrically charged grid, may be put between an ani-mal and various goals, such as water, food, mate, etc. Then the strength of the electric charge required to keep the animal from crossing the grid to the goal may be used as a measure for comparing strength of motives.

Various goals may be paired, and an animal given a choice between them, thus comparing the strengths of the motives.

The strength of a response to a particular stimulus may be measured by its resistence to extinction.

Various measures of autonomic nervous system activity may indicate the de-gree of excitement or tension present with various motives.

And, finally, the speed of learning with various rewards can be used as a basis for inferring the strengths of motives.

Emotion

The term "emotional states" refers to total organismic posture or sets. The ost notable of these are anger (a readiness to attack), fear (a readiness to flee), ove or delight (a readiness to approach), and grief or gloom (a readiness to stop l response).

It is not easy to distinguish some emotional states from motivational states, nd in fact, some emotions do seem to have a "drive" quality to them. And, as e shall see, each emotional state is clearly correlated with chemical and neural rocesses from which it cannot be separated. Nevertheless, the term *emotion* ersists in psychology because it refers to aspects of behavior and experience that ave distinctive qualities demanding the use of a separate term.

Emotion is the awareness of bodily changes. As we mentioned earlier, William ames in 1890, equated emotion with our experiencing or feeling the bodily nanges that occur in response to a stimulus.

> My theory . . . is that the bodily changes follow directly the percep-
> tion of the exciting fact, and that our feeling of the same changes as
> they occur *is* the emotion.[35]

this view were diagrammed, it might appear as follows:

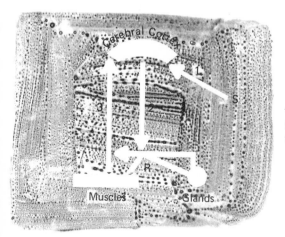

The feedback to the brain, is thought to be emotion.

1. a stimulus is perceived
2. a reaction to the stimulus occurs (largely involuntary)
3. the bodily changes are felt

Step 3 is the emotion

ames saw the response to stimuli as being partly innate, partly learned or habit- al, and partly willful or voluntary. A practical application of his view, suggested by James, was that if we want to do something about our emotions, the best way to do so is to change, as much as we can, the response that we make to stimuli. He suggested that we feel the way we do because of the way we act. Thus he saw emotion as the result of behavior rather than as the cause of behavior.

Emotion as thalamic activity. In 1927, W. B. Cannon criticized James' theory on the basis of newer knowledge of the brain. Studies of subcortical centers, especially in the hypothalamus, led Cannon to the conclusion that what we call emotional experience is mostly due to activity in these nerve centers. Diagrammed, Cannon's theory would be:

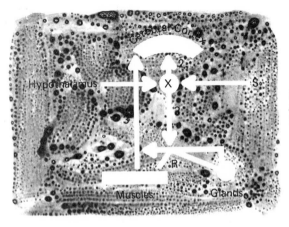

Emotion is viewed as activity in the hypothalamus.

1. stimulus is received
2. the reaction is triggered in the hypothalamus
2'. simultaneously the activity of these nerve centers is felt in the cerebral cortex
3. the bodily changes are felt

Step 2' is the emotion

Cannon saw emotion primarily as an emergency reaction of the organism to important stimuli. He tested this theory on decorticated cats, which could not experience bodily changes because the spinal cord was cut. He found that these cats displayed the same kind of emotional response as normal cats.[36]

Practically, Cannon's theory would lead to essentially the same conclusion as that advanced by James: emotions are not controlled by something called "will power," but are affected by the response we habitually make to a stimulus. The subcortical centers to which Cannon pointed are, in fact, the mediating centers for conditioned or learned responses, as well as being centers for the autonomic nervous systems that are so involved in emotional responses. Thus, James and

Cannon would agree that emotional responses will change as we learn new re-responses to emotion-inducing stimuli.

Emotion as a signaling system. O. H. Mowrer, in 1960, related emotional states to his theory of learning, which he calls a "two-factor" theory. He includes four emotional states in his scheme: fear, disappointment, relief, and hope. He hypothesizes that fear and disappointment are associated with tension-increasing stimuli or punishment, while relief and hope are associated with tension-reducing stimuli or reward.

Fear is the state characterized by the coming on of the danger signal, leading to increased tension through the arousal of the sympathetic nervous system and the suppression of the parasympathetic system.

Disappointment is the state characterized by the going off of the safety signal, leading to increased tension through the suppression of the parasympathetic nervous system adn the arousal of the sympathetic system.

Relief is the state characterized by the going off of the danger signal, leading to reduced tension through the suppression of the sympathetic nervous system and the arousal of the parasympathetic system.

Hope is the state characterized by the coming on of the safety signal, leading to reduced tension through the arousal of the parasympathetic nervous system and the suppression of the sympathetic system.

To Mowrer, emotions then, serve as signals for impending reward or punishment and, as such, take on reinforcement qualities. In other words, we tend to do things which lead to the going off of the danger signal or the coming on of the safety signal, and to avoid doing things which lead to the opposite.[37]

Emotion as an interpretation of events. In 1962, Schachter presented a view that not only fits our commonsense ideas, but integrates the previous theories of emotion. According to him the emotion that we feel is an interpretation of the stirred–up bodily states. We receive stimuli, a bodily state results, and then we interpret the bodily state to suit the way we perceive our situation.

In one experiment, Schachter found that subjects injected with adrenaline and then put in a pleasant situation experienced pleasant emotions in connection with the changed bodily states, while subjects injected with adrenaline and then put in an unpleasant situation experienced unpleasant emotions in connection with the changed bodily states.

Thus Schachter would integrate the incoming stimuli, the subcortical activity, the changed bodily states, and the cortical awareness of them into an experience that fits the cognitive interpretation of the situation.[38]

BEHAVIOR HAS ENVIRONMENTAL CORRELATES

So far we have concentrated our attention on behavioral correlates within the organism, although we have touched on environmental characteristics in our discussion of motivation and emotion. Now we must recognize that all behavior is inextricably related to an environment which not only sustains our life and serves as a place in which to act but also provides the stimuli that are necessary to cause behavior.

Physical Stimuli

Physical stimuli are related to behavior in a wide variety of ways. We shall note three examples.

Imprinting. Goslings follow their mother as soon after hatching as they are able to walk. Instinct used to be the usual explanation. But in 1935 Konrad Lorenz conducted an experiment in which he demonstrated that goslings will follow whatever moves in their vicinity soon after they are hatched. .He called this phenomenon "imprinting."[39] E. H. Hess, in 1958, reported further studies of this process. He found that goslings, as well as ducklings and certain other birds and insects, manifest this tendency, and that it occurs only during a certain critical time. He found that imprinting can occur for ducklings only within the first 30 hours after hatching, and that those imprinted between 13 and 16 hours show the maximum effect.[40]

Mating behavior. The mating behavior of animals is affected by a large variety of physical stimuli, including climatological factors (such as length of day, temperature, or rainfall), as well as physical features of other members of the species, such as sound made, coloration, bodily shape, and odors.[41] Timbergen has reported some of the most interesting findings in connection with his studies of the mating behavior of the stickleback fish. In a study reported in 1942, he found that nest-guarding males displayed courtship reactions when confronted with a rough model of a female stickleback in which the abdominal region was enlarged, while very accurate models of the female produced no reponse if the abdominal area was slim.[42]

Homing Behavior. Bees, butterflies, birds, and salmon are notable for their ability to return to their place of departure. All studies of this behavior reveal that the so–called instinct is actually an example of great sensitivity to certain physical stimuli. Recently (1955) Hasler and Larsen discovered that "the salmon identifies the stream of its birth by odor and literally smells its way home from the sea."[43]

Social Stimuli

It might be said that social stimuli, defined as the presence of other members of the species, are actually physical stimuli. But we distinguish this class of stinuli because, while certainly physical, they seem to represent a complexity that amounts to a qualitative difference.

Sexual behavior in monkeys. We have already noted that the sexual behavior of animals is markedly affected by various kinds of physical stimuli, most especially stimuli associated with the body of the prospective mate. However, the Harlowes (1962) found that if monkeys are deprived of any social contact during the first two years of their lives, they will show no sexual behavior after this even if they are confronted with opposite-sexed members of the species. In other words, the sexual "instinct" will not manifest itself in behavior unless, at the crucial time, contact with other members of the species has occurred.[44]

Social behavior in baboons. Washburn and De Vore (1961) reported a careful study of African baboons which described a patterned social life. Many insects and animals have a social life, but the baboons show an unusually interesting example of how the behavior of one animal is affected by the behavior of another. Particularly important for the baboons is the dominance scale, which, once established, seems to be quite persistent. This study makes it clear that the social structure, even for animals other than man, is a significant factor in determining the behavior of individual members.[45]

Social influences on human perception. There is no great need to convince human beings that social influences importantly affect behavior, but we may not be aware how very pervasive this influence is. Asch (1955) reported an experiment that showed that such a simple task as judging the lengths of lines could be markedly influenced by social pressure. Subjects that made few, if any, errors in judgment when working alone, made as many as 32 percent errors when put in a group where three other people, following instructions, were judging the lines erroneously.[46] And Sherif (1956) found that boys in a camp behaved either competitively or cooperatively, dependent on whether the situation was structured one way or the other.[47]

SUMMARY

We have found behavior correlates in organismic conditions, in chemical processes, in neural processes, in motivational and emotional states, and in environmental conditions.

While the causal relationship between these factors and behavior is quite complex, the inevitable presence of these factors in behavior is incontrovertible.

QUESTIONS FOR STUDY AND CLASS DISCUSSION

1. Does it change your view of man to think of him as an organism? If so, how?

2. What do we mean when we speak of correlates of behavior? How do they differ from causes?

3. Imagine that one of the endocrine glands is either overactive or under active. What personality changes would you expect?

4. What benefits can you see in the chemical control of behavior? What problems?

5. Why do you think that the sense of smell is less important for man than for lower animals?

6. Why do we say of a very intelligent person, "He has lots of gray matter"? Is there a relationship between amount of gray matter and intelligence?

7. What can you learn about man by studying the relative proportion of the brain involved in motor and sensory processes for various parts of the body?

8. If the homeostatic theory of motivation is basically true, would it follow that we tend to want what we need? Do we ever want something we don't need? If so, why?

9. Do you understand why James said, "I feel sad because I cry"?

10. Do you think the word "instinct" is still useful?

SUGGESTIONS FOR FURTHER READING

Asimov, Isaac. *The Human Brain.* New York: New American Library, 1963.

Delgado, Jose, M. R. *Physical Control of the Mind.* New York: Harper & Row, 1969

Eiseley, Loren. *The Immense Journey.* New York: Random House, 1957.

Morris, Desmond. *The Naked Ape.* New York: McGraw-Hill, 1967.

Simeons, A. T. *Man's Presumptuous Brain.* New York: E. P. Dutton & Co., 1960.

PART IV
THE ART OF PSYCHOLOGY

If philosophy is the effort to see things whole, and science is a systematic study of detailed processes, then art is the skilled use of knowledge by persons for human goals.

The art of psychology is, of course, far older than the science of psychology, just as the art of agriculture is older than the science of botany. Yet, as science progresses, the related arts are given new knowledge and new tools to be used by skilled practitioners.

Psychological knowledge is today being applied in many areas. In the commercial world, psychologists serve as consultants in advertising, consumer research, and public relations. In industry, the principles of psychology are applied to human engineering, personnel selection, and executive training. In education, teaching methods, special programs for exceptional children, and guidance programs utilize psychological knowledge. In social work and penology, psychologists are deeply involved in both theory and practice. In the Armed Forces, psychologists have taken part in research programs, classification programs, training programs, propaganda and counter propaganda, rehabilitation and counseling. In medicine, psychologists have worked in mental hospitals and in clincs as members of therapeutic teams. And, finally, clinical psychologists practice the art of psychotherapy in offices where they seek to help a wide variety of troubled people.

Psychology is a growing profession, and many states now issue licenses to qualfied people with adequate training in psychology, while making it illegal for unlicensed people to offer psychological services to the public.

The field of applied psychology is so broad that, rather than try to survey all of it, we shall limit ourselves here to considering three psychological arts.

> Psychotherapy – The Art of Healing (chapter 10)
> Persuasion – The Art of Influencing (chapter 11)
> Being – The Art of Living (chapter 12)

These chapters are called art in the spirit expressed by John Ciardi, when he wrote, "Where Science touches man, it turns to art."[1]

The final test for any of us is not our philosophy, nor our science, important as they are, but the artfulness with which we solve our human problems.

10

PSYCHOTHERAPY—THE ART OF HEALING

CHANGING ONE'S PHILOSOPHY
UNCOVERING UNCONSCIOUS CONFLICTS
ALTERATIONS OF "LIFE STYLE"
REORGANIZATION OF LIFE SITUATION
FINDING ONE'S SELF, OR SELF-DISCOVERY
BEHAVIOR MODIFICATION OR TRAINING
RECONDITIONING OR DESENSITIZATION
AN ASSESSMENT OF THE ART OF HEALING

In chapter 5 we surveyed the field of problem behavior.

Now, in this chapter, we speak of efforts to help troubled people–the art of healing, or psychotherapy. We should remember that the approaches taken by many psychologists in helping troubled people would be more aptly called education, behavior modification, or guidance. The more neutral terms, therefore, would be counseling, or psychological consultation, but we use the term psychotherapy because it is most widely used.

In this chapter we shall not go into the strictly medical approaches. These include, most especially, the use of many drugs, tranquilizers, and energizers. Besides drugs, or chemotherapy, there are electroshock and insulin shock, psychosurgery, nutritional therapy, and other physical methods.

We shall limit ourselves to what are more strictly psychological arts, and shall do so descriptively rather than analytically. In other words, rather than attempt a careful study of the various schools of psychotherapy, we shall try to get a feel for the kinds of things which have been done and are being done to help disturbe people. The order in which we shall present the material has no special signifi-

cance except that it roughly corresponds to the historical sequence in which these approaches were first used.

A great many psychological methods have been used in the attempt to help people, and, because only seven were selected for discussion here, many interesting and possibly important methods will be left out. We will briefly consider the following seven kinds of psychological processes: (1) changing one's philosophy, (2) uncovering unconscious conflicts, (3) altering one's life style, (4) reorganization of the life situation, (5) self-discovery, (6) behavior modification, and (7) reconditioning or desensitization.

CHANGING ONE'S PHILOSOPHY

Perhaps the oldest and most persistent approach to helping people is that of trying to bring about changes in their basic attitudes toward life. It is the approach of the great philosophers, of religion, and of common sense. Intuitively we feel that many people are in trouble because they are looking at things wrongly, and that if they would only change their ways of seeing and doing things, everything would be different.

From ancient times to the present, thousands of books have been written, and millions of words have been spoken, whose aims have been to tell people how to live. We think of Solomon and his Proverbs in the Bible, and of the Greek philosophers. The philosophies of the East, such as Hinduism, Buddhism, and Confucianism aim at helping men to function effectively by thinking correctly and doing rightly. Yoga in India and Zen in Japan are particularly noted examples of Eastern psychotherapy.

Popular books have asserted that we can be happy, successful, and healthy if we will change our ways of thinking and of doing. Our forefathers were instructed by Benjamin Franklin, our grandparents by the stories in McGuffey's *Reader,* and our generation by Liebman, (*Peace of Mind*), Carnegie (*How to Stop Worrying and Start Living*), and Peale (*The Power of Positive Thinking*).

Psychologists too have taken this approach, which we might call the didactic (or teaching) approach. The first of the American psychologists, William James, stressed the importance of *habit* in his famous *Principles of Psychology,* and the power of *ideals* in his *Talks to Teachers.* In fact, while only a few psychotherapists would call themselves directive or didactic, most include some elements of this approach in their work.

The following statements are frequently made by psychologists of many different points of view and are illustrations of a didactic approach:

Try looking at it this way.
That sounds reasonable; that's unreasonable.
Try to be more cooperative; you're not cooperating.

Be realistic.
You'll just have to try.
It's up to you.
I can't help you unless you trust me.
It will take time.
Try and be constructive or positive.
That won't work; that won't get you anywhere.
I think you're doing fine; I feel you're resisting.
Be more open.
Don't be afraid of your feelings.

Implied in such expressions are several ideas that are practically axiomatic to most psychologists. One such idea is the importance of *habits* and the difficulty in changing them. So it is explained to patients or clients that it takes time to break old habits and to form new ones. Another axiom has to do with *reality*. We must look at things realistically; we must set realistic goals; our expectations of others must be realistic. Patients are encouraged to distinguish between reality and fantasy. A third axiom stresses the importance of *openness*. It is assumed that it is good for people to be open to their own feelings and to their memories. An effort is made to teach people not to be afraid of their own feelings, and to talk more freely about how they feel and how they see things. Equally unquestioned is the notion of *individual responsibility*. Indirectly and directly, therapists teach patients that they must accept responsibility for themselves, that they must take the initiative, that they must make their own decisions, that only they can really help themselves. Other axioms have to do with *cooperativeness*, and *constructiveness*. The positive attitudes of working with people, especially with the therapist, and of really making the effort are encouraged, while such attitudes as uncooperativeness and destructiveness are labeled as negative. Finally, it is assumed that *flexibility* is good, while rigidity is bad. Clients are encouraged to try other ways of seeing and acting.

Besides teaching patients by means of such direct expressions as those we have mentioned, therapists indirectly, and perhaps more importantly, teach by means of what they themselves are and by what they themselves do. The therapist's genuine interest in the client and the warm, caring feelings he shows are an example of unselfishness and love. His own realism and honesty are demonstrations of what it means to be realistic and open. His ability to listen patiently and to remain unperturbed when the client is upset serves as a model of the constructive attitude he hopes the client can achieve. His own confidence, good humor, and faith have a contagious quality which is often caught by the client. The therapist's way of speaking and the language he uses show the client a realistic, reasonable, and responsible way of looking at and talking about a situation.

The didactic or directive approach in therapy has obvious drawbacks. Preaching at people or lecturing to them is notoriously ineffective. It is especially difficult to teach people when they are emotionally upset. Intense fear, burning anger, and passionate love are known to blind our perceptions and to make us unreceptive to what someone tells us is reasonable. We do not talk a paranoiac out of his delusions; we do not persuade the victim of phobias that he can, if he wants to, stop being afraid; we do not convince the addict that, with more will power, he can do without his drugs; and we seldom are able to give a depressed suicidal patient a reason for living.

The problem, of course, is *how* do we teach those who most need to be taught. The answer seems to be that teaching is an art, and in chapter 11 we shall propose some answers to the problem. But, even some one who is most skilled in this art is clearly limited in how much he can do for disturbed people in this way. We must conclude that *some* people apparently are helped by learning from the therapist new ways of looking at things and new ways of doing things. Education, in this broad sense, would seem to be a part of the therapeutic process, a part of the art of healing.

UNCOVERING UNCONSCIOUS CONFLICTS

It was Sigmund Freud who advanced the theory that mental illness has its source in the unconscious, and it was he who developed techniques for uncovering these hidden problems. Freud's ideas and techniques are embodied in the system called psychoanalysis, which forms the frame of reference also for therapists who are not strict followers of Freud but who nevertheless follow him in assuming that most mental and emotional problems have their roots in the unconscious.

While the concept of the unconscious as a region of the mind is quite problematical, many degrees of awareness no doubt exist; and such phenomena as dreams and hypnotic states clearly involve levels of awareness that differ from wakeful consciousness. Freud felt that memories of important experiences in early childhood are carried in the unconscious and that, since they may involve strong sexual and aggressive drives, they threaten to break out in various ways. This causes the anxiety and the symptoms seen in the neuroses.

The three methods developed by Freud to get at unconscious conflicts are *free association, dream interpretation,* and *the transference relationship.* These still constitute the heart of the psychoanalytic method and are used in modified form by many other psychotherapists as well.

By *free association* Freud meant that the patient lies on a couch and says everything that comes into his mind. This method was developed to replace hypnosis, which Freud had first used. Some therapists still use hypnosis and, sometimes, sodium pentathol or sodium amytal to get at unconscious memories. But for most therapists, talking things out is by far the most frequently used method. The emotional release gained from this is called *catharsis,* and there is widespread agreement that talking freely to a trustworthy person who is interested and who understands is a helpful experience. It is also true that such free talking also leads, in time, to forgotten memories coming back into awareness, making it possible to reinterpret childhood experiences in the light of a more mature way of looking at them. Cases have also been reported where dramatic cures have followed the uncovering of some traumatic experience in childhood which had been, apparently, repressed into the unconscious. Most readers are no doubt familiar with the case of Eve White, made famous by the book and movie, *The Three Faces of Eve.*

Another route to the unconscious is *dream interpretation.* Freud called dreams "the royal road to the unconscious." He believed that all dreams are an expression of wish fulfillment, and that the often difficult symbolism is due to a process of disguise made necessary by a censoring mechanism in the ego. While Freud's particular theory of dreams is not shared by psychologists in general, many do feel that dream interpretation is a useful way of getting at conflicts of which a person may not be aware. There is, at present, no science of dream interpretation, though scientific study of dreams is now being undertaken by several researchers.[2] But there is an art of dream interpretation which many therapists consider useful. Generally, the patient is asked to "free associate" to each element of the dream, and an interpretation is suggested which seems to make some sense. Most clinicians would feel that a correct interpretation has not been found until the patient recognizes it himself as the right one.

A third route to the unconscious is the *transference.* By this Freud meant that the patient comes to see the therapist as an authority figure, usually a parent, and begins to act out with him some of the feelings he had as a child. The patient may begin to make demands on the therapist, act rebelliously, or he may love or hate the therapist. If the theory of transference is adopted, the therapist will not take personally this behavior of the patient but will interpret it as regressive or childish. As with other Freudian ideas, the concept of transference is highly controversial. Yet most therapists would agree that patients tend to become emotionally dependent, and that this tendency is likely to result in problems between the patient and the doctor which, when understood, can shed important light on the developmental history of the patient.

No other therapeutic approach is as controversial as psychoanalysis. Most thorough have been the criticisms of Eysenck[3] and Mowrer.[4] Yet, aside from the research generated by his ideas, Freud's influence is felt by most psychotherapists, and a great many act on the assumption that people can be helped by getting at conflicts that involve early childhood experiences of which the patient may not be aware. Acting on this assumption therapists work to have the patient achieve insight, to outgrow childish fears, and to throw off inappropriate inhibitions.

ALTERATIONS OF LIFE STYLE

Alfred Adler was a contemporary of Freud, in fact a one-time associate. It was Adler's view that mental and emotional problems are related to an unhealthy style of life which is developed by a person as his way of overcoming feelings of inferiority. Adler agreed with Freud that early childhood experiences are crucial, but he felt that, rather than these experiences passively causing specific behaviors, people actively develop a way that seems to work best for them in dealing with things. This he called one's style of life, and he interpreted later difficulties in the light of this. His method of helping people involved techniques for making them aware of their style of life and of changing it to a more appropriate one.

Though Adler's view is not as controversial as Freud's, the number of therapists who consider themselves to be followers of Adler is not great. Nevertheless, there are very few therapists who do not, to a greater or lesser extent, work with patients on their life style. Recently, this way of looking at problem behavior was popularized by Eric Berne in his book, *Games People Play.*

This way of helping people pays more attention to what people do than to what they say. It is assumed that people develop habitual ways of dealing with situations, and that these habitual ways were developed and have been continued because they have worked. To use a technical word, we would say that these ways of acting have been *reinforced* by being rewarded. Berne would say that people play games that they have found they can win. The problem is that games we played as children may not work so well for us as adults, or, even if they do work, we have to pay too high a price for the results we get.

Much of the group psychotherapy being practiced today aims at helping people to become aware of their behavior and to work out better ways of achieving their goals.

Three techniques are most frequently used in the effort to help people alter their life style. First, we try to help them become aware of what they are doing and to evaluate it in terms of their goals. Notice that we regard behavior, in this approach, as something that people *do* rather than as something that *happens.* Whether the approach is individual or group therapy, the key is honest, sensitive feedback. We tell the person what he seems to be doing and what consequences seem to be resulting, as we see it. We then ask if this is what he wants to happen; and, if it is not, whether he might find some other way to better reach his goal. In this connection, Rudolf Dreikurs, a disciple of Adler, suggests a helpful rule: "If you want to know the purpose of someone's behavior, look at what results from it."[5] Most of us like to pretend that we really don't make things happen, that we are the victims of what others do. If Dreikurs is right (and when we see a certain kind of behavior repeatedly occur, it is hard to deny that he is), then we can confront people with what they are doing and help them to recognize their style of dealing with problems and to evaluate it.

Second, we can help people to alter their style of life by refusing to reward or reinforce it. Berne would say that we can refuse to play their game, and they must either give the game up or find someone else to play it with them. A style of life is always developed with the cooperation of others and continues because other people, wittingly or unwittingly, make it rewarding.

Finally, we help people to alter their life style by giving them opportunities to practice different, more effective ways of behaving. It is in this connection that group therapy, and especially so-called marathon therapy, has been unusually effective. Once a person has decided that he wants to stop acting like a baby, for example, the group can refuse to respond to infantile tactics while warmly reinforcing adult ways of talking and acting.

Many therapists who use this approach also use such techniques as role-playing and psychodrama in helping people to become aware of how they act in specific situations and to try out different ways.

Many people learn to relate to other people more effectively after being confronted in therapy by honest feedback. The major questions about this approach have to do with how much pressure to put on a person, especially in a group situation, and how deep and lasting changes may be if they are worked out at this conscious level.

REORGANIZATION OF LIFE SITUATION

Another way of helping people involves working with them to relieve sources of stress in their lives. The work of Selye has made us aware that stress, especially if prolonged, can lead to serious mental and physical breakdown.[6] Soldiers in battle, civilians in times of catastrophe, and anyone whose life situation is extremely stressful—such people can break under the strain and need help.

Many times such people can be helped by prescribing rest or vacation, and this is probably the most time-honored therapeutic device we have. The organism has amazing powers of renewal and, if it can be relieved of noxious influences, will move toward re-establishing equilibrium and health.

Other people are helped by exploring with them possible sources of help—legal, financial, social—and by cooperating with them in dealing with real problems that are putting crushing pressures on them. Still other people may be suffering from real guilt because their behavior has alienated them from people who are important to them. Sometimes pastoral counselors can help restore such people to the community or fellowship in which their lives have meaning. Then there are those who need the support of someone who will stand with them as they find their way through a divorce, struggle to achieve independence from parents, or work through a maze of legal or ethical problems.

Sometimes the only way people can be taken out from under pressure is by hospitalization, and it is not unlikely that many take the route of illness to escape psychological pressures.

The growing field of psychiatric social work demonstrates that many disturbed people can be aided most effectively when a trained social worker helps them to resolve some of the practical problems that are causing stress.

The problem in this approach is to distinguish between persons who have psychological problems because of circumstances in their life situations, and persons who have practical problems because of psychological disturbances. Every social worker has felt the futility of trying to help people who seem to create new problems faster than the old ones can be solved.

FINDING ONE'S SELF, OR SELF-DISCOVERY

A radically different way of helping people rests on the assumption that people do not *have* problems, but that people *are* problems and that real changes and growth must come from within the person himself. Sometimes called non–directive or client–centered counseling, this way of helping people does not involve analyzing people, advising people, teaching people, or doing things for people. Rather, it is an effort to provide a relationship in which the client can best find himself. Jung, Maslow, and Rogers, among others, have used the term self–actualization, to refer to this process of self-discovery and self-affirmation. We shall describe Rogers' way of relating to clients.

Rogers does not deny that many different approaches may prove helpful to a person, but he feels that the way for a psychologist to be most helpful is: (1) to have an unconditional positive regard for the client; (2) to empathically understand what the client is expressing; (3) to accept the client as he expresses himself; and (4) to be congruent within himself as he relates to the client. It is Rogers' hypothesis that as much as the counselor is able to be these things and to the extent that this is experienced by the client, the relationship will facilitate his healing and growth.[7]

By *unconditional positive regard*, Rogers means a genuine interest in the person, a real caring about him. Obviously, if we are not interested, if we don't care about him, and if we're not for him, it is not likely we can be of much help to him. In fact, if we're not really for him, the most helpful thing would be to tell him we aren't so he can watch out! This kind of caring does not come easily, but it seems to begin with a sincere interest in and a deep respect for the uniqueness of the individual. It seems to be experienced by the client as both warm and safe.

Empathic understanding can be contrasted with analytic understanding. The latter involves understanding what is in a person by interpreting what he says and does, while the former concentrates solely on trying to understand or get the feel of what the person is trying to express. Empathic understanding does not come from sitting back and trying to figure out a person, but from leaning forward to catch all that a person is trying to express. It is a very special way of listening, and of checking one's understanding by asking, "Is this what you're saying, is this what you're feeling?"

To *accept* a person as he expresses himself means to refrain from all judgment or evaluation. Acceptance is a profound respect for the person as he is, and as he is trying to be, including what he is expressing in this particular moment. Perhaps the closest most of us have come to experiencing this kind of acceptance is with our best friends, the ones with whom we feel we can really be ourselves. Acceptance involves neither approval nor disapproval, and thus neither threatens nor supports a person. Acceptance is not only a willingness for the person to be himself, but also leaves him with the necessity of being himself, of evaluating himself, of affirming himself.

By *congruence* Rogers means that what the therapist is expressing is what he is feeling. He is not *pretending* to be interested, to be understanding, to be accepting. He tries to express only what he actually is in relationship to the client. If he is not interested, he will say so. If he does not understand, he will say so. If he cannot accept, he will say so. Rogers feels that only as the therapist is transparently genuine with the client can he provide the kind of relationship which best facilitates self-discovery and growth, both for the client and for the therapist.

Most therapists would agree that Rogers has put his finger on some of the most important aspects of the helping relationship. Questions about this approach center on whether *all* kinds of mental and emotional disturbance can be helped in this way. Will this approach work with psychotics? Is this the best way to work with anti-social or psychopathic persons?

BEHAVIOR MODIFICATION OR TRAINING

Similar to what we have called alteration of lifestyle, but working with smaller behavioral units, is the effort to help people by modifying their behavior. This approach utilizes the techniques of operant conditioning and is based on the assumption that abnormal behavior has been learned. If this is so, then such behavior should be susceptible to being extinguished, and more desirable behavior should be acquirable through reinforcement.

Most people are familiar with the essential principles involved in behavior modification, for they have long been used in training children and animals. Essentially, desirable behavior is rewarded or reinforced and undesirable behavior is ignored (not reinforced) or is punished.

There are published reports on successful application of behavior modification techniques in changing the behavior of patients in mental hospitals,[8] in reaching autistic children who did not respond to any other approach,[9] in getting rid of specific symptoms, such as tics,[10] and in providing parents and teachers with a means of changing the behavior or problem children.[11]

Three kinds of behavior modification are attempted: (1) extinguishing undesirable behavior; (2) increasing the frequency of or reinstating desirable behavior which a person has already acquired; and (3) shaping new desirable behavior. Extinction is accomplished by withholding reinforcement or by providing unpleasant consequences. Behavior is reinstated or its frequency increased by providing positive reinforcement. And new behavior is shaped through the method of approximation, which involves positively reinforcing any behavior which even barely approaches that desired, then demanding closer and closer approximation to the desired behavior before reinforcement is provided.

Several factors are important to the success of these methods. In extinguishing behavior, it is necessary to discover what has been serving as the reward for the undesirable behavior and to determine what the schedule of reinforcement has been. For example, if the behavior has been maintained by a 100 percent reinforcement schedule, it may easily be extinguished by simply ignoring it. But if the behavior has been maintained by a variable ratio reinforcement, then it may be necessary to use unpleasant consequences to discourage the behavior, while being careful to positively reinforce desirable alternative behaviors. In extinguishing behavior as well as in establishing it, we must see that consequences occur consistently, that they are specifically related to the behavior being treated, and that they occur rapidly.

Questions related to this approach include: Is it really enough just to change behavior? Will these methods work for all age ranges and for all types of disturbed persons?

RECONDITIONING OR DESENSITIZATION

Also based on conditioning techniques, but this time on the Pavlovian or classical, is an approach that seeks to change the emotional response to specific stimuli. Perhaps best known is the work of Wolpe, who calls his method reciprocal inhibition.[12] Briefly, his theory is that two incompatible responses to a stimulus cannot occur simultaneously.

Typically, Wolpe will train the subject in relaxation procedures, then, when the person has learned to relax completely, the problem stimulus will be presented in gradually increasing intensity until the person can remain completely relaxed in the presence of that most intense stimulus.

For example, if a person has a phobia toward cats, after he has learned to relax he will be told to think about a little kitten. When he can do this and remain relaxed he will progressively be told to think of what are to him more and more frightening pictures of cats until finally he can play with a cat in his lap and remain relaxed. This, of course, is almost exactly what Watson did with the little boy who was afraid of white rabbits.

Wolpe has apparently had best results in working with phobias and other emotional problems such as frigidity and impotence as well as homosexuality.

This approach leaves us with such questions as: Is getting rid of the symptoms enough? How many of the problems of disturbed people are amenable to this approach?

AN ASSESSMENT OF THE ART OF HEALING

We have surveyed many different ways in which psychotherapists attempt to be helpful to people with mental, emotional, and behavioral problems. If one is interested in learning what really helps or the right way to help people, the picture is most confusing. However, if we were to visit the offices of a cross-section of therapists and watch them at work, we might be surprised to notice that they don't seem to act as differently as we would expect. While only some of them would admit to being eclectic, which means to select what seems best from the various approaches, we would observe that few, if any, of these therapists treat all patients alike or use only one of the approaches we have described. Like artists using all the colors on the palette, most therapists respond to the needs of a client by drawing on all the resources at their command: common sense, philosophy of life, skill in relating to people and in influencing them, all of their own experiences, and all that they have studied and practiced in training. While a therapist may take one particular school of thought as his point of departure, he will probably modify this approach by mixing into it elements he has picked up from many others. The decisive factors are likely to be his own inner security as a person, his warm caring for others, his strong desire to be helpful, and his wisdom about human life.

And how consistently helpful is any therapist? We are not able to give a decisive answer to this question. Some who have carefully studied the reports of various therapists are quite skeptical of the value of most current psychotherapy. Others feel that there is reliable evidence supporting the claim that certain specific approaches are consistently effective.[14] Still others feel that the very nature of psychotherapy makes extremely difficult an evaluation of its effectiveness.

This chapter was included in this section of the Art of Psychology rather than in the section on the Science of Psychology because the author considers psychotherapy more art than science.

The attempt to justify psychotherapy does not require that it be claimed scientific or that we discount medical, social, or religious approaches. We are not interested in proving that psychotherapy alone can do the job; we only want to know how, and how much, psychotherapy may help.

QUESTIONS FOR STUDY AND CLASS DISCUSSION

1. How much awareness of self is good? Is ignorance sometimes really bliss? Can there be too much self-consciousness?

2. How much intervention in a person's life by another is good? Should this intervention occur only at the request of the person himself, or may others request it?

3. How much can one person help another person by listening to him and talking with him? How can talking help?

4. How much can people be helped by dealing with them at the conscious level? How much must the unconscious be probed?

5. How much does it help to get rid of undesirable symptoms or to change behavior without getting at underlying factors?

6. Can people be helped in groups, or must they receive individual treatment?

7. Is there a danger that too much dependency on either an individual or a group can occur?

8. How much should the person of the therapist, his values, his feelings, become involved in the helping process?

9. How much can we help a person who does not want to be helped?

10. If a way can be found to change people against their will, how do you feel about using this method to further socially desirable goals?

SUGGESTIONS FOR FURTHER READING

Axline, Virginia. *Dibs in Search of Self.* New York: Ballantine Books, 1964.
Laing, R. D. *The Politics of Experience.* New York: Ballantine Books, 1963.
Mowrer, O. H. *The Crisis in Psychiatry and Religion.* New York: D. Van Nostrand Co., 1961.
Sutherland, Robert I., and Smith, Kruger. *Understanding Mental Health.* New York: D. Van Nostrand Co., 1965.
Watts, Alan W. *Psychotherapy East and West.* New York: New American Library, 1961.

11

PERSUASION—THE ART OF INFLUENCING

SOME PRELIMINARY QUESTIONS

It is sometimes said that the aim of science is prediction and control. If this is so, and if psychology is a science, then the principles of psychology should be useful to those who would control the behavior of others.

In fact, we can find this assumption at both the professional and popular levels. It is not uncommon to hear someone say that someone else has ued psychology to get his way, or that someone else has been psyched out. In *The Hidden Persuaders*,[1] Vance Packard has documented some of the possibilities and problems of using psychological principles in advertising and selling. And in *Walden Two*,[2] the eminent experimental psychologist, B. F. Skinner, seriously explores the kind of society that might be possible if known principles of conditioning were carefully and consistently used. Finally, there is the more sinister use of psychological techniques in what has come to be called brain washing.

Clearly, this matter of the use of psychological knowledge, psychological skills, and even of the psychological profession, for the purpose of influencing the behavior of people raises not only technical questions about the most effective way of doing this, but also it raises profound ethical questions in view of some of the values to which we have traditionally been committed.

The technical questions are, of course, the only truly psychological questions. Whether it is wise or good to use certain techniques for influencing people is, strictly speaking, beyond psychology. But it is not beyond the responsibility of psychologists as men, and therefore, though a science of psychology may not be required to deal with ethical questions, a professional psychologist cannot escape such a responsibility.

Let us pose some hypothetical situations.

> Parents, teachers, or church personnel consult with a psychologist about how to get children (or adults) to think a certain way or to act a certain way. The psychologist is not convinced it is good for people to be influenced in this way. What is his responsibility?

> Some government agency consults with a psychologist about how to influence people to accept a certain proposal, to favor certain action, or to think a certain way. What is the psychologist's responsibility?

> Some corporation consults with a psychologist about how to keep employees more content, or about how to sell some product, or about projecting a certain public image. What is the psychologist's responsibility?

> In law enforcement, a psychologist is consulted on how best to get a confession from a suspect, or on whether someone should be held responsible for his acts, or on whether a prisoner should be paroled. What are the psychologist's responsibilities?

The key issue in all such cases involves respect for the privacy of individuals. Is it ethical for the psychologist to bypass the public presentation of a person and get facts, or supposed facts, about people and then supply these facts to other persons who want to use them as the basis for doing something to, or something with, this person?

No one has attacked this question more forthrightly than Sidney Jourard, whose position we quote at some length:

> When researchers are transparently pledged to further freedom and self-actualizing of their subjects, rather than be unwitting servants of the leaders of institutions, then they will deserve to *be* and to *be seen* as recipients of the secrets of human being and possibility. I envision a time when psychologists will be the guardians of the most intimate

> secrets of human possibilities and experience and possessors of know-
> ledge as to how man can create his destiny because man has shown
> him; and I hope that if we "sell" these secrets to advertisers, business-
> men, politicians, mass educators, and the military, we shall not do so
> until *after* we have informed our subjects, after we have tried to "turn
> them on," to enlarge their awareness of being misled and manipulated.
> I hope, in short, that we turn out to be servants and guardians of indi-
> vidual freedom, growth, and fulfillment, and not spies for the institu-
> tions that pay our salaries and research costs in order to get a privileged
> peep at human grist. Indeed, we may have to function for a time as
> counterspies, or double spies—giving reports about our subjects to
> our colleagues and to institutions, and giving reports back to our sub-
> jects as to the ways in which institutions seek to control and predict
> their behavior for their (the institutions') ends.[3]

We do not want to be naive or hypocritical. The answers to these ethical
questions are not easy. There are times when all of us want to influence someone else, and we are often convinced that it is important both for him and for
the general good that we succeed. In chapter 10 we touched on this issue in connection with psychotherapy, which certainly includes an effort to influence behavior. Parents are eager to influence their children to be good citizens, as are
teachers. It is important for the safety of the community that law enforcement
officials have ways of apprehending and influencing lawbreakers. There are times
when the national good seems to justify unusual efforts to influence other nations
or the people in our own country.

Because of the complexity of these ethical questions, and because they involve
all citizens rather than just psychologists, we do not propose to answer them here.
The issues are raised so that thoughtful people may be aware of the problems and
share in the discussions which, hopefully, will provide working answers.*

Now, then, let us turn to the psychology of persuasion. What are some of the
principles of influencing other people?

Motivational Factors

The simplest approach to influencing people is the application of principles of
motivation. Traditionally, this has involved the use of the carrot and the stick—
dangling something desirable in front of the subject or goading him from behind.

In chapters 8 and 9, in connection with our survey of some of the studies of
behavior and of the correlates of behavior, we noted some theories of the relationship between motivation and behavior. Without forgetting that many unan-

---

*The complexity of the issue may be seen in the fact that the author is using the most per-
suasive writing techniques to influence the readers to share his concern about this. Nor is it
difficult to ascertain the bias of the author in the way he has treated the question, even as he
leaves it to "thoughtful" readers to come to their own conclusions.

swered questions remain in this area, we shall nevertheless take the position that behavior is motivated and that to influence people, motives must be activated.

According to Maslow's theory of the hierarchy of motives, we would expect unsatisfied physical needs to be the most potent movers, followed by the safety needs, social and ego needs, and, finally, the growth or actualization needs. It is instructive to look at advertising to see what Madison Avenue thinks will move people. Until recently there was little deprivation of air, so we did not see this need appealed to. Now, however, the need for clear air is increasingly being appealed to. Thirst, hunger, and sex play central roles in advertising, as do the desires to be free from pain, to be safe and secure, and to be comfortable. But the social and ego needs are, if anything, appealed to even more in this affluent society. Particularly intense is the appeal to the need for social approval and the desire to avoid social ostracism. The ads tell us that if we use the right toothpaste, the right hair-grooming product, the right deodorant, and the right mouthwash, people will want to be with us; while if we don't, we are likely to be left out in the cold. Growth needs are not appealed to nearly so much as these others.

The art of influencing people by appealing to motivational factors involves two stages. First is the identification of the needs many people are feeling, and second is the effort to convince them that a need can be met by doing what we suggest or by buying what we suggest. And this works best when the person honestly feels that what he is doing is what he himself genuinely wants to do and not something that someone else wants him to do.

Effective teachers, successful salesmen, and skilled propagandists never leave people with the feeling that they have been manipulated, or that they have done something that was really someone else's idea. Rather, a well-taught student will feel that he has discovered an idea himself, a well-sold customer will feel that he bought just what he himself really wanted, and a well-propagandized person will feel that he is taking the only logical point of view.

Sometimes we distinguish between what is called push motivation and what is called pull motivation. By *push* we mean the goad (or stick) and by *pull* we mean the carrot. By and large, pull is far more effective than push, especially if we want the person to feel that he has made up his own mind and has done what he wanted to do. Nevertheless, sometimes push can be quite persuasive, as the slang name for a pistol suggests, i.e., "the persuader." The trouble with such persuasive tactics is that their results are not long-lasting. This is true, also, of the difference between extrinsic and intrinsic motivational factors. *Extrinsic* factors are reasons outside the activity itself which serve as motivators, while *intrinsic* factors are part of the activity itself. Eating, for example, is intrinsically motivating, while working in order to get money is responding to extrinsic motivation. Both types are used in influencing people, but whenever something can be presented as intrinsically satisfying, it becomes more deeply established as a goal.

The distinction between push and pull, and between extrinsic and intrinsic factors, provides a frame of reference for understanding the limitations in trying to make people do things or of convincing people against their will. There is a saying that it is possible to win an argument but lose a friend. Ordinarily, argument is considered a poor way of convincing or of persuading someone. It tends to evoke resistance and to cause the person we are arguing with to have a vested interest in maintaining his position. When we are skillful in persuasion we will agree with the opponent and convince him that what we are saying is in agreement with what he has said.

In contrast to pressure tactics of the push type are the pull methods. At their best they are called inspiring or contagious, while at their worst they are called seductive and "conning." In inspiring people we appeal to what are considered high motives, while in seducing them we appeal to what are considered low motives. In either case, there is no felt pressure; the person responds to that which appeals to him.

Perhaps the most effective pressure is the power of the group. So eager are most people for group approval that, while group pressure is most intense, people often are unaware that they have been swayed by the group. If asked about it they are likely to say, "I made up my own mind." For this reason, many efforts to influence people are either done in a group situation or the suggestion is given that a group feels a certain way. Called the band-wagon technique, the appeal is to the desire not to be left out or left behind.

Similar to group pressure is that of the appeal to authority and prestige. Most people are unsure enough of themselves that they like the reassurance that famous or successful people are on their side. Utilizing what is called the halo effect, the assumption is made that if such-and-such a movie star, or athlete, or scientist uses a certain product or thinks a certain way, then it must be right.

For most people, there is nothing so persuasive as the appeal to their pride, their sense of self-worth. In other words, most people are largely motivated by their ego needs. When people are convinced that doing something, or thinking a certain way, makes them look better or smarter, they are likely to do it. Effective leaders have a way of making the people around them feel important and needed. Most of us view being needed as being important.

If we are to influence the most mature people, we will have to appeal in the long run to what Maslow calls the growth motives. The opportunity to be creative, to express oneself, to face challenges—these are what appeal to the mature. He who would influence such people will do so by providing opportunities for this kind of activity. Increasingly, the larger corporations are finding that, if they are to attract and hold the most competent men, they must not only offer good monetary incentives but also provide working conditions in which such men can meet their needs for growth and self-expression.

Emotional Factors

As pointed out in chapter 9, it is not easy to distinguish between factors which we call motivational and those which we call emotional. The distinction becomes even more difficult when we find that emotions can act as motivators.

Nevertheless, while a strict science of psychology must be concerned with very precise distinctions, the art of persuasion does not require that we be sure whether we are using motivation or emotion or both. People who are effective influencers of other people would agree that emotions play a crucial role in determining whether people are moved.

Some examples come quickly to mind.

> Salesmen report that it is more by appeal to emotions than by appeal to reason that people can be persuaded to buy. Sometimes it is anger, sometimes it is pity, at other times it may be fear that moves people to buy.

> Persuasive speakers find it effective to get people to laugh and cry, or to feel anger, fear, or love.

> A Japanese friend told me of an experience during World War II. He had grave misgivings about the war, he was old enough not to be drafted, and he was sure he didn't want to volunteer. Yet, one day there was a parade; the bands were playing and the flags were waving. At a recruiting booth an officer said to my friend, "And you, Uncle, don't you want to sign up?" And my friend said he stepped up proudly and with great emotion said, "Yes, I want to go!" His emotions had been stirred.

What, then, are some of the principles involved in the appeal to emotions as a means of influencing people?

First, emotions act as energizers. Whether emotions actually cause the energizing, or whether both the emotions and the energizing are caused by something else, we can say that when our emotions are stirred, we are stirred, and behavior of some kind is likely to occur. It is almost as if the emotions long to be expressed in action. Seldom, if ever, do we see a great expenditure of energy by people who are not emotionally aroused. The practical consequences of this are utilized by people who want to move others to such expenditure of energy. They find out what stirs people emotionally and they use this knowledge to get the action they want. For example, if the sight of victimized women and children stirs people to angry action, then pictures of such atrocities are shown and we say that our enemy is doing such things. The result is that people want to go and destroy such an enemy. Of course, the enemy is probably showing similar pictures to people on his side.

Second, emotions act as inhibitors of the rational. There is evidence that as emotions are stirred up, careful rational processes are inhibited. Emotions, in a sense, make us drunk. We do things when we are emotionally aroused that we might not do when we are calm. Thus, if we want people to think very carefully, we avoid stirring them up emotionally. But if we want them to be uncritical, to act without thinking, then we do all that we can to get them emotionally aroused.

Third, where there is ego involvement, emotions are more easily stirred. McDougall called the self-regarding sentiment the master sentiment.[4] The fact that the emotions are activated in the part of the nervous system called the old brain suggests that they are closely related to the organismic processes which have favored the survival of the species. In other words, that which is most related to self-survival is likely to stir up the strongest emotions. We all know from experience that people are emotional about themselves. It is difficult to talk about ourselves without getting emotional, and our emotions begin to stir as soon as someone else starts to talk about us. This emotionality about ourselves spreads out to all with which we identify—our name, our family, our friends, our church, and on and on. This means that if we can be appealed to on the basis of this self-regarding sentiment, we are more easily moved. Those who are good at influencing people take an interest in those things in which they know a person has invested his ego. We often hear such advice as, "If you want to get to him, just talk about his children," or "He's proud of his dogs; notice them and talk about them," or "She's crazy about her rose garden; say something nice about it." By touching on these areas of ego-involvement, we are often able to get people's emotions aroused and they are more likely to be influenced.

Among the so-called negative emotions, perhaps the most frequently used in persuasion are *fear, anger,* and *hatred.*

The emotion of fear arouses people for flight or for fight. When used in persuasion, fear is used to make people uncomfortable, and then a way out is offered to them. We arouse the fear of medical and hospital bills, then sell health insurance. In some cases, we arouse the fear of death and hell, then offer a particular religion. We arouse the fear of social ostracism, then sell deodorant and mouthwash. We arouse the fear of punishment in someone, and then persuade him to do the "right" thing.

Anger is, in many ways, similar to fear, but the arousal is to fight rather than to flee. Thus, when we want to move people to aggressive action we find it useful to stir up anger in them. In sports and in the military, men have been prodded into action by coaches or officers who say things to make them angry. Sometimes, especially in sales work, anger is used to unsettle people and, at times, to make them feel guilty so that they are more amenable to pressure. The author knows one high-pressure salesman who delights in making people mad because, he says, he invariably makes the sale.

The emotion of hatred is an anger rooted in a severe wound to the ego, which results in an emotion that sustains a long-time hostility. This emotion is appealed to, therefore, to persuade people to maintain hostile action over a long period of time. It is commonly used in war, where hatred of the enemy is constantly reinforced through indoctrination. It is used to maintain cohesiveness in groups which have their reason for existence in being separated from, or opposed to, some other group. Examples of this are racial prejudice, religious prejudice, and political prejudice. Where such hatreds have been deeply implanted, there exists a ready instrument for moving people which is gladly exploited by demagogues and other opportunists.

Among the positive emotions, the most frequently aroused for persuasive purposes are *love* or *affection, laughter* or *the sense of the ridiculous,* and *tears* or *pity.*

The poets have often reminded us that men will do nearly anything for love. The love of men and women for each other, the love of parents for their children, the love of people for their country, the love of a man for his God—all of these are appealed to by those who would influence others. And, when it can be demonstrated that what we are suggesting is a sure proof of a person's love, there is a strong incentive to do what is suggested. A man's love for his wife is aroused (or perhaps sometimes it is his guilt), and we tell him to buy her flowers or a diamond, or, perhaps, to take her with him the next time he flies out of town on business. A man's love for God or his church is aroused, and we tell him to show this love by a monetary contribution. Parents' love for their children is aroused, and we sell them expensive toys or a trust fund for a college education.

The emotion of laughter moves people in at least two ways. Most frequently it is used just to relieve tension and lower resistance so that people will be more receptive to suggestions. Speakers, salesmen, and supervisors of workers have long used a timely joke as an introduction to people they are trying to influence. But another use of humor is to subtly undermine a person's commitment to an idea or a way of life. If the humorous attack is too blatant, it will backfire. But, if an idea can be lightly and good-naturedly laughed at, there is a real weakening of the commitment to the idea. This is why it is usually considered taboo to make fun of the sacred, that toward which the group wants no weakening of commitment. On the other hand, many a rigid person has been gently teased out of a position that was causing trouble for him or others.

People who are moved to tears are vulnerable to suggestion. Not angry tears, but the tears that spring from sorrow or pity are effective in persuasion. Many a husband or wife has found that, if the other can be moved to tears, he can be influenced. Effective platform speakers have developed the ability to tell the kind of stories that leave few dry eyes, and while people are emotionally open in this way, ideas are planted that might otherwise be resisted.

The most insidious use of emotions to influence people is brain washing. The process has been succinctly summarized as the use of three D's: dependency, debilitation, and dread.[5] Subjects are systematically weakened, physically and emotionally, by deprivation, fatigue, and separation from comrades. They are made dependent because of weakness and the need for survival. And, perhaps most important of all, they are kept in a state of dread through uncertainty, threats, and the loss of contact with dependable clues to what is real.

There is no more effective tool of persuasion than the arousal of emotions.

By the same token, there is no more problematical aspect for those who are concerned with the integrity of persons.

Cognitive Factors

By cognitive factors in persuasion we mean, primarily, the appeal to logic or reason. How much are we influenced by the force of reason?

In areas of little ego involvement, reason and logic are likely to be the determining factors. Here persuasion refers to the clarity and reasonableness of the presentation. Ideally, those who are dedicated to the pursuit of truth would not want to persuade anyone in any other way. Dispassionate objectivity is the professed mistress of scientists and academicians alike. Few, of course, are always loyal to this commitment, but many people are open, in wide areas of their mind to the persuasion of reason. Indeed, most of us would like to think of ourselves as such people.

More often, however, logic and reasoning are used in a process called rationalization. This, of course, is quite different from a dispassionate pursuit of truth. Rather it is a quite passionate effort to appear reasonable to ourselves or others. Festinger has described the phenomenon of cognitive dissonance,[6] which is the experiencing of tension when we find ourselves inconsistent and the effort to reduce that tension, usually by rationalization. Other studies have supplemented Festinger's and suggest that the tension is experienced, not so much when we find that we are inconsistent in the area of ideas as when we are made aware of inconsistent action. We shall assume that any felt inconsistency leads to some tension but that having to face inconsistency in action will lead to a greater tension. In either case, we are most likely to try to reduce the tension through rationalization.

So-called logic-tight compartments are quite common in us all, but we are usually bothered about this only when we are confronted by our inconsistency through a person for whom we have great respect, or we are confronted by the demand for action which brings into conflict the positions hitherto kept separate For example, let us say I think of myself as a liberal in matters of race, but I have no real contacts with black people. Then one day my daughter announces that she is marrying a black man (as in *Guess Who's Coming to Dinner*). I am no longer able to avoid the dissonance between the two inconsistent positions.

In persuasion we apply this principle in two ways. On the one hand, if we are trying to persuade people to act on the basis of inconsistency, we help them to better maintain the logic-tight compartments by giving them better rationalizations. In other words, we support the inconsistency by saying that it is really not inconsistent at all but quite reasonable. Or we belittle its importance by noting that those who consider us inconsistent are actually much more inconsistent than we are. On the other hand, if we want to influence someone to give up his inconsistency and to follow through on the implications of some position he professes, we try to maneuver him into a situation where the conflict is increased until it must be resolved. This strategy, however, has risks, inasmuch as there are three things a person can do when faced with such a conflict: he may do as we hope, resolving the inconsistency in favor of what we are pleading for; he may decide to go the other way, resolving the inconsistency by giving up the position we are urging him to live up to; or, if the pressure is great, he may do what Lewin calls leaving the field. The last course of action is very likely to occur if our importance to him is not great and if there are no compelling reasons why the conflict must be resolved.

Another cognitive factor is quite different from the reasoning process. Called suggestion, it is most dramatically seen in hypnotic phenomena. We are not yet able exactly to explain how suggestion works, so far as the underlying processes are concerned, but that it does work is well known, and many of the principles by which it may be used in influencing people can be stated.

First, people are put into an uncritical mood. This can be done through relaxation, through emotion-arousing music, through social contagion, or by appeal to prestige and authority.

Second, monotonous repetition further deadens the critical capacities and focuses the unresisting mind.

Third, the suggestions are very specific, in this sense similar to stimuli used in the classical conditioning process.

Fourth, a linkage is established between specific clues, usually verbal, and thoughts, feelings, or actions which are being suggested.

Fifth, there is never any argument, no appeal to the analytic processes. There is only the confident expectation that the subject will accept the suggestion; in fact, that he has already accepted it. And all of this is done in an atmosphere of supportiveness for the subject and a persistent pushing out of all other considerations from mental focus.

There is evidence that TV advertising works on these principles of suggestion. This is why, often to our amazement, they work. It does not matter that the commercials are monotonous or repetitious or irrational. In a semidarkened room, slouched drowsily before our sets, we are highly susceptible to suggestion. The commercials drone on and ideas are planted in us which will affect our behavior when we go to the store.

Other advertising, while not working so hypnotically, also uses techniques of suggestion. By various means, the name of a product is presented to us in association with some stimulus that gets our attention. The two become linked so that when we "think beer," we think such-and-such; or we hum a catchy little tune and think of a certain cigarette.

Religion has made much use of the power of suggestion. In the more sophisticated churches, quiet music, darkened, serene surroundings, and repetitious ceremony may be used to implement suggestions. In the less formal churches, especially those favoring highly charged emotional experiences, the closeness of people crowded together, the repetition of well-known phrases, the music which throbs with monotonous beat, and the confident dogmatism of the speaker make people highly receptive to suggestion.

Teaching, psychotherapy, medicine, and most group management make use of suggestion. A teacher confidently tells her pupils, "You will like this." A counselor, especially one who is more directive, quietly says, "You will feel different." A doctor, standing beside a sickbed, says firmly to his patient, "You'll be all right." Parents, too, have long used quiet, firm, repetitious suggestions in shaping their children's behavior.

One problem related to cognitive factors is of special interest and has been the subject of research. It is the question of whether persuasion is more effective when both sides of an issue are presented, or whether it works better when only one side is given. The research suggests that it depends on the specific situation. When we are trying to build enthusiasm and morale in people, we usually present only "our" side of issues. A good example of this is a speaker at a political convention. But if we want to indoctrinate people in such a way that they are less vulnerable to being changed when they hear the "other" side, we can do this better by telling them what they can expect to hear from the other side, then giving them the best answers we have to this counter position. It has been found that people who have heard only one side are very susceptible to being changed when they are presented with a contrary position.[8]

Communication Factors

From the field of information theory come other factors important to an understanding of persuasion. It is hypothesized that all communications systems involve five parts: source, transmitter, channel, receiver, and destination.[9] A schematic representation of this would be as follows:

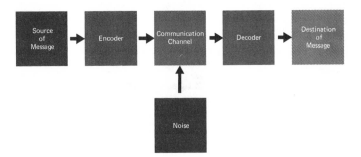

Using this frame of reference, we may identify some of the communications factors involved in persuasion.

Factors in the source. Sometimes persuasion is ineffective because of uncertainty or confusion in the person who is trying to do the persuading. Mixed feelings or ambivalence about purposes can prevent one from having influence. In the author's experience as a counselor, he has often found that a husband or wife fails to persuade the other because he or she is not really sure about what is wanted. Supervisors, coaches, or military officers may be ineffective for the same reason. Nothing is more essential in command than that the commander be very certain of what he wants others to do.

Factors in the transmitter. Transmission of information requires that the message be encoded, put into a form capable of transmission. The most common transmitter among men is the spoken or written word—language. The most basic skill in persuasion is effective use of the language. The choice of words and the style of expression can, in themselves, make or break the influence one has on others. In a complex society, such as ours, he who commands the language is likely to command people. This power has been recognized and exploited by several extremely popular training programs stressing the speaking skills.

Factors in the channel. If we are to persuade people, we must reach them with the message. Because ours is a bustling, noisy world, the effective persuader takes two main steps to avoid having his message lost through interference. One is to repeat his message often enough so that if it is not heard at one time, or only dimly heard the first time, it can be heard at another time. Secondly, he uses many different channels, knowing that one channel may be closed for some people. Among individuals, if communication is important, we will not be content to mumble one time the message we are sending.

Factors in the receiver. The receiver, in information theory, is that which picks up the message. In the area of our concern, the receiver is the hearing apparatus of people. We are not thinking only of ears, but of the entire capacity to hear and understand a message. Key factors are attention (receiver turned on), capacity to understand or decode the message, and whether or not the receiver has been keyed to distort. We know that in frightened, insecure people (like the paranoid personality), there is a terrible distortion in the receiving or perceiving processes. Certainly one who is trying to persuade such a person would have to take such distorting tendencies fully into account if he were to get the message through effectively.

Factors in the destination. Even after the message gets through, without serious distortion or misunderstanding, there are factors in the person being addressed that will determine whether he will be influenced. One is whether he sees the source of the message as credible. This includes not only the general credibility of the source but, in particular, how this specific effort at persuasion is viewed.

Propaganda, for example, is seldom labeled as propaganda, and many advertisers would be happy if they did not have to label their message as an advertisement, for we tend to discount a message that is clearly related to the interests of its author. Most important, however, are the interests and goals of the person to whom the message is addressed. No one is likely to pay much attention to a message totally unrelated to his interests and goals.

Feedback. While not a necessary part of a communications system, the use of feedback greatly increases its effectiveness. When we can find out how much of our message is being received we can quickly make changes to ensure better reception. Speakers use many audience reactions to gauge the reception their message is getting. Salesmen make it a point to ask questions designed to provide feedback from potential customers. Wise teachers provide ample opportunities for responses from students. Advertisers, public relations firms, and politicians make extensive use of surveys to get this feedback.

Concluding Statement

In the beginning of this chapter we raised serious questions about the use of persuasive techniques in interpersonal relationships. Then we explained the most effective methods of persuasion. We must now come back to the questions about the place of the art of influencing people in a healthy society.

It is the author's conviction that the only real protection for the individual is to be found in a free society in which a commitment to human values is nourished as the highest good. In such a society, the use of persuasive techniques will be limited by the self-restraint of men dedicated to encouraging the growth of individuals and by the discipline free men can bring to bear on one another through criticism and the marshaling of an educated public opinion. Perhaps, too, if more of us know about the techniques of persuasion, we can recognize when they are being used on us.

QUESTIONS FOR STUDY AND CLASS DISCUSSION

1. How would you distinguish between persuasion and manipulation?

2. When is managing people justified and when is it not justified?

3. Do you think a psychologist should get information from people without their being aware of what he is doing?

4. Would you rather be pulled or pushed into doing something?

5. What place is there for highly emotional behavior in the life of a mature person?

6. Is there a place for inconsistency in mature living, or should we strive for consistency at all costs?

7. What limits do you feel should be put on advertising?

8. Are there any limits that ought to be imposed on the press, on TV?

9. What is the best protection we have against government propaganda?

10. Can you find any examples of true brain washing in our society?

SUGGESTIONS FOR FURTHER READING

London, Perry. *Behavior Control.* New York: Harper, 1969.

McLuhan, Marshall. *Understanding Media.* New York: New American Library, 1964.

Packard, Vance. *The Hidden Persuaders.* New York: Pocket Books, 1958.

Riesman, David. *The Lonely Crowd.* New Haven, Conn.: Yale University Press, 1950.

Skinner, B. F. *Walden Two.* New York: Macmillan Co., 1948.

12

BEING—THE ART OF LIVING

TO BE OR NOT TO BE
BEING ONESELF RATHER THAN SOMEONE-ELSE BEING
BEING ALL THAT ONE IS OR ALL-THAT-ONE-IS BEING
BEING WHAT ONE CAN BE
BEING WITHIN LIMITS
BEING WITH OTHERS
BEING FREE OR FREELY BEING

We have noted that part of psychology is still more philosophical than scientific, especially that part that is most concerned with persons. But we have found, also, that although young, psychology is a thriving science of behavior. We have briefly summarized the most important experimental evidence in chapters 6 through 9, and have looked at some of the applications of psychological knowledge, particularly the art of healing and the art of influencing.

Now we must ask the question of concern to most people: How can psychology help me to live a better life—one that is more happy, effective, and meaningful? We shall not ignore this question but shall present, as best we can, the implications for living that are to be found in psychology as philosophy, science, and art. As much as possible, we shall distinguish between the facts as we see them and our personal interpretations of these facts. The reader will, no doubt, discern some unwarranted conclusions on the part of the author. This should only sharpen the reader's critical capacity and make him even more aware than he is that, in the final analysis, each of us must construct his own philosophy of life and artfully make his own applications of the available knowledge.

TO BE OR NOT TO BE

The novelist, Camus, has said that there is only one ultimate philosophical question and that is the question of suicide.[1] From the standpoint of psychology, this question is not faced directly except when we confront a person who says, "I don't want to go on living." But, indirectly, the question of whether to live or not can be seen in much of the troubled behavior with which we deal, as in a strangely withdrawn autistic child, the desperate self-destructive behavior of an angry adolescent, and the deeply discouraged alcoholic or drug addict.

Most of us take life for granted and find it difficult to comprehend anyone who doesn't want to live. This is not strange, for, as we have noted, living things have an amazing adaptive capacity, and for most of us life is reasonably good and certainly preferable to death.

But there are conditions which can, for any of us, raise questions about whether living is worth the cost. And apparently, individuals differ among themselves in their capacity to cope with the frustrations and pains of life. Individual differences are partly genetic, partly learned, and partly rooted in the mystery of individual selfhood. As yet we do not understand these differences very well, although, as noted in chapter 9, we do know some factors, such as chemical and neural conditions, that can dramatically affect the capacity to cope with life's problems.

Whatever the cause, and however directly or indirectly the question of living or dying is raised, it requires of each person his own individual answer.

Why should we live rather than die? There is, of course, no easy answer. Sometimes we hear the answer that it is our destiny to live, or that we just have to. Or, there is the religious answer that it is a sin to take one's life, that God gives life and only God has the right to take it away.

But the question is really broader than that of taking one's life or not taking it. The principle involved has to do with accepting life or rejecting it. We may stay alive and yet reject life. We can, in many ways, defeat life without ceasing to live.

In the broader sense, then, why should one accept life, why should one live? Psychologists, as men, must grope together with other men for their own answers. But psychologists have found some of the factors associated with a loss or a recovery of the will to live.

Factors that are related to the will to live include: being loved, or cared about, for oneself; discovering some meaning in continuing to live; the ability to perceive possibilities for oneself in the future or to hope; and the insight (or is it faith?) that one is a part of a process that can be trusted, a process that is supportive of the essence of oneself rather than a threat to it. These factors, at times, appear to be very much related to chemical and neural factors, and at other times seem to be psychological or spiritual in nature.

The will to live can be much affected by whether we are loved. For the infan
this is radically important, but it remains largely true throughout life. The feelin
that one is not loved, whether or not the feeling is valid, can drastically reduce tl
will to live. When one feels that he is not loved by others, it is difficult to love
oneself.

Nietzsche is credited with the statement, "Man can bear any *what* if he has a
why."[2] When life loses its meaning, the will to live is reduced. One definition c
meaning is purposeful behavior.[3] Life is meaningful if it appears that what one
does will make some difference, be significant in some way. When what one doe
seems to make no difference at all, it is difficult to find a will to live. Victor
Frankl, in *Man's Search for Meaning*, recounts that some of his fellow inmates
in the concentration camps during World War II found that the only freedom
they had was that of deciding for themselves how they would accept their death
But those who took even this very limited purposeful action seemed to discover
a meaning that made a great difference in the quality of their lives.[4]

Related to purposeful action is the ability to perceive some possibilities in the
future, the ability to hope. The old saying, "Where there is life, there is hope,"
might be turned around with equal truth—"Where there is hope, there is life."
There is, of course, a false hope which can cruelly disappoint. Hope, also, can
act as a narcotic so that we do not face reality. For this reason, some philosophers have recommended that we learn to live without it.[5] But psychologists, as
well as medical doctors, cannot so lightly discount the life-supporting power of
hope. At its best, hope is neither wishful thinking nor delusion, but an affirma-
tive response to life's promise.

But most basic of all and transcending all sciences including the science of
psychology is one's identification with the life process. It is difficult to speak of
this without sounding mystical, but the final answers to the reason for living seen
to come from life itself. We live because it is our nature to live.

We live because life lives in us. We find that we are living a life that in a way
is all our own, yet we sense that the life is really not ours to do with as we please
for the life in us has its own nature and is a part of all life. So the life in us is ou
and yet we belong to it.

Life is partly under our control and we are partly under life's control, and ou
destinies, for a time, are inextricably bound together: we are stuck with life and
the life in us is stuck with us.

For some strange reason, life has risked itself in us. Is it so that life might expand and be enriched in us? Is the cry of the infant life's cry or our own cry?

Life can be taken as a gift or a burden. If we take it as a gift, a trust, we worl
with it and for it, and it brings to us the energies of the universe and the accumu
lated adaptive capacities of millions of years of life's struggles to be. If we take
life as a burden, we labor under the load of incomprehensible drives and demand
and, in turn, stifle and choke life's potential.

BEING ONESELF RATHER THAN SOMEONE-ELSE BEING

Popeye the Sailor Man was neither philosopher nor psychologist, but his bold affirmation, "I am what I am and that's all I am," shows both profound insight and sound mental health. Because, for persons, the problem of *being* inevitably becomes the problem of whether to be or not to be oneself.

On the surface, nothing could be more absurd than the idea that a person could be someone other than the person he is. Yet, as we all know, this is precisely what we are constantly tempted to try. And the language with which we speak of the self reflects the confusion which results.

We say such things as, "I am not myself today"; "This is not the real me"; "I must get hold of myself"; or "I don't dare be myself."

In psychology we call this the problem of identity or of self-affirmation. It involves knowing oneself and accepting the self that one discovers himself to be.

To know oneself is to become aware that one has inherited a particular biochemical system, that one has been put in a particular time and place, and that one has been subjected to a particular set of circumstances. But it is also to become aware that "I" have been active in this interaction between organism and environment; that I have a past, a present, and a probable future—a continuity in time; that I am this particular self and no other; and that I am only one self but, at the same time, am capable of making myself the object of my awareness, and also strangely susceptible to feeling that there is more than one "I" in me.

As pointed out in chapter 2, we know some of the factors associated with a more reliable self-awareness. Overwhelmingly important seems to be the way in which people on whom we are dependent interact with us. If the significant people in our lives are able to see us as we are, accept us as we are, and cooperate with us as we are, then it is much easier for us to be aware of ourselves as we are. But we often find that those whom we need are unwilling to see us as we are and unable to accept certain aspects of our being. A girl may find that her father wanted a boy and just won't see her and treat her as a girl, so she finds it hard to be the girl she is. It may be that our real feelings of anger, fear, or lust are unthinkable to our parents, so they are never recognized by them or by us.

But one thing is certain: that which is, does not depend for its existence on someone's recognizing it. It *is* whether or not we know it, whether or not we like it. Denial does not change anything that is; it only affects what can be done about it. So we are what we are, whether we know it or admit it.

To be oneself is to know oneself and to accept oneself. They are, of course, related because if we are unwilling to accept ourselves we will probably also not know ourselves. Yet self-acceptance goes beyond self-knowledge to self-affirmation. To accept oneself is to genuinely like oneself, to be glad that one is oneself. There are many who say, "But I could never like myself, never!" And there are many more who cannot like some parts of themselves. Then there is the idea, sometimes supported by unfortunate religious teaching, that it is wrong to like ourselves.

No doubt self-love can be unhealthy. Freud called one kind "narcissism," from the Greek myth of the boy who spent all his time looking in the pool at his own reflection and admiring his own beauty. Another kind is the ugly selfishness that calculatingly uses other people for one's own goals. But there is a self-love which has nothing in common with narcissism or selfishness.

To accept oneself is to delight in the life that is in oneself; therefore, it is an expression of the love of life. To hate oneself is the same as hating life, and the two go together. To accept oneself is to work with the life that is in us, to be a friend of that life rather than its enemy.

Soren Kierkegaard, the father of Existentialism, wrote that the ultimate sin is the refusal to be ourselves. He felt that we refuse to be the selves we are in either pride or despair, and that pride, too, is a form of despair. We can also see despair as a form of pride. The point is, we feel that we ought not to have to be who we are; we should have been someone else. He concludes his book, *The Sickness Unto Death*, with these words, "By relating itself to its own self and by willing to be itself, the self is grounded transparently in the Power which constituted it."

Kierkegaard puts his finger on the key to the issue when he relates self-acceptance to power or energy. When we accept ourselves, our energies flow, we experience vitality. When we reject ourselves, our energies are blocked, we discover that our fictional self has little access to the engines of our life. For, as we said earlier, we can only partly control life, and if life's energies are to be directed by us, we must go in the general direction that life wants to go. We can't separate out the power of life and use it very long for goals that are opposed to life.

BEING ALL THAT ONE IS OR ALL-THAT-ONE-IS BEING

Self-acceptance already implies the acceptance of *all* that one is. But the matter is of such importance that we shall deal with it in yet greater detail.

Harry Stack Sullivan was one of the first to describe the processes by which, as infants, we learn to distinguish between the me and the not me, and the good me and the bad me.[7]

Briefly, his theory is that ordinarily the difference between me and not me is perceived as we experience our world, largely by what we put into our mouths, then by what we touch. But if we are made very anxious by the reactions of the important people in our lives, this process is disturbed and it is possible for us not to include all the body in the concept me. Later, the same thing can happen with respect to feelings, and we may fail to recognize certain feelings as our own, relegating them to the not me.

So, also, with the distinction between good me and bad me. While it is theoretically possible for us to discover that certain ways of acting lead to bad consequences and thus might be called bad in a purely empirical or descriptive sense, we usually make the distinction on the basis of the reactions of the significant people in our lives. And, as often as not, rather than limiting themselves to labeling certain *actions* as bad and other *actions* as good, they tell us *you* are bad or *you* are good. So, sometimes we experience ourselves as bad. The good me is accepted; the bad me is rejected.

Thus, when I come to think of myself, and to be myself, there is a tendency for the self to be limited to the me that leaves out or only dimly senses the body parts and emotions and ideas that were not acceptable. I then find it difficult, if not impossible, to be all that I am. If I have experienced much anxiety in my early life, as an adult I am likely to be seriously alienated from much that is really me, feeling strange about some of the ideas, feelings, and behavior that come out of me ("I just don't understand why I acted that way"), and considering it unthinkable that *all* of me should be accepted and somehow admitted into my being.

Why not reject part of myself? Is there not a part of me that is bad? Should it not be sternly repressed? These questions raise the most serious philosophical, theological, and psychological questions. They relate to our view of the nature of man, the problem of evil, and the issue of dualism (the idea that there are two kinds of ultimate reality). Obviously, it would be presumptuous to try to settle such questions in a paragraph or two. Nevertheless, there are some relevant points which we can make from the standpoint of our psychological knowledge, and some tentative reformulations of traditional religious concepts which can be suggested.

From the psychological point of view, it is important to distinguish between *feeling* something and *doing* something, both of which are involved in being. I can feel angry enough to kill someone, but I can choose not to do it. I can feel sexual attraction for someone and yet decide not to engage in sexual behavior. Am I a murderer, an adulterer? The psychological answer is clear: No, I *felt* like killing, but I did not; I *felt* like engaging in illicit sexual behavior, but I did not. Psychological health is not served by blurring this distinction. No realistic good is served by my saying, "If I felt like killing, it is the same as if I did. I am a killer." But neither is it psychologically healthy to deny the feeling of murderous anger just because I manage to keep from acting it out. Being all that I am involves being fully aware of the intense emotion and being fully able to act in the way that I decide best expresses what I really want to do.

It seems to this author that this kind of honesty about oneself has ethically positive consequences and should be consistent with the religious ideal of openness before a God of holiness. For, not only are the words whole and holy related linguistically, but the ideas are similar. That which is most whole is most holy, and the most holy is wholeness. If this is so, there should be no conflict between a psychology which encourages man to own all his feelings, all his ideas, and all his behavior, and a religious commitment to a God who is said to know us as we are.

BEING WHAT ONE CAN BE

Being all that one is always involves the discovery that there is change within the self. One experiences parts of oneself as belonging more to the past than to the present. One finds also movement toward new ways of being which are glimpsed only as desirable possibilities. All these pulls and drives mingle, separate and wax and wane in their strengths. They are not rigidly organized into some clear system. Yet the result is not chaos and, when trusted, experience tends to be a dependable basis for self-identity and for self-directed action.

One author has referred to this movement toward new ways of being as "becoming."[8] Whatever we call it, it is an important complement to the concept of being oneself. Many seem to think that being oneself is a static state, and that we should carefully evaluate that self, identifying and cultivating the good in it while ignoring or suppressing the bad. In the idea of becoming we have a radically different idea of how change may occur.

Becoming is a process of growth, more a happening than a doing. And as we grow we find ourselves changing, but the changes are not accomplished by rejecting parts of ourselves or by imposing something not of ourselves upon ourselves. I do not hate what I outgrow, because it was me; I do not hate what I become, because it is me.

We have said that growth is a happening and not a doing. Yet we can do things that will favor growth, and we can do things that will hinder growth. Being what one can be, is facilitated by our seeing possibilities, and by responding to them according to our ability.

Teilhard de Chardin wrote, "To see more is to be more."[9] He was pointing to the relationship between openness to experience and growth. When we open our eyes and our hearts, we see not only what is, but what can be. We see possibilities. Among these possibilities, some seem peculiarly inviting, really right for us. We find ourselves responding to these possibilities with our whole being. We say yes to that which invites us, and this yes is genuine will power—the power we feel when we want something with our whole heart.

Being what one is, leads to becoming what one can be. Openness to perceived possibilities leads to responsible action (that is, acting according to our response ability). This kind of responsible action is purposive behavior, and it is commitment. But, in this context of surrendering ourselves to that which we want with all our heart to do, responsibility, commitment, will power, and purpose lose the artificial, strained quality they have when they reflect our being what others say we are to be.

When *to will* means *to want,* when *commitment* means really *being with,* when *responsibility* means *doing what we can,* then being what one can be is life at its best. It is what Maslow calls a peak experience,[10] and what Ortega calls living up to the height of the times.[11]

BEING WITHIN LIMITS

When we are willing to be what we can be, we open ourselves up to an increased awareness of what we cannot be. We discover our limits.

Few themes are older in literature than that of man's reluctance to accept limits, to be finite. In the Bible, the story of Adam and Eve is the story of man's desire to be more than man, to be like God.[12] In contemporary literature no one has captured the feeling better than Robert Frost in the poem, "The Road Not Taken."[13] As Frost suggests, we are always coming to forks in the road and, forced to choose, we take one road, but forever after we wonder what was down the other road.

Our lives are lived within limits—limited time and space, limited resources, limited capacities, and limits set by others. Each individual experiences his own limits, his own personal frustrations. But being limited does not always lead to frustration. The way we deal with our limitations is one of the keenest tests of our artfulness in living.

There are at least four kinds of limits: (1) limits set by our physical environment; (2) limits set by the social environment; (3) limits found in our capacities; and (4) the limits we set for ourselves.

Of course, we react in different ways when we run into limits. The most common reaction is to feel frustrated and become angry or depressed (anger turned inward). Some pout or cry, while others become physically ill or mentally disturbed. But all of us at times experience limits as supportive and turn to them for security, for definition, and as the very world in which we can work out our possibilities.

A limit is frustrating if it happens to be a barrier between us and a goal we seek. The same limit may be a protection for another person if that barrier keeps others away from his possessions. Some of our worst nightmares have to do with limitlessness—falling forever, time going on and on and on, etc. It is surely significant that we can experience *both* claustrophobia (the fear of being closed in) and agoraphobia (the fear of no enclosure).

What, then, are some of the principles in the art of living within limits?

One principle has been adopted by Alcoholics Anonymous. It is expressed in the prayer, "Lord, give me the patience to accept what cannot be changed, the courage to change what can be changed, and the wisdom to know the difference."

Another principle has to do with realistic expectations. Frustration is not a simple function of barriers. The degree to which we are frustrated is partly a function of the level of aspiration or expectation. We can guarantee for ourselves a life of continual frustration by setting unrealistic goals. It is *not* true that our possibilities are limitless. Every boy in the country *cannot* be president some day. Maybe there is always room at the top, but there is not room for all of us there.

Most important, however, is a refusal to spend one's life vainly kicking against limits or crying in self-pity, and to work with limits as the materials out of which we build a real life, imperfect but exciting and satisfying. This philosophy has been handed down for countless generations in all cultures in myths, legends, proverbs, and literature. The facts of modern psychology can do no more than reinforce this wisdom. Start where you are; use what you have; do what you can with it.

And with this constructive attitude will come also a new appreciation for one-self, a new delight in living. Like spoiled children, many of us not only give up on life and other people because they disappoint us, but we give up on ourselves. When people get married, we ask that they take one another "for better or for worse" and vow to love one another "in sickness and in health." It is precisely this kind of commitment to ourselves that will lead to the richest possible life. Why should we not take ourselves for better or for worse, and why should we not be faithful to ourselves in sickness and in health?

Being within limits is being human. The way we respond to these limits will determine the kind of human being we will be.

BEING WITH OTHERS

Human being is always social being. From birth to death our lives are tied to other lives whose love we need and who need our love. It is one of the ironies of human life that other people constitute the major support of our being and, at the same time, the major threat to our being. We can't live without other people and we often find it so difficult to live with them.

At first, as infants, our being with others is primarily a being dependent on their care. Gradually, however, though remaining dependent, we learn the ways of being with other people that make for the least anxiety and the most satis-faction. We learn the language, the facial expressions, the gestures, and the be-havior that enable us to maintain the cooperative contacts with others without which we could not survive.

The social skills we first learn are, then, to use Maslow's phrase, "deficiency motivated."[14] In other words, we first learn to get people to help us. We need certain people and, if they cooperate with us, we love them.

As we mature, we learn to respond to the needs of others and to feel good about ourselves because we are able to do this. At first, this too is a deficiency need, the need to feel important and worthwhile. We do not cease to need others, but there is a move toward mutuality, the meeting of one another's needs. Most human relationships involve much deficiency–motivated behavior, which is to say, most people act within relationships that have been structured to meet needs.

Since this is so, it is imperative that we learn how to be with people in such a way that our needs for companionship, being loved, belonging, identity, worth, and loving are satisfied. But here we run into one of the many paradoxes of life: we must learn not to need people too much or they will feel so threatened that they will withdraw from us and our needs will go unmet. Kierkegaard put it this way, "We love people who do not need our love because they do not need our love, and we do not love people who need our love because they need our love."[15] The art of being with people requires that we need people, but not too much; that we try to please people, but not too much; that we be a part of our group, yet separate from it.

Perhaps these paradoxes can be understood if we see that being with others is really being with other beings. We are being and others are being and we are trying to be together. Social being is complex because there are three kinds of being at once. We are being with others; other are being with us; and they and we are being together. Good relationships require that we be true to ourselves, accepting of others, and aware of what is going on between us.

In the long run, we cannot afford to be other than ourselves with significant others. If the price of someone's love is that we betray ourselves, the price is too high. We pay for this self-betrayal with psychosomatic symptoms, depression and irritability, or loss of genuine feeling. We do not need to pay such a price, but most people who do so mistakenly think that they must and they feel that, if the alternative is to be alone, there just isn't any other way for them. But it is only when we can risk losing a relationship that we can dare to be ourselves in it. We are not suggesting a daily ultimatum to the effect that we can live perfectly well without this or that particular person. Rather we are saying that we must learn to be alone if we are to have the courage to be ourselves with those who love us.

Neither, however, is a relationship satisfying if it requires that the other not be himself. When others are not themselves with us, they are really not with us and we are actually alone.

But a real relationship is not simply the summation of our being ourselves and others being themselves; it is something which happens, as Buber says, "between man and man."[16] And the only satisfying relationships come into being between one man and another when two face one another as "I and Thou," another of Buber's terms.[17] In the I-Thou relationship, each affirms himself and each speaks to and listens to the other.

As pointed out in chapter 11, there are techniques by which people can be manipulated. Perhaps many of our relationships will be predominantly deficiency-motivated and will require the effective use of these social skills. But, as we move toward intimacy, to the kind of closeness in which we do not so much meet needs as enjoy the self-expression of each other, we will want to give up our anxious games and mutual exploitation.

BEING FREE OR FREELY BEING

No adjective seems more fitting for describing our ideal of being than the word "free." Its meaning is best felt when we contrast it with ideas like rigid, constricted, bound, or compulsive. To be free is a dream that is shared by people in all ages and all places, and it is an ideal especially dear to those who are dedicated to the worth of the individual.

Psychologically speaking, however, it must be said that real freedom has not so much to do with external conditions as with internal conditions. We would not deny the reality of political and economic tyrannies which are capable of making it so hard for people to be free. We are only saying that there is a freedom which no man can give to another, and which no man can take from another. And, while we work for greater freedom in the social order, we do not want to neglect even more important freedoms.

Being free is, on the one hand, an insight and, on the other, it is an achievement.

Jesus said, "Ye shall know the truth and the truth shall make you free."[18] Freud, in his way, said much the same thing: discover the truth hidden in your unconscious and you will be free of neurosis. What we mean, however, is the change that takes place in us when we know, deep within ourselves, that we *are* free—free to know ourselves, free to be ourselves. Once we know this, not intellectually but emotionally, it becomes clear that freedom is not a right but a responsibility; not something we ask of another, but something we do ourselves. To be free is to act freely.

Often, however, it is not enough to see that one is free, important as this is. If one is to act freely he must have some strength and skill. In other words, freedom is also an achievement. This is the kind of freedom seen in, for example, the smoothness of the disciplined violinist, the freedom of playing easily because one has built habits that support the playing. Being free also takes practice or habit formation, such as the practice of being alone, of thinking for oneself, of carrying through on decisions, etc.

Whether from insight or achievement or both, being free is the basis of our most effective behavior. In Eastern philosophy, much is said about being unencumbered and unattached, and of "effortless effort." Our own expressions such as "hanging loose" and "sitting light in the saddle" seem to be getting at much the same thing. The idea is that to try too hard is to stifle vital processes, to be too serious is to lose perspective, to try to hang onto life is to have it slip through one's fingers.

Being free is to move with the rhythm one finds in himself, to march to the cadence of one's own drummer. It is to be committed to that which takes hold of one, to respond to one's own visions.

Finally, being free is being unafraid—not that fear is absent but that fear does not control behavior. What a grand vision of being it is, to walk through life with a quiet, confident step, choosing one's own directions, speaking the truth as one sees it, in tune with the nature within and without, loving and being loved, treating success and failure alike.

QUESTIONS FOR STUDY AND CLASS DISCUSSION

1. Our society treats attempted suicide as an illness. Can you find reasons for this point of view?

2. Can you see the relationship between suicide and achieving far below one's potential?

3. Can we be anything we want to be?

4. Does it make any difference what one believes? Why should we tamper with a person's beliefs?

5. What are the psychological implications of a belief in life after death?

6. How much choice do we have about what we will be?

7. Should we really accept all of ourselves, or should we reject some parts of ourselves as bad or undesirable?

8. Is it possible to socialize our children without training them to reject some of themselves?

9. What limits on free being do you think are necessary? How do you justify any limits imposed from without?

10. How are need and love related?

SUGGESTIONS FOR FURTHER READING

Allport, Gordon. *Becoming.* New Haven, Conn.: Yale University Press, 1955.

Fromm, Erich. *Man for Himself.* New York: Holt, Rinehart and Winston, 1947.

Kurtz, Paul, ed. *Moral Problems in Contemporary Society.* Englewood Cliffs, N.J.: Prentice-Hall, 1969.

Rogers, Carl R. *On Becoming a Person.* Boston: Houghton Mifflin Co., 1961.

Scheibe, Karl E. *Beliefs and Values.* New York: Holt, Rinehart and Winston, 1970.

PART V
THE GROWING EDGES
OF PSYCHOLOGY

An introductory text emphasizes the older, more classical knowledge in the field at the expense of the newer, less settled. This is advisable if one is to get a feel for the field as it has developed.

But an introductory text can also point out areas in which important current work is being done which is likely to shape the field for the future. To do this an author must exercise his judgment with respect to material which is still controversial and has not yet been assimilated into the main body of the discipline.

In this last part of the book we briefly note seven areas that appear to the author as growing edges of psychology.

Ethology, the study of the characteristic behavior of a species, is a relatively new and vital academic area that raises questions which psychologists cannot ignore. In particular, we look at the work of Konrad Lorenz.

Physical Control of the Mind draws on the work of Jose M. R. Delgado, who pioneered in the implanting of electrodes in the brains of cats, monkeys, and men.

Principles of Behavior Modification introduces a body of knowledge about techniques by which behavior may be modified through the manipulation of environmental factors.

Altered States of Consciousness summarizes the new interest in cognitive changes associated with drugs, meditation, and hypnotism. Special attention is given to studies relating EEG alpha waves with the meditation states.

Sensitivity Training, a new and controversial area of study is illustrated by Esalen.

Toward a Science of the Person shows how one thoughtful psychologist, Carl Rogers, feels about the possibilities of developing a science that does justice to the complexity of persons.

General System Theory describes the theoretical underpinnings for a new way of conceptualizing not only man and his behavior but all observable phenomena. Our material is taken from the work of Ludwig von Bertalanffy.

13

SEVEN CURRENT TRENDS
IN THE BEHAVIORAL SCIENCES

I. ETHOLOGY

Three recent books focusing attention on the biological basis for behavior typify a renewed interest in what used to be called instincts.

As an explanation of behavior, "instinct" fell into disfavor largely due to an indiscriminate use which ascribed just about every form of observable behavior to some separate instinct.

But Ardrey's *The Territorial Imperative,* Morris's *The Naked Ape,* and

Lorenz's *On Aggression* remind us that instinct theory is not dead and stimulate us to take another look at what is now called species-specific characteristics.

Ethology, which literally means the science of character, concerns itself with descriptions of the traits which characterize a species. The work of a careful researcher such as Konrad Lorenz is a brilliant example of the scientific method at its best, though most of his data is collected by the field study method rather than the experimental method (see chapter 1 for discussions of these methods).

The most famous study reported by ethologists has to do with a phenomenon called *imprinting.* It was Konrad Lorenz of Austria who first brought widespread attention to this phenomenon in 1935 and who gave it the name imprinting.[1] Eckhard Hess has done detailed experimental studies of imprinting in the United States. The facts about imprinting are simple, but the implications are far-reaching. It had long been known that baby ducks tend to follow their mothers in train-like fashion. Lorenz found that this is not an instinct but an innate tendency to become attached to anything that moves around the newly-hatched ducks during a critical period of a few hours. If nothing moves around them during this time, they become attached to nothing. If the experimenter, or a puppy, or a box on a string moves near them during this critical period, they became attached to this moving object and followed it. Usually, of course, it is the mother duck. Lorenz called this tendency to become attached to a moving object *imprinting,* and he called the object a *releaser,* since it triggered or released the behavior.

Another famous ethological study was that of Tinbergen's description of the mating behavior of the stickleback fish in 1942. He found, for example, that it is the red coloring on the male stickleback's abdomen that attracts the female during the mating season. A male without this coloring does not attract; a red wooden model fish or even a red toy truck will attract. In order for the female who has been lured into the nest to lay her eggs she must be prodded at the base of her tail. The male stickleback usually does the prodding, but it may be done by the experimenter with a glass rod. Tinbergen concluded that the innate sexual behavior of the stickleback is released by very specific sign stimuli, such as the color red or a hard prod.[2]

The work of ethologists has tremendous implications for psychological theory, especially in the area of learning and development. Advanced students in psychology must come to grips with these implications. But the introductory student will be more excited by the less precise but more relevant research into the possible genetic basis for violence and war in man. It is in this connection that Ardrey's *The Territorial Imperative* and Lorenz's *On Aggression* are claiming wide attention.

It is Lorenz's contention that intra-species aggressive behavior has been carefully and intricately controlled in the process of evolutionary development. This had to be if the species was to survive. The most effective inhibitions against intra-species aggression may be seen in animals which are armed with the means to seriously damage one another, as in wolves for example. Those species not capable of great damage to one another have not developed innate inhibitions against intra-species violence.

Man does not come with sharp teeth or claws and so carries no biologically based inhibitions against intra-species violence. Man's invention of weapons of violence necessitates that the same mental ability utilized for inventing weapons shall be used for setting up social inhibitions against intra-species aggression. So far man has not done well in this area, but he must if the human species is to survive.[3]

Suggestions for Further Reading

Ardrey, Robert. *The Territorial Imperative.* New York: Dell Publishing Co., 1966, 1971.

Handler, Philip. *Biology and the Future of Man.* New York: Oxford University Press, 1970.

Hess, Eckhard H. "Ethology," in *New Directions in Psychology.* New York: Holt, Rinehart and Winston, 1962.

Lorenz, Konrad. *On Aggression.* New York: Bantam Books, 1966, 1967.

Morris, Desmond. *The Naked Ape.* New York: McGraw–Hill Book Co., 1967.

II. PHYSICAL CONTROL OF THE MIND

It is painfully true that we as yet know very little about how the mind works (see remarks quoted from William James, p. 29). But some things we do know, and one of them is that there is an unquestionable relationship between the brain and observed behavior as well as conscious states reported or inferred.

It may seem unnecessary to say it, but without a brain there is nothing of man: no life, no behavior, no thought. The control center for thought and behavior is not in the bowels, as ancient people said, nor in the heart, as was more recently thought, but in the brain. This, it is safe to say, we know.

Our task, then, is to discover *how* the brain works. One line of research has been the direct physical stimulation of the brain and nervous system. What have we learned and what are we learning from these studies?

Delgado, who is in the forefront of this movement, summarizes what we have learned:[4]

Table 1

Experimental Facts	*Implications*
Frog muscle contracted when stimulated by electricity (Volta, 1800; Galvani, 1791; Dubois-Reymond, 1848).	Electrical stimuli under man's control can initiate and modify neural processes.

Table 1 (cont)

Experimental Facts	*Implications*
Electrical stimulation of the brain in anesthetized dog evoked localized body and limb movements (Fritsch and Hitzig, 1870).	The brain is excitable. Electrical stimulation of the cerebral cortex can produce movement.
Stimulation of the diencephalon in unanesthetized cats evoked well-organized motor effects and emotional reactions (Hess, 1932).	Motor and emotional manifestations may be evoked by electrical stimulation of the brain in awake animals.
In single animals, learning, conditioning, instrumental responses, pain, and pleasure have been evoked or inhibited by electrical stimulation of the brain in rats, cats, and monkeys (Delgado et al., 1954; Olds and Milner, 1954).	Psychological phenomena may be controlled by electrical stimulation of specific areas of the brain.
In colonies of cats and monkeys, aggression, dominance, mounting, and other social interactions have been evoked, modified, or inhibited by radio stimulation of specific cerebral areas (Delgado, 1955, 1964).	Social behavior may be controlled by radio stimulation of specific areas of the brain.
In patients, brain stimulation during surgical interventions or with electrodes implanted for days or months has blocked the thinking process, inhibited speech and movement, or in other cases has evoked pleasure, laughter, friendliness, verbal output, hostility, fear, hallucinations, and memories (Delgado et al., 1952, 1968; Penfield and Jasper, 1954).	Human mental functions may be influenced by electrical stimulation of specific areas of the brain.

To recapitulate, there is ample evidence that the nervous system, including the brain, can be activated or inhibited by direct electrical stimulation. This electrical stimulation results in a wide range of behavior including motor movements, perceptions, emotional reactions, well-organized behavior such as social interactions, and the experience of pain and pleasure.

One of Delgado's experiments will illustrate his methods and suggest some of the implications of this approach. We quote from a description of a monkey in which electrodes had been implanted in a part of the brain called the caudate nucleus.

The old dream of an individual overpowering the strength of a dictator by remote control has been fulfilled, at least in our monkey colonies, by a combination of neurosurgery and electronics, demonstrating the possibility of intraspecies instrumental manipulation of hierarchical organization. . . . A monkey named Ali, who was the powerful and ill-tempered chief of a colony, often expressed his hotility symbolically by biting his hand or by threatening other members of the group. Radio stimulation in Ali's caudate nucleus blocked his usual aggressiveness so effectively that the animal could be caught inside the cage without danger or difficulty. During stimulation he might walk a few steps, but he never attempted to attack another animal. Then a lever was attached to the cage wall, and if it was pressed it automatically triggered a five seconds' radio stimulation to Ali. From time to time some of the submissive monkeys touched the lever, which was located close to the feeding tray, triggering the stimulation to Ali. A female monkey named Elsa soon discovered that Ali's aggressiveness could be inhibited by pressing the lever, and when Ali threatened her, it was repeatedly observed that Eli responded by lever pressing. Her attitude of looking straight at the boss was highly significant because a submissive monkey would not dare to do so, for fear of immediate retaliation. The total number of Ali's aggressive acts diminished on the days when the lever was available, and although Elsa did not become the dominant animal, she was responsible for blocking many attacks against herself and for maintaining a peaceful coexistence within the whole colony.[5]

In other experiments Delgado was able to both excite and inhibit a wide variety of behavior in cats, bulls, and monkeys.

More recently, implantation of electrodes in human brains is being used in an effort to treat such ailments as epilepsy, Parkinson's disease, narcolepsy, and schizophrenia. Some favorable results are being obtained, and, as a by-product, many patients are giving themselves pleasure through pressing the button that triggers the electrical stimulation to the selected area of the brain.

Delgado states the hypotheses that underlie his work:[6]

1. There are basic mechanisms in the brain responsible for all mental activities, including perceptions, emotions, abstract thought, social relations, and the most refined artistic creations.
2. These mechanisms may be detected, analyzed, influenced, and sometime substituted for by means of physical and chemical technology.
3. Predictable behavioral and mental responses may be induced by direct manipulation of the brain.
4. We can substitute intelligent and purposeful determination of neuronal functions for blind, automatic responses.

Some control of the mind through direct electrical stimulation of the brain is definitely possible. The extent of possible control is still unknown. However, the work already done opens the door for more far-reaching control of the mind and raises questions of the greatest theoretical and practical importance.

Suggestions for Further Reading

Delgado, Jose M. R. *Physical Control of the Mind,* New York: Harper & Row, 1969.

London, Perry. *Behavior Control.* New York: Harper & Row, 1969.

Olds, James. "Pleasure Centers in the Brain." *Scientific American,* October 1956.

Penfield, W., and Jasper, H. *Epilepsy and the Functional Anatomy of the Human Brain.* Boston: Little, Brown and Co., 1954.

Woolridge, Dean E. *The Machinery of the Brain.* New York: McGraw-Hill Book Co., 1963.

II. BEHAVIOR MODIFICATION

The reader will recall our discussion of John Watson and the behaviorist school of psychology in chapter 1, the behavioristically oriented studies in chapter 8, and the discussion of behavioral therapy in chapter 10. Why, then do we bring up behavior modification in this section on the growing edges of psychology?

While a behavioristic approach in psychology goes back to the turn of the century and the basic principles of classical and instrumental conditioning were formulated by Pavlov and Thorndike, there is a current revival that merits new attention. To speak of behavior modification today is to point to the application of old principles to new problems and to note refinements of these principles as a result of the more precise work of B. F. Skinner.

Behavior modification is now being used with autistic children, patients in mental hospitals, children in classrooms, parent-child relationships, and in general psychological counseling. Advocates of this approach are enthusiastic about its possibilities, and critics raise questions either about the adequacy of the approach or the ethics of using it. However these questions are answered, the principles of behavior modification need to be understood by anyone interested in psychology today.

The major principles on which behavior modification rests are deceptively simple. They may be summarized as follows:

1. Behavior is primarily a function of stimuli.
2. Some behavior, usually of a reflexive type, may be consistently elicited by certain stimuli. This behavior is called "respondent."
3. When some neutral stimulus is consistently associated with a stimulus which elicits a response, the neutral stimulus usually comes to elicit that response. This is called classical or Pavlovian conditioning.
4. Some behavior is emitted in response to stimulus situations and increases or decreases in frequency depending on the *consequences* of the behavior. This behavior is called "operant."

5. Operant behavior may be influenced by controlling the consequences that follow it. There are four basic reinforcement patterns:
   a. Giving positive reinforcement (increases frequency of responses)
   b. Withholding positive reinforcement (decreases frequency of responses)
   c. Giving negative reinforcement (decreases frequency of responses)
   d. Withholding negative reinforcement (increases frequency of responses)

There are, of course, many more specific variables that must be understood and utilized if one is to be effective in using behavior modification techniques. But the key ideas are found in the above five principles.

By far the majority of behavior modification work is in the area of operant behavior. Two examples will illustrate how this is done.

In one study, in an effort to teach four-year-olds how to read, it was found that with praise alone the children became bored and restless after 15 to 20 minutes and asked to leave. At this point

> tangible rewards, consisting of candy treats, trinkets, and tokens that could be exchanged for attractive toys, were introduced. Under the influence of the positive reinforcers, made conditional upon reading achievements, the children's limited attention span suddenly expanded, and they not only worked enthusiastically at the reading tasks for 45 minutes, but participated actively in additional sessions.[7]

Withholding reinforcement in order to alter behavior has been used successfully in the classroom. Let us say that John is disrupting the class with his misbehavior. Observation reveals that every time he misbehaves he gets scolded by the teacher. It is hypothesized that this scolding is reinforcing the misbehavior and the teacher is instructed to ignore John's disruptive acts. There is a dramatic decrease in the misbehavior. To test the hypothesis further, the teacher is instructed to again scold every disruptive act by John. John's misbehavior increase to the original level. Convinced that the scolding really is the reinforcing agent, the teacher and the researcher agree that ignoring John's misbehavior will effectively reduce its frequency.

Both of these examples are extracted from more complicated programs of behavior modification. An extensive literature is now available and interested students will want to consult it.

Suggestions for Further Reading

Ayllon, T., and Azrin, N. *The Token Economy; A Motivational System of Therapy and Rehabilitation.* New York: Appleton-Century-Crofts, 1968.

Bandura, Albert. *Principles of Behavior Modification.* New York: Holt, Rine-Hart, and Winston, 1969.

Buckley, N. K., and Walker, H. M. *Modifying Classroom Behavior.* Illinois: Research Press, 1970.

Rogers, C. R., and Skinner, B. F. "Some Issues Concerning the Control of Human Behavior." *Science*, 1956, pp. 1057–66.

Wenrich, W. W. *A Primer of Behavior Modification.* Belmont, Calif. Brooks/Cole Publishing Co., 1970.

IV. ALTERED STATES OF CONSCIOUSNESS

In chapter 1 we noted that modern psychology began with Wundt's efforts to study the structure of the mind through observing various states of consciousness. With the shift in emphasis toward organismic function and behavior, the detailed work of the structuralists (as Wundt's followers were called) ceased to interest psychologists.

In the last few years, however, we are seeing a renewed interest in states of consciousness. This time the goal is not to learn about the structure of the mind. States of consciousness, themselves, are considered sufficiently interesting for study.

Among the states of consciousness being studied are relatively old ones such as hypnotic states and dream states as well as the newer drug-induced states and so-called meditation states similar to those achieved in Yoga and Zen.

The reader will remember that Wundt used introspection as the major tool for research into states of consciousness. The newer psychophysics also utilizes introspection, but modern researchers have been able to introduce several objective tools into their studies of subjective. One example is the use of REMs (rapid eye movements) as an indication that people are dreaming. Most dramatic has been the use of EEGs (electroencephalographs or brain wave graphs).

In his book, *Altered States of Consciousness*, Charles Tart reviews the whole spectrum of conscious states as we know them. Most of the studies rely largely on the verbal reports of subjects (introspection), but in the last section of his book he presents three studies based on the use of EEGs which shed important light on the psychophysiology of some altered states of consciousness.

The first is by Kassamatsu and Hirai[8] and is an electroencephalographic study of Zen meditation. These researchers report several interesting findings. First, they found that the Zen meditation state produces a distinct EEG pattern which can be distinguished from sleep, hypnotic states, and ordinary wakefulness. Zen meditation produces changes in four stages: (1) a slight change which is characterized by the appearance of alpha waves in spite of opened eyes (2) the increase in amplitude of persistent alpha waves (3) the decrease of alpha frequency (4) the appearance of the rhythmical theta train, which is the final change of EEG during Zen meditation but does not always occur.

Secondly, Kasamatsu and Hirai found this distinct pattern to correlate with years of experience in Zen meditation. And, thirdly, they found that during Zen meditation there is a different EEG response to a clicking sound. In ordinary states, as the clicking sound is repeated the EEG response is less and less, indicating habituation. In the Zen meditation state no such habituation occurs.

Following Kasamatsu and Hirai's study, Tart presents Anand, Chhina, and Singh's electroencephalographic studies of yogis.[9] They found much the same results as in the studies of Zen. Again there was the prominent alpha activity and the lack of habituation to external stimuli.

In view of the finding that both Zen and Yoga meditation show pronounced alpha activity, the study of Kamiya[10] (the third of the three studies reported by Tart) is especially interesting.

Kamiya did two things: first he demonstrated that subjects could be taught to distinguish states in which the alpha rhythm was present from states in which it was not; and, more exciting, he was able to train (condition) subjects to produce more alpha activity or to suppress it.

It is intriguing to find that Kamiya's subjects found the high alpha state very pleasurable, and the verbal reports of the subjects are amazingly similar to the reports of subjects in Zen and Yoga meditation.

From Kamiya's work we are tempted to conclude that Zen and Yoga training are essentially methods for increasing the alpha activity of the brain. But one thing is certain; now that EEGs are being correlated with introspection, the study of states of consciousness has entered a new phase.

Suggestions for Further Reading

Boisen, Anton. *The Exploration of the Inner World.* New York: Harper and Row, 1952.

Castaneda, Carlos. *The Teachings of Don Juan: A Yaqui Way of Knowledge.* New York: Ballantine Books, 1968.

Huxley, Aldous. *The Doors of Perception.* New York: Harper & Row, 1954.

King, C. *The States of Human Consciousness.* New Hyde Park, N.Y.: University Books, 1963.

Tart, Charles T., ed. *Altered States of Consciousness.* New York: John Wiley & Sons, 1969.

V. SENSITIVITY TRAINING

The term "sensitivity training" is actually not so new. It was first used by the National Training Laboratory in connection with its work in T-groups (training groups) and pointed to an emphasis on the here and now in the training approach.[11] Recently, however, sensitivity training has come to mean many different things and much controversy and a great deal of emotion have surrounded it.

The name Esalen is most widely associated with the newer methods of sensitivity training. Started in 1962 and located in Big Sur, Esalen has been the center of a movement that has spread through the psychological community. Alan Watts, Fritz Perls, Virginia Satir, William Schutz, and Ida Rolf are among those who typify the newer sensitivity training.

The major thrust of this movement is the awakening of the senses and feelings so that oneself, other people, and the world may be experienced more fully and more directly. This grows out of a theory that Westerners in general, and Americans in particular, have developed their rational, analytic powers at the expense of the more intuitive, nonrational sensibilities.

Though the various people associated with this movement do not agree too well among themselves and, in fact, relish the lack of agreement, there are threads which run through all their work.

One thread is the emphasis on the here and now, and this is perhaps the most significant thread tying the newer sensitivity movement to the older T-groups. Persons in the sensitivity (or encounter) groups are urged to stay in the room. If something in the past is bothering one, he is urged to talk about how he is now bothered rather than the past event. If one reports a dream, as in a Perls dream workshop, the dream must be told in the present tense: "I am in a big house, etc."[12]

A second thread is the primacy of feelings over ideas. A favorite expression is "gut-level feelings." Participants are urged not to go on "head trips." Explanations are devalued in favor of simply accepting and owning one's feelings and behavior. Once it is clear to a person *what* he is doing, he then may be asked how he feels about it. Does he like it? Is he comfortable with it? If not, what is he going to do about it?

The emphasis on feelings leads to the senses and to the body, for emotions are felt in the body, not in the brain. A person may be asked, "Where do you feel that?" or "What does your body want to do?" This has led to interest in nonverbal communication and body-language. People are made aware of what they are saying with their body posture, with their facial expression, with their tone of voice. Some workshops aim at getting people in touch with each other through actual touching.

The most dramatic work with the body is being done by Ida Rolf. Her approach is properly called structural integration, but more frequently one will hear it called Rolfing. Rolf and those whom she has trained manipulate or massage the body in an effort to get the person back in shape by getting his body in shape. For Rolf believes that emotional difficulties lead to a misshapen body and a misshapen body leads to emotional difficulties. One of her axioms is that body and character form a unity.[13]

Esalen is frankly experimental. Michael Murphy, its founder, says:[14]

> It is hard for us at Esalen to assess our impact on the scientific com-
> munity. We are aware that Esalen is controversial. While many peo-
> ple respect what we are doing, and some might agree with Abraham
> Maslow, who called Esalen "in *potential*, the most important educa-
> tional institution in the world," many others consider us little more
> than kooks and cultists.

> There are risks in an organization like Esalen, but we prefer risks to
> the status quo. Some of our approaches will hold up with passage of
> time, others will be discarded as foolish or useless. But no approach
> is too far out to be tried here. We intend to be on the cutting edge.

Murphy's self-analysis may be applied to the sensitivity movement as a whole.
More time must elapse before its permanent contributions can be identified.

Suggestions for Further Reading

Golembiewski, Robert T., and Blumberg, Arthur. *Sensitivity Training and the
   Laboratory Approach.* Itasca, Ill.: F. E. Peacock Publishers, 1970.
Gunther, Bernard. *Sense Relaxation: Below Your Mind.* New York: Collier
   Books, 1968.
Keen, Sam. *To a Dancing God.* New York: Harper & Row, Publishers, 1970.
Perls, Frederick S. *Gestalt Therapy Verbatim.* Lafayette, Calif.: Real People
   Press, 1969.
Murphy, Michael. "Esalen: Where its At," in *Readings in Psychology Today.*
   Del Mar, Calif.: CRM Books, 1969.

VI. TOWARD A SCIENCE OF THE PERSON

Since publishing *Counseling and Psychotherapy*, in 1942, Carl Rogers has been
a significant influence both in the field of psychotherapy and in the field of personality theory. His work has combined to a rare degree warm sensitivity to persons with a rigorous commitment to science.

Chapter 2 noted that some psychologists would argue that we can study persons, in all their complexity, scientifically. Rogers is one who passionately believes this, and in a chapter written in 1964, entitled "Toward a Science of
Persons," he argues persuasively for a view of science that is congenial to the
study of persons.[15]

First he points out that there are three ways of knowing: subjective knowing,
objective knowing, and interpersonal knowing. It is his opinion that "even the
most rigorous science has its origin in the subjective mode of knowing." As for

objective knowing, which is based on an external frame of reference, he points out that while the hypotheses are checked by externally observable operations, they are also checked with a trusted reference group. Interpersonal knowing has to do with knowing what another person thinks or feels, and this is best done with empathic understanding and interpersonal skill.

Rogers then suggests that a mature psychological science will make use of each of these ways of knowing and of all three appropriately interwoven.

> Whatever approximations to the truth we are able to achieve in the behavioral sciences will not come automatically through following one approach to knowledge. There is no such thing as a "scientific methodology" which will see us safely through. . . (and) it is of the utmost importance to be entirely clear as to the mode we are using at any particular moment or in any particular enterprise. . .[16]

The adoption of this approach, which Rogers calls a phenomenological-existential trend, will, he thinks, have the following consequences:

1. A more inclusive science—"the trend of which I am speaking will attempt to face up to *all* of the realities in the psychological realm."
2. New classes of variables explored. Psychology will not shy away from using such variables as meaning, the self, and other variables found in psychotherapeutic interaction.
3. A new mode in psychological theories—"there will be more concern with process, or as Bridgeman (1959) says, with 'doings or happenings,' rather than with 'static elements' and abstractions."

Rogers then addresses himself to two issues, and rather than attempt to paraphrase him, we shall let his own words speak for him:

> *Science and the "Unreal."* I should like to turn for a moment to the uneasiness which such thinking creates in the minds of many psychologists and perhaps in the minds of other scientists as well . . . What is to become of psychology if it turns its attention to such ephemeral, vague wisps of fog as experiencing, the self, becoming? What has happened to the solidity of a science which was built on a tangible stimulus, an observable response, or a visible reward? To such uneasy ones, I would like to point out the course of the physical sciences . . .
>
> It seems quite clear that most of the recent striking advances in these sciences have come about, not through following the channel of logical positivism and operationism—though their continuing contributions cannot be denied—but through the fantastic imaginings of experienced, insightful, thoughtful men . . .
>
> If I may draw a cautious conclusion from this for the field of psychology, it would be this: There is no special virtue attached to the

policy of limiting our theories to observable behaviors . . . A theory that postulates relationships between inner subjective phenomena not directly measurable may, like theories regarding non-Euclidean space, prove to be more valuable in advancing our knowledge than theories regarding observable behavior.

The Philosophical View of Man. There is one other consequence of this phenomenological-existential view in psychology. It caries with it a new philosophical underpinning for psychological science, which is, I believe, more fruitful and more human than the presently held philosophies.

Each current in psychology has its own implicit philosophy of man. Though not often stated implicitly, these philosophies exert their influence in many significant and subtle ways. For the behaviorist, man is a machine, a complicated but nonetheless understandable machine, which we can learn to manipulate with greater and greater skill until he thinks the thought, moves in the directions, and behaves in the ways selected for him. For the Freudian, man is an irrational being, irrevocably in the grip of his past and the product of that past, his unconscious.

It is not necessary to deny that there is truth in each of these formulations in order to recognize that there is another perspective. From the existential perspective, from within the phenomenological internal frame of reference, man does not simply have the characteristics of a machine; he is not simply a being in the grip of unconscious motives; he is a person in the process of creating himself, a person who creates meaning in life, a person who embodies a dimension of subjective freedom.

It is my judgment, as I try to understand the vigorous thrust of this phenomenological-existential movement in a variety of other fields, as well as in psychology, that it represents a new philosophical emphasis. Here is the voice of subjective man speaking up loudly for himself. Man has long felt himself to be but a puppet in life—molded by economic forces, by unconscious forces, by environmental forces. He has been enslaved by persons, by institutions, by the theories of psychological science. But he is firmly setting forth a new declaration of independence. He is discarding the alibis of *un*freedom. He is *choosing* himself, endeavoring, in a most difficult and often tragic world, to *become* himself—not a puppet, not a slave, not a machine, but his own unique individual self. The view I have been describing in psychology has room for this philosophy of man.

Suggestions for Further Reading

Allport, Gordon W. *The Person in Psychology.* Boston: Beacon Press, 1968.
Bakan, David. *On Method: Toward a Reconstruction of Psychological Investigation.* San Francisco: Jossey-Bass, 1968.

Jourard, Sidney. *Disclosing Man to Himself.* Princeton, N.J.: D. Van Nostrand Co., 1968.

Rogers, Carl R. *On Becoming a Person.* Boston: Houghton Mifflin Co., 1961

Ruitenbeek, Hendrik N., ed. *Varieties of Personality Theory.* New York: E. P. Dutton and Co., 1964.

VII. GENERAL SYSTEM THEORY

If there be a third revolution (i.e., after psychoanalytic and behavioristic), it is in the development of a general theory.[17]

In the history of psychology, many different models have been used in the effort to conceptualize man and his behavior. The *tabula rasa* (blank tablet), the machine, the electrical circuit, and the hydraulic system come immediately to mind. In 1964, the dean of personality psychologists, Gordon Allport, said, "I am most hopeful that systems theory, properly developed, may yield the comprehensive solution we seek."[18]

The name most closely associated with the development of systems theory is that of Ludwig von Bertalanffy, who is credited with originating the approach in 1947. We shall use his 1968 book, *General System Theory,* as the basis for our confrontation with this approach.

The systems approach differs most markedly from the commonly used analytic approach in the way it treats causality. Ever since Aristotle, Western thought has used a linear approach in which antecedent events were seen as causes of succeeding events. The reader will remember how this led to hypotheses about a first cause, a concept adaptable to certain theological ideas about God as creator or prime mover.

Using this linear approach, however, increasingly led to a deterministic position which excluded such ideas as purpose, freedom, organization and other wholistic concepts favored by so-called humanistic psychologists.

Von Bertalanffy points out that the older analytic approach is valid when two conditions are present: (1) interactions between parts are non-existent or weak enough to be neglected for certain research purposes; and (2) the relations describing the behavior of parts must be linear. He then notes that these conditions are not met in *systems.*

The term *system* refers to organizations in which the resulting functions depend on a complex interaction of parts. These parts working together "cause" events to happen, but the causality here is quite different from the old linear cause and effect relationship.

There are basically two kinds of systems: the closed system, as a machine; and the open system, as in organisms. The open system differs from the closed system in that it is able to exchange elements with the environment and grow as a result.

But systems can also be distinguished in terms of whether they are goal-directed (teleological) or not. Most machines are not goal-directed: they perform operations for which they were designed but they cannot be assigned a goal in terms of which they adjust their operations. So-called servomechanisms, however, are closed systems which are goal-directed. By making use of feed-back information they can adjust their operations so that the goal is reached or maintained. A thermostatically controlled temperature system is an example of such a system. Open systems, such as organisms, are goal-directed.

Von Bertalanffy states two other important principles that characterize open systems.

One is the *principle of equifinality*, first formulated by the biologist Driesch. To quote from von Bertalanffy:

> In any closed system, the final state is unequivocally determined by the initial conditions: e.g., the motion in a planetary system where the positions of the planets at a time t are unequivocally determined by their positions at a time t_o. Or in a chemical equilibrium, the final concentrations of the reactions naturally depend on the initial concentrations. If either the initial condition or the process is altered, the final state will be changed. This is not so in open systems. Here, the same final state may be reached from different initial conditions and in different ways. This is what is called equifinality, and it has a significant meaning for the phenomena of biological regulation.[19]

The second principle has to do with what von Bertalanffy calls the problem of "immense" numbers. Systems, as we noted, involve interactions among many factors. In a strictly mechanistic model, the number of possible interactions between a given number of factors is expressed mathematically as $2^{N(N-1)}$. If there are only twenty factors, the number of possible connections exceeds the estimated number of atoms in the universe. Thus it seems impossible to account for the self-restoring tendencies of organisms in mechanistic terms. There must be some directional quality in open-system processes which acts differently from the chance happenings postulated by a mechanistic model.[20]

Applying his ideas to psychology, von Bertalanffy concludes that if we are to do justice to the complexities of human behavior we must utilize the principles found operating in open systems rather than the principles found in machines and closed systems.

Suggestions for Further Reading

Gray, W., Duhl, F. J., and Ruzzo, N. D., eds., *General Systems Theory and Psychiatry*. Boston: Little, Brown, & Co., 1969.

Buckley, Walter, ed., *Modern Systems Research for the Behavioral Scientist*. Chicago: Aldine Pub. Co., 1968.

Koestler, Arthur. *The Ghost in the Machine.* New York: Macmillan Co., 1967.
von Bertalanffy, Ludwig. *Robots, Men and Minds.* New York: George Braziller, 1966.
—— *General System Theory.* New York: George Braziller, 1968.

NOTES

NOTES TO PART I AND CHAPTER 1

1. Will Durant, *Our Oriental Heritage* (New York: Simon and Schuster, 1954), pp. 195, 196. Used by permission of the publisher.

2. Isaiah Berlin, *The Hedgehog and the Fox*, New York: The New American Library, 1957, p. 1.

3. Edwin G. Boring, *History, Psychology, and Science* New York: John Wiley & Sons, 1963), p. 93. Used by permission of the publisher.

4. Nicholas H. Charney, *Psychology Today* 2, no. 2 (July 1968): 33.

5. Ibid., p. 33.

6. John Dollard, et al., *Frustration and Aggression* (New Haven: Yale University Press, 1939).

7. Boring, *History, Psychology, and Science*, p. 130.

8. Ibid., p. 166.

9. Fred S. Keller, *The Definition of Psychology* (New York: Appleton-Century-Crofts, 1937).

10. Boring, *History, Psychology, and Science*, p. 132ff. Used by permission of John Wiley & Sons.

11. Ernest Jones, *The Life and Work of Sigmund Freud*, abridged edition by Lionel Trilling and Steven Marcus (Garden City: Anchor Books, Doubleday & Company, 1963), pp. 26–37.

12. Keller, *The Definition of Psychology*, p. 237.

13. Ibid., p. 56.

14. Boring, *History, Psychology, & Science*, p. 176.

15. Keller, *The Definition of Psychology*, pp. 89, 90.

16. Edna Heidbreder, *Seven Psychologies* (New York: Appleton-Century-Crofts, 1933). p. 360.

17. S. Ross and R. F. Lockman, *A Career in Psychology* (Washington D.C.: American Psychological Association, 1963).

NOTES TO PART II AND CHAPTER 2

1. Goethe (Taken from Wilhelm Reich, *Selected Writings* (New York: Farrar, Straus and Giroux; 1960), p. 17.)

2. Gordon Allport, *The Person in Psychology* (Boston: Beacon Press, 1968), p. 23.

3. Harry K. Wells, *Ivan P. Pavlov: Toward a Scientific Psychology and Psychiatry* (New York: International Publishers, 1956), p. 67.

4. William James, *Psychology: The Briefer Course* New York: Harper Torchbooks, 1961), p. 335. Used by permission of Harper Torchbooks.

5. Sidney M. Jourard, *Disclosing Man to Himself* (Princeton: D. Van Nostrand, 1968), p. 10. Used by permission of Van Nostrand Reinhold Company.

6. Gertrude Ezorsky, "Wishing Won't—But Wanting Will," in Sidney Hook, ed., *Dimensions of Mind* (New York: Collier Books, 1960), p. 228.

7. Thomas H. Howells, *Hunger for Holiness* (Denver; World Press, 1940).

8. Abraham Maslow, *Toward a Psychology of Being* (Princeton: D. Van Nostrand Co., 1962).

9. Rollo May, *Psychology and the Human Dilemma* (Princeton: D. Van Nostrand Co., 1967), p. 195.

NOTES TO CHAPTER 3

1. Loren Eiseley, "An Evolutionist Looks at Modern Man," in Richard Thruelsen, and John Kobler, *Adventures of the Mind*, First Series (New York: Vintage Books, 1958), p.8. Used by permission of The Saturday Evening Post 1958 Curtis Publishing Co.

2. Will Durant, *Our Oriental Heritage* (New York: Simon and Schuster, 1935), p. 73. Copyright © 1935 by Will Durant, used by permission of the publisher.

3. Charles H. Southwick, *Primate Social Behavior* (New York: D. Von Nostrand Co., 1963), p. 72.

4. August Kroch, "The Language of the Bees," in Stanley Coppersmith, *Frontiers of Psychological Research* (San Francisco: W. H. Freeman and Co., 1964), p. 5.

5. Durant, *Our Oriental Heritage*, p. 73. Used by permission of Simon and Schuster.

6. Ibid., p. 76.

7. David Krech, et al., *Individual in Society* (New York: McGraw-Hill Book Co., 1962), p. 273.

8. Orvis C. Irwin, "Infant Speech," in Stanley Coppersmith, *Frontiers of Psychological Research* (San Francisco: W. H. Freeman and Co., 1964), pp. 33–35.

9. Theadora Kroeber, *Ishi* (Berkeley: University of California Press, 1962), p. 38.

10. Gordon Allport, *Personality* (New York: Holt, Rinehart and Winston, 1937).

11. Albert Camus, Speech accepting Nobel Prize, 1957, in Bergen Evans, *Dictionary of Quotations* (New York: Delacorte Press, 1968), p. 781.

12. David Riesman, *The Lonely Crowd* (New Haven: Yale University Press, 1950).

13. A. Bavelas, "Communication Patterns in Task Oriented Groups," *Journal of the Acoustical Society of America* 22 (1950): 725–30.

14. J. L. Moreno, *Who Shall Survive? Foundations of Sociometry, Group Psychotherapy and Sociodrama*, 2nd ed. (Beacon, N.Y.: Beacon House, 1953).

NOTES TO CHAPTER 4

1. Martin Buber, *Between Man and Man* (Boston: Beacon Press, 1955), p. 200.

2. Ibid., p. 202.

3. H. S. Sullivan, *The Interpersonal Theory of Psychiatry* (New York: W. W. Norton, 1953.

4. Fritz, Heider, "On the Reduction of Sentiment," in Sidney Hook, *Dimensions of Mind* (New York: Collier Books, 1961), p. 181.

5. Ernest Becker, *The Birth and Death of Meaning* (New York: Free Press of Glencoe, 1962), pp. 95, 101, 103, 104.

6. *Webster's New Collegiate Dictionary* (Springfield, Mass.: G. & C. Merriam Co., 1961), 1961), p. 860.

7. Erich Fromm, *The Art of Loving* (New York: Bantam Books, 1963).

8. Erik Erikson, *Childhood and Society* (New York: W. W. Norton, 1950), p. 220.

9. Eric Berne, *Games People Play* (New York: Grove Press, 1964), p. 50.

10. Everett Shostrum, *Man the Manipulator* (Nashville, Tenn.: Abingdon Press, 1967).

11. Erving Goffman, *The Presentation of Self in Everyday Life* (New York: Doubleday and Co., 1959).

12. C. G. Jung, *Modern Man in Search of a Soul* (New York: Harcourt Brace Jovanovich, 1933).

13. Anders,Nygren, *Agape and Eros*, trans. Philip S. Watson (London: S.P.C.K., 1953).

14. Fromm, *The Art of Loving*, pp. 38-69.

15. Sullivan, *The Interpersonal Theory of Psychiatry*, p. 246.

16. Austin Wright, *Islandia* (New York: New American Library, 1966), p. 531.

17. *The New Testament (Letters to Young Churches)*, trans. J. B. Phillips (New York: Macmillan Co., 1948, p. 58), I Corinthians, 13th Chapter.

18. Goethe, in Becker, *Birth and Death*, p. 98.

19. Bruno Bettelheim, *Love is Not Enough* (New York: Free Press, 1950).

20. Carl R. Rogers, *On Becoming a Person* (Boston: Houghton Mifflin Co., 1961)

21. Jung, *Modern Man*, p. 34.

22. Rogers, *On Becoming a Person*, p. 339.

23. Gregory Bateson, et. al., "Toward a Theory of Schizophrenia," in Warrn G. Bennis, et. al., *Interpersonal Dynamics* (Homewood, Ill.: Dorsey Press, 1964), p. 145.

24. Goffman, *Presentation of Self*, p. 2.

25. Bateson, *Toward a Theory of Schizophrenia*," p. 148.

26. John Ciardi, *Saturday Review*, 3 February 1968, p. 10.

27. Jung, *Modern Man*, pp. 31-36.

28. O. H. Mowrer, *The New Group Therapy* (New York: D. Van Nostrand Co., 1964, pp. 65-71).

29. Rudolf Dreikurs, *Psychology for the Classroom* (New York: Harper & Row, 1957).

30. Thomas Szasz, "Entropy, Organization and the Problem of the Economy of Human Relations," *International Journal of Psychoanalysis* 36 (1955): 289-97.

31. Bernard Steinzor, *Psychiatry and Social Science Review* 2, no. 7 (July 1968): 25.

NOTES TO CHAPTER 5

1. John Dollard, et al., *Frustration and Aggression* (New Haven: Yale University Press, 1939).

2. Anna Freud, *The Ego and the Mechanisms of Defense* (New York: International Universities Press, 1946).

3. James C. Coleman, *Abnormal Psychology and Modern Life* (Chicago: Scott-Foresman, 1956), inside back cover.

4. Ibid.

5. Ibid.

6. Arthur P. Noyes, and Lawrence C. Kolb, *Modern Clinical Psychiatry* (Philadelphia: W. B. Saunders Co., 1963), p. 62.

7. Mary Alice White, and Myron W. Harris, *The School Psychologist* (New York: Harper & Row, 1961), p. 241.

8. Ashley Montagu, "Chromosomes and Crime," in *Readings in Psychology Today* (Del Mar, Calif.: CRM Books, 1969), p. 371ff.

9. Robert G. Heath, "A Biochemical Hypothesis on the Etiology of Schizophrenia," in Don D. Jackson, ed., *The Etiology of Schizophrenia* (New York: Basic Books, 1960), p. 146ff.

10. Jan A. Böök, "Genetical Aspects of Schizophrenic Psychoses," in Don D. Jackson, ed., *The Etiology of Schizophrenia* (New York: Basic Books, 1960), p. 23ff.

11. Clyde Kluckhorn, Henry A. Murray, and David M. Schneider, *Personality in Nature, Society, and Culture* (New York: A. Knopf, 1953).

12. T. S. Szasz, *The Myth of Mental Illness* (New York: Harper & Row, 1961).

13. Robert R. Sears, et al., *Patterns of Child Rearing* (Evanston, Ill.: Row, Petersen and Co., 1957).

14. Sigmund Freud, *The Ego and the Id*, trans. Joan Rivierre, and James Strachey (New York: W. W. Norton, 1962).

15. Heinz Ansbacher, and Rowena Ansbacher, *The Individual Psychology of Alfred Adler* (New York: Basic Books, 1956).

16. H. S. Sullivan, *The Interpersonal Theory of Psychiatry* (New York: W. W. Norton, 1953).

17. Ernest Becker, *The Revolution in Psychiatry* (New York: Free Press of Glencoe, 1964).

18. Don D. Jackson, "The Monad, the Dyad, and the Family Therapy of Schizophrenics," in Arthur Burton ed., *Psychotherapy of the Psychoses* (New York: Basic Books, 1961).

19. Carl R. Rogers, *On Becoming a Person* (New York: Houghton Mifflin Co., 1961).

NOTES TO CHAPTER 6

1. Edwin G. Boring, *History, Psychology, and Science*, New York, John Wiley & Sons, 1963, p. 147. Used by permission of the publisher.

2. *Encyclopaedia Brittannica*, Chicago, Encyclopedia Britannica, 1957 ed. vol. 3, p. 473.

3. Boring, *History, Psychology, and Science*, p. 153. Used by permission of John Wiley & Sons.

4. Clifford T. Morgan and Richard A. King, *Introduction to Psychology* (New York: McGraw-Hill Book Co., 1966), p. 461.

5. Anne Anastasi, *Psychological Testing*, 2nd ed. (New York: Macmillan Co., 1961), p. 343ff.

6. J. P. Guilford, *The Nature of Human Intelligence* (New York: McGraw-Hill Book Co., 1967).

NOTES TO CHAPTER 7

1. James C. Coleman, *Psychology and Effective Behavior*, Chicago: Scott, Foresman, 1969, pp. 73–77.

2. Erik Erikson, *Childhood and Society*, New York: W. W. Norton, 1950, p. 234.

3. Ribble, Margaret "Infantile Experience in Relation to Personality Development," in J. M. V. Hunt, *Personality and the Behavior Disorders*, vol. 2 (New York: Ronald Press Co., 1944), p. 621ff.

4. Arnold Gesell and Frances L. Ilg, *Infant and Child in the Culture Today* (New York: Harper & Row, 1943).

Gesell and Ilg, *The Child from Five to Ten* (New York: Harper & Row, 1946).

Gesell and Louise B. Ames, *Youth: The Years from Ten to Sixteen* (New York: Harper & Row, 1956).

5. Rolf E. Muns, *Theories of Adolescence* (New York: Random House, 1962), p. 111.

6. Gesell and Ilg, *The Child from Five to Ten*, 1943, p. 20. Used by permission of Harper & Row, Publishers.

7. Ibid., p. 29.

8. Barbel Inhelder, in Hans Furth, *Piaget and Knowledge*, (Englewood Cliffs, N.J.: Prentice-Hall, 1969), p. 33.

9. Taken from Coleman, *Psychology and Effective Behavior*, p. 80, by permission of David McKay Co.

10. Carl R. Rogers, "The Concept of the Fully Functioning Person," *Psychotherapy: Theory, Research and Practice* 1, mo. 1 (August 1963): 18-20. Reprinted by permission of *Psychotherapy: Theory, Research, and Practice.*

11. Ibid., p. 22.

NOTES TO CHAPTER 8

1. From, *The Definition of Psychology* by Fred S. Keller. Copyright © 1937 by D. Appleton — Century Company, Inc. Renewed 1965. Reprinted by permission of Appleton-Century-Crofts, Educational Division, Meredith Corporation.

2. J. R. Millenson, *Principles of Behavioral Analysis* (New York: Macmillan Co., 1967), p. 51.

3. Ernest R. Hilgard and Gordon H. Bower, *Theories of Learning* (New York: Appleton-Century-Crofts, 1966), pp. 19–20.

4. Keller, *Definition of Psychology*, p. 71.

5. Hilgard and Bower, *Theories of Learning*, p. 75.

6. Ibid., p. 113.

7. Ibid., p. 113.

8. Ibid., p. 115.

9. O. H. Mowrer, *Learning Theory and Behavior* (New York: John Wiley & Sons, 1960), pp. 380-381.) Used by permission of the publisher.

10. Hilgard and Bower, *Theories of Learning*, p. 195.

11. Ibid., p. 196.

12. Ibid., p. 196.

13. Ibid., p. 232.

14. Ibid., p. 233.

15. Breger and James L. McGaugh, "Critique and Reformulation of 'Learning Theory' Approaches to Psychotherapy and Neurosis," *Psychol. Bull.* 63 (1965): 355.

16. J. F. Dashiell, *Fundamentals of General Psychology* (Boston: Houghton Mifflin, 1949), p. 26.

17. Helen E. Durkin, "An Experimental Study of Problem Solving," in Theodore L. Harris and Wilson E. Schwahn, *Selected Readings on the Learning Process* (New York: Oxford Univ. Press, 1961), pp. 41–52.

18. Ibid., p. 52.

19. Wilbert S. Ray, *The Experimental Psychology of Original Thinking* (New York: Macmillan Co., 1967), pp. 8–9.

20. Karl Duncker, "The Solution of Practical Problems," in Theodore L. Harris and Wilson E. Schwahn, *Selected Readings on the Learning Process* (New York: Oxford Univ. Press, 1961), pp. 53–59.

21. J. P. Guilford, "Intelligence: 1965 Model," in Wayne H. Bartz ed., *Readings in General Psychology* (Boston: Allyn and Bacon, 1968), p. 530.

22. J. P. Guilford, "Creativity: Its Measurement and Development," in James A. Dyal, *Readings in Psychology: Understanding Human Behavior* (New York: McGraw-Hill Book Co., 1967), pp. 275–285.

23. Ray, *Experimental Psychology*, p. 23.

24. Ibid., p. 12.

25. Ibid., p. 122.

26. From *Creativity and Personal Freedom* by Frank Barron, pp. 201-2, copyright ©1968 by Litton Educational Publishing, Inc.

27. Ibid., pp. 208–11.

28. Ibid., p. 210.

29. Ibid., pp. 212–13.

NOTES TO CHAPTER 9

1. J. W. Kimball, *Biology* (Reading, Mass.: Addison-Wesley, 1968), pp. 497–99.

2. Ibid., pp. 491–94.

3. Daniel H. Funkenstein, "The Physiology of Fear and Anger," in *Psychobiology: The Biological Bases of Behavior*, Readings from *Scientific American* (San Francisco: W. H. Freeman Co., 1967), p. 196.

4. Kimball, *Biology*, pp. 501–3.

5. Ibid., pp. 503–5.

6. Isaac Asimov, *The Human Brain* (New York: New American Library, 1963), p. 6.

7. Ibid., p. 58.

8. Richard E. Whalen, *Hormones and Behavior* (Princeton, N.J.: D. Van Nostrand Co., 1967), p. 12.

9. Ibid., p. 12.

10. Ibid., p. 13.

11. Ibid., p. 11.

12. Ibid., p. 15.

13. Richard P. Michael, "Oestrogens in the Central Nervous System," in Whalen, p. 127.

14. Lawrence Z. Freedman, " 'Truth' Drugs," in *Psychobiology*, Readings from Scientific American (San Francisco: W. H. Freeman and Co., 1967), p. 350.

15. Harold E. Himwich, "The New Psychiatric Drugs," in *Psychobiology*, p. 342.

16. Issac Asimov, "That Odd Chemical Complex, the Human Mind," in Robert V. Guthrie, ed., *Psychology in the World Today* (Menlo Park, Calif.: Addison-Wesley Publishing Co., 1968), p. 42.

17. James R. Weeks, "Experimental Narcotic Addiction," in *Psychobiology*, p. 351.

18. James V. McConnell, "Memory Transfer through Cannibalism in Planarians," *Journal of Neuropsychiatry* 3 (1962): 42–48.

19. G. Ungar and L. N. Irwin, "Transfer of Acquired Information by Brain Extracts," *Nature* 214 (1967): 453–55.

20. James L. McGaugh, "Analysis of Memory Transfer and Enhancement," *Proceedings of the American Philosophical Society* 3, no. 6 (1967): 350.

21. Alan E. Nourse, *The Body*, *Life* Science Library (New York: Time Incorporated, 1964), p. 158.

22. Kimball, *Biology*, pp. 511–29.

23. Ibid., pp. 553–67.

250

NOTES FOR PAGES 175–85

24. D. O. Hebb, "Introduction to Dover Edition of: Brain Mechanisms and Intelligence, by K. S. Lashley," in Richard A. King, ed., *Readings for an Introduction to Psychology* (New York: McGraw-Hill Book Company, 1966), p. 512.

25. Peter Milner and Stephen Glickman, *Cognitive Processes and the Brain* (Princeton, N.J.: D. Van Nostrand Co., 1965), p. v.

26. Elinor S. Brush, M. Mishkin, and H. E. Rosvold, "Effects of Object Preferences and Aversions on Discrimination Learning in Monkeys with Frontal Lesions," in Milner and Glickman, *Cognitive Processes*, pp. 1–17.

27. Waclawa M. Lawicka, "The Effect of the Prefrontal Lobectomy on the Vocal Conditioned Reflexes in Dogs," in Milner and Glickman, *Cognitive Processes*, pp. 18–24.

28. Clifford T. Morgan and Richard A. King, *Introduction to Psychology* (New York: McGraw-Hill Book Co., 1966), p. 704.

29. Ibid., p. 703.

30. James Olds, "Pleasure Centers in the Brain," in *Psychobiology*, p. 183.

31. Jose M. R. Delgado, *Physical Control of the Mind* (New York: Harper & Row, Publishers, 1969).

32. Neal E. Miller, "Central Stimulation and Other New Approaches to Motivation and Reward," in Richard A. King, *Readings*, 498.

33. Abraham H. Maslow, *Toward a Psychology of Being* (Princeton, N. J.: D. Van Nostrand Co., 1962), p. 20.

34. Floyd L. Ruch, *Psychology and Life*, 7th ed. (Chicago: Scott, Foresman and Co., 1966), p. 378.

35. William James, *Psychology: The Briefer Course* (New York: Harper Torchbooks, 1966), p. 378.

36. W. B. Cannon, "The James-Lange Theory of Emotions: A Critical Examination and an Alternative Theory," in Richard A. King, *Readings for an Introduction to Psychology* (New York: McGraw-Hill, 1961), p. 86ff.

37. O. H. Mowrer, *Learning Theory and Behavior* (New York: John Wiley & Sons, 1960) p. 213.

38. Stanley Schacter, "The Interaction of Cognitive and Physiological Determinants of Emotional State," in Joseph F. Perez, Richard C. Sprinthall, George S. Grosser, and Paul J. Anastasion, *General Psychology: Selected Readings* (Princeton, N.J.: D. Van Nostrand, 1967), p. 177ff.

39. Eckhard H. Hess, "Ethology," in *New Directions in Psychology* (New York: Holt, Rinehart and Winston, 1962), p. 225.

40. Ibid., pp. 224ff.

41. S. S. Stevens, *Handbook of Experimental Psychology* (New York: John Wiley & Sons, 1951), pp. 393–95.

42. Ibid., pp. 392–93.

43. Arthur D. Hasler, and James A. Larsen, "The Homing Salmon," in *Psychobiology*, p. 21.

44. Harry F. Harlow and Margaret K. Harlow, "The Effect of Rearing Conditions on Behavior," in Richard A. King, *Readings*, pp. 54–62.

45. S. L. Washburn and Irven De Vore, "The Social Life of Baboons," in *Psychobiology*, pp. 10–19.

46. Solomon Asch, "Opinions and Social Pressure," in *Frontiers of Psychological Research*, Readings from *Scientific American* (San Francisco: W. H. Freeman and Co., 1964), p. 110.

47. Muzafer Sherif, "Experiments in Group Conflict," in *Frontiers of Psychological Research*, p. 112.

NOTES TO PART IV AND CHAPTER 10

1. John Ciardi, "Lines from the Beating End of the Stethoscope," *Saturday Review*, 18 November, 1967, p. 12.

2. C. Fisher and W. C. Dement, "Studies on the Psychopathology of Sleep and Dreams," *American Journal of Psychiatry* 119 (1963): 1160-68.

3. H. J. Eysenck, "The Effects of Psychotherapy," in Eysenck, *Handbook of Abnormal Psychology* (New York: Basic Books, 1961).

4. O. H. Mowrer, *The Crisis in Psychiatry and Religion* (Princeton, N.J.: D. Van Nostrand Co., 1961).

5. Rudolph Dreikurs, *Psychology in the Classroom* (New York: Harper & Row, 1968, pp. 6, 61.

6. Hans Selye, *The Stress of Life* (New York: McGraw-Hill Book Co., 1956).

7. Carl R. Rogers, "The Characteristics of a Helping Relationship," *Personnel and Guidance Journal* 37 (1958): 6-16.

8. H. H. Schaefer and P. L. Martin, *Behavioral Therapy* (New York: McGraw-Hill, 1969).

9. O. I. Lovaas, B. Schaeffer, and J. Q. Simmons, "Building Social Behavior in Autistic Children by Use of Electric Shock," *J. exp. Res. Personality* 1 (1965): 99-109.

10. Aubrey Yates, *Behavior Therapy* (New York: John Wiley & Sons, 1970).

11. Albert Bandura, *Principles of Behavior Modification* (New York: Holt, Rinehart and Winston, 1969).

12. J. Wolpe, *Psychotherapy by Reciprocal Inhibition* (Stanford: Stanford University Press, 1958).

13. Eysenck, "The Effects of Psychotherpy."

14. C. Rogers and Rosalind Dymond, eds., *Psychotherapy and Personality Change* (Chicago: University of Chicago Press, 1954).

NOTES TO CHAPTER 11

1. Vance Packard, *The Hidden Persuaders* (New York: Pocket Books, 1958).

2. B. F. Skinner, *Walden Two* (New York: Macmillan Co., 1948).

3. Sidney Jourard, *Disclosing Man to Himself* (Princeton, N.J.: D. Van Nostrand Co., 1968), p. 8.

4. William McDougall, *The Energies of Men* (New York: Scribners, 1933).

5. I. E. Farber, H. F. Harlow, and L. J. West. "Brainwashing, Conditioning, and DDD." *Sociometry* 20 (1957): 271-85.

6. Leon Festinger, "Cognitive Dissonance," *Scientific American*, October 1962.

7. C. I. Hovland, A. A. Lumsdaine, and F. Sheffield. *Experiments on Mass Communication* (Princeton: Princeton University Press, 1949).

8. C. E. Shannon. "A Mathematical Thing of Communication." *Bell System Technical Journal* 27 (1948): 379-423, 623-56.

NOTES TO CHAPTER 12

1. Albert Camus, *The Myth of Sisyphus, and Other Essays,* New York: Knopf, 1955.

2. Frederick Nietzsche quoted in Victor Frankl, *Man's Search for Meaning.* New York: Washington Square Press, 1963, p. 164.

3. E. V. Pullias, *A Search for Understanding,* Dubuque, Iowa: Wm. C. Brown Co., 1965, p. 104.

4. Victor Frankl, *Man's Search for Meaning,* New York: Washington Square Press, 1963, p. 123.

5. Nikos Kazantzakis, *The Odyssey: A Modern Sequel,* TV. by Kimon Friar. New York: Simon and Schuster, 1958. From translators introduction, p. xix.

6. Soren Kierkegaard, *The Sickness Unto Death,* translated by Walter Lowrie, Princeton, New Jersey: Princeton University Press, 1941, p. 19.

7. H. S. Sullivan, *The Interpersonal Theory of Psychiatry,* New York: W. W. Norton and Co., 1953.

8. Gordon Allport, *Becoming,* New Haven, Conn.: Yale University Press, 1955.

9. Teilhard de Chardin, *The Phenomenon of Man,* New York: Harper Torch Books, 1961, p. 33.

10. Abraham Maslow, *Toward a Psychology of Being,* Princeton, New Jersey: Van Nostrand Co., 1962, p. 67.

11. Jose Ortega y Gasset, *The Revolt of the Masses,* New York: W. W. Norton and Co., Inc., 1932, p. 31.

12. The Bible, Genesis 3:5.

13. Robert Frost, "The Road Not Taken" in Bergen Evans, *Dictionary of Quotations,* New York: Delacorte Press, 1968, p. 595.

14. Abraham Maslow, *Op. Cit.,* p. 19.

15. Soren Kierkegaard, *Training in Christianity,* translated by Walter Lowrie, Princeton: Princeton University Press, 1947.

16. Martin Buber, *Between Man and Man,* Boston: Beacon Press, 1955.

17. Martin Buber, *I and Thou,* translated by Ronald Gregor Smith, 2nd Ed., New York: Scribner's, 1958.

NOTES TO CHAPTER 13

1. Eckhard H. Hess, "Ethology," in New Direction in Psychology (New York: Holt, Rinehart and Winston, 1962), p. 225.

2. N. Tinbergen, "The Curious Behavior of the Stickleback," *Scientific American,* December 1952.

3. Konrad Lorenz, *On Aggression* (New York: Bantom Books, 1966, 1967), p. 228ff.

4. Jose M. R. Delgado, *Physical Control of the Mind* (New York: Harper & Row, Publishers, 1969), pp. 70 and 71. Copyright © 1969 by Jose M. R. Delgado, Reprinted by permission of Harper & Row, Publishers.

5. Ibid., p. 166.

6. Ibid., p. 68.

7. Albert Bandura, *Principles of Behavior Modification* (New York: Holt, Rinehart and Winston, Inc., 1969, p. 226.

8. Charles T. Tart, ed., *Altered States of Consciousness* (New York: John Wiley and Sons, Inc., 1969), p. 489ff.

9. Ibid., p. 503ff.

10. Ibid., p. 507ff.

11. Robert T. Golembiewski and Arthur Blumberg, *Sensitivity Training and the Laboratory Approach* (Itasea, Ill.: F. E. Peacock Publishers, Inc., 1970), p. 4.

12. Frederick S. Perls, *Gestalt Therapy Verbatim* (Lafayette, California: Real People Press, 1969).

13. Keen, Sam, "Sing the Body Electric," *Psychology Today*, 4, no. 5 (October 1970): p. 58.

14. Michael Murphy, Esalen: Where It is At," in *Readings in Psychology Today*, (Del Mar, Calif.: CRM Books, 1969), p. 415.

15. Carl R. Rogers, "Toward a Science of the Person," in T. W. Wann, ed., *Behaviorism and Phenomenology: Contrasting Bases for Modern Psychology* (Chicago: University of Chicago Press, 1964), pp. 109-40. Reprinted by permission of University of Chicago Press.

16. Ibid.

17. R. R. Grinker, ed., *Toward a Unified Theory of Human Behavior*, 2nd ed. (New York: Basic Books, 1967) p. ix.

18. Gordon Allport, *The Person in Psychology* (Boston: Beacon Press, 1968), p. 22.

19. Ludwig von Bertalanffy, *General System Theory* (New York: George Braziller, 1968), p. 40.

20. Ibid., pp. 25, 26.

INDEX